To, with love,

Sal

PSYCHOTECHNIQUES

PSYCHOTECHNIQUES
How to Help Yourself or Someone You Love

Dr. Salvatore V. Didato

METHUEN, NEW YORK

Library of Congress Cataloging in Publication Data

Didato, Salvatore V.
   Psychotechniques, how to help yourself or someone
you love.

   Bibliography: p. 277
   Includes index.
   1. Success. 2. Behavior modification. I. Title.
BF637.B4D53   158'.1   80-15636
ISBN 0-416-00761-9

Manufactured in the United States of America by
Fairfield Graphics, Fairfield, Pennsylvania
Designed by David Miller

First Edition

Published in the United States of America by
Methuen, Inc.
733 Third Avenue
New York, N.Y. 10017

I dedicate this book to my dear and loving wife, Dr. Paulette Didato, whose editorial skill and verbal acumen were of invaluable help in writing it.

Contents

Preface

Behavior therapists, many of whose methods are intended to be self-administered, claim that professionals waste too much time using therapy to cure symptoms. They argue vigorously that often all the sufferer needs is a retraining method to bring relief.

Psychotechniques is a collection of such methods, distilled from many sources, with discussion of theories or abstract rationales kept to the barest minimum. The book describes briefly and in step-by-step fashion dozens of techniques for coping with a wide variety of problems and difficult interpersonal situations.

Although it is directed primarily toward the lay reader, it will be valuable to the professional person in the helping arts, especially to those at intermediate stages of training.

Introduction

Because part of my job is to counsel people having personal problems and to deal with such difficulties in books, talks, and in our publication work, it is important that I be able to refer individuals to competent sources of help.

For this reason, I hail the new book *Psychotechniques,* by Dr. Salvatore V. Didato, with enthusiasm. In reading the manuscript of this excellent book by a distinguished psychologist, I became at once aware that here is one of the most comprehensive sources of practical help in the many problems facing adults and children that has come to my attention.

The book covers a wide range of personal problems, indeed, fifty-seven of them—practically every sort of human situation encountered by the counselor who is called upon to give helpful advice. This book, therefore, is bound to become a valuable tool for psychologists, pastors, teachers, or anyone who is called upon to counsel and guide people in trouble. But beyond that, it will be of value to lay readers who desire to improve their own understanding of personality. Because the book is written in a highly readable style and communicates clearly with the nontechnical reader, it will be a popular work in helping persons everywhere with specific problems.

Dr. Didato's practical, self-directive emphasis should enable the reader to put into practice for himself or herself workable techniques that are designed to result in personal improvement. Indeed, the book is actually a library of information on exactly what to do in a given situation. The specific steps to take will prove of help in handling a fear, relaxing tension, overcoming self-doubt, losing weight, or whatever problem may confront an individual. That one can help oneself with the problems that come to most of us—and just how to go about doing it—comes through clearly and with practical helpfulness in this book. For this reason Dr. Didato, through *Psychotechniques*, will surely be accounted a helpful friend by many who use his practical and valuable book.

Norman Vincent Peale

Prologue

There is a fable about a man who was surrounded by all the people of the world. He was eating junket, and he asked the curious world, "Can you guess what I'm thinking about? But first," he said, "let me tell you what I am not thinking about. I am not thinking about a year-old lion blowing out the candle on his birthday cake, nor about a walrus balancing an apple on his back." On the basis of this useful information, the people then tried to guess what was on the man's mind. They suggested it might be a kangaroo jumping over a glass of orange juice, or a rabbit wondering if a bunch of grapes was tied to its tail, or any of a number of other interesting capers involving animals. When they finished guessing, he finally told them the answer—he was thinking about eating junket.

This charming fantasy by Dorothy Kunhardt suggests the present state of affairs in the field of human relations. We sometimes spin unnecessary theories about human beings while the most obvious facts soar over our heads. And one of these facts is that *people can help themselves more than they think they can.*

Man's capacities have never been measured; nor are we to judge . . . what he can do by any precedents, so little has been tried.—*Henry David Thoreau*

Divine is the work to relieve pain.—*Hippocrates*

PSYCHOTECHNIQUES

WE ALL HAVE THE POWER TO HELP OURSELVES

Prior to the introduction of behavior therapy, mental health experts held firmly to the belief that psychological problems stemmed from unconscious motivation. This thinking, which prevailed from about 1910 to the early 1960s, wrested some of the initiative from the human spirit in its quest for self-mastery. It held that habits, feelings, and attitudes are largely directed by inner forces beyond our awareness and control. Man thus becomes dependent upon others to rescue him from his difficulties. The sublime rationalization for failure was: It is not I who am responsible for my destiny, it is my unconscious urges.

But modern psychology has changed most of this. Man is no longer relegated to psychic impotency. He is now viewed as an active participant in his own growth. The change began with the work of B. F. Skinner, psychologist at Harvard University. Skinner argues that many of our actions can be explained in terms of our environment, and the basis for human behavior is not instincts and unconscious drives, but conditioning and learning. The way to alter behavior is to teach adequate responses to old problems through repeated successes (reinforcements). His discoveries go back to the 1940s. They paved the way for a host of self-help techniques in psychology (operant conditioning), medicine (biofeedback), and education (automated learning).

The Behavior Therapists

In the late 1950s, Joseph Wolpe, a psychiatrist from South Africa who is now at Temple University, drew on Skinner's findings and showed that it wasn't necessary to psychoanalyze the unfathomed recesses of the unconscious mind to correct a faulty behavior pattern. Simpler methods, many of them self-applied, can be used; scene rehearsal, desensitization, and emotive imagery are a few. The appeal is made directly to consciousness. A person is told what causes his faulty behavior, and a plan of reeducation (through what has since been called *behavior modification*) is laid out and followed.

Unlike those myopic observers of the man eating junket, who missed the obvious, we can now see that human beings, despite their historical frailty, do have the capacity to help themselves if they learn the proper methods to do so.

Here are three typical examples:

Although attractive Nancy Miller of Boston was a good student, she grew unbearably self-conscious and nervous when she faced her college classmates to deliver a talk. One day she read about a method of using fantasy scene-rehearsal to overcome fears. Being highly motivated to help herself, she decided to try it out. She followed the instructions carefully. First, she took deep breaths and then relaxed completely. Slowly, she began imagining the scenes that would lead up to her speaking to the class. She saw herself giving the speech easily and receiving the group's approval. Somehow, just imagining herself succeeding made her feel more confident.

Later, when she actually gave the talk, she felt calm and composed and was pleased with her performance. Now, each time she must speak before the class, she prepares herself by using the same method (*consolidated desensitization*) that worked so well for her. She learned a skill she will never forget.

A well-adjusted suburban housewife suffered from a recurring nightmare. She dreamed she was lost in a huge train station. She felt confused and panic-stricken about where she was going, what time to leave, and which train to board. After many months of this nightmare, an idea finally struck her. She asked her husband, who was a commuter, to bring home as many train schedules as he could find. She poured over them for hours, until she reassured herself that she knew the departure times and routes of all trains leaving the depot.

For a few nights, she dreamed that she calmly took trains on time to specific destinations. Soon after that, her nightmares stopped completely and never recurred. She sensed what her therapy should be and proceeded to help herself with a solution.

Wally Stone, a postman from Toledo, Ohio, worked in the same locality for fourteen years and knew everyone along his route. He always considered himself to have an average memory. When he was transferred to a new neighborhood, however, he began having difficulty memorizing names and remembering faces. He was puzzled and concerned. One day, a friendly co-worker who heard of his plight told him about a method of recall that a college instructor had taught him. The technique was to associate a person's name with some unusual or even bizarre image of that person. Wally tried it, focusing on a Mrs. Barker, a widow who lived in a blue frame house with a white fence. He closed his eyes, relaxed, and then visualized a huge blue circus tent with a white fence around it, and Mrs. Barker out front, dressed as a sideshow barker.

The next day when he met her, he had no trouble recalling her name or the house where she lived. He tried it for several other residents along the route and the technique worked equally well for them, too. Wally still uses the method when he needs it. Now he can remember names and faces much better than he ever thought he could.

These are examples of average people who used a self-help method to overcome a personal problem. Such people always make scientists sit up and take notice. Many prominent authorities on the psyche have alluded to this inherent capacity of humans to solve many of their own problems. Psychoanalyst Karen Horney has told us, "Only the individual himself can develop his potentialities. But like other living organisms, the human individual needs favorable conditions for his growth from acorn to oak tree." And psychologist Carl Rogers has said, "Therapy . . . relies much more heavily on the individual drive toward growth, health, and adjustment. [It] is not a matter of doing something *to* the individual (or of inducing him to do something about himself). It is, instead, a matter of freeing him for normal growth and development, or removing obstacles so that he can again move forward."

Although some behavior experts express similar optimism

about man's capacity to grow, somehow they have never taken self-help techniques too seriously. They view them with hesitation. For the most part, patients are seen as too unmotivated to benefit from a self-help program of personal improvement. But the fact remains, virtually all of us at one time or another have benefited from a specific self-help psychotechnique, which we followed cook-book fashion because we had faith in it.

In part, the erroneous notion that behavior change must demand long, arduous years of struggle for both doctor and patient is engendered by those who come for help. To the chagrin of many physicians, patients tend to deify the doctor. The 1973 Pacific Medical Center Symposium on the Medical Mystique saw doctors as the most unassailable of all professionals in our society. It reported that "for the past 20,000 years, man has placed the healer in a special role, both honored and feared and almost always, cloaked in mystery." One strong voice who calls for a change in this distorted view is Dr. Marvin Belsky of New York City. He states: "The demystification of the medical mystique is a job for both doctor and patient. The assertive and informed patient must identify and join with those doctors who want to do away with the priestly, authoritarian aspects of the mystique."

In a sense, all do-it-yourself books crusade against this mystique of priestly authority within the fields in which they are written. This volume could be considered in that same light.

2

PSYCHOTECHNIQUES: AN ARSENAL OF TOOLS FOR BETTER LIVING

This book is a collection of strategies. We use the term *psychotechniques* to describe them, and we define them as follows: *A psychotechnique is a special step-by-step system of self-help, presented in printed form and administered, monitored, and verified by the person using it, without the assistance of a professional.*

We have chosen the term psychotechnique because it is the best single word to deliver the message of this book quickly. It is an approach to solving problems in daily living and it involves skills we can all learn. When properly applied, psychotechniques can give a person control over an entire range of psychological difficulties that he might encounter in the course of his life.

All societies esteem the person who can overcome obstacles to his growth. Such is the self-made man, that rare creature who does not allow the stresses of life to buffet him about on a tempestuous sea. A good argument can be made for the conclusion that, somehow, the self-made man has grasped and applied the principles of a large variety of psychotechniques, which are available to all of us if only we would search them out.

Fortunately, psychotechniques are not as unattainable as they were a generation ago. Each day, therapists discover new ones, which they teach their clients. Those presented in this book are the result of much research and clinical experience in the fields of education, medicine, psychiatry, and psychology.

Learning psychotechniques is as important as learning all the other skills we need for a smooth passage through life—reading, writing, and so forth. Once we are familiar with these skills and know when to choose and apply them as tools, we can confront obstacles and gain the upper hand with them. Without these skills, our problems may well gain control over us and eventually lead to symptoms or even make us patients in need of psychiatric treatment.

A good psychotechnique has two characteristics:

1. *It increases awareness of ourselves and others.* One of the main reasons we have adjustment problems is that we are not aware of the cause-and-effect connections between what we do wrong and our symptoms. In the next chapter, we will look at ten examples of this lack of awareness.

Awareness is the cornerstone of all learning. Dr. Edmund Jacobson taught patients to be *aware* of the difference between tense and relaxed muscles and thereby enabled them to learn self-relaxation (see chapter 6). Dr. Samuel Renshaw taught his subjects to be *aware* of minute differences in the silhouettes of airplanes and thus enabled them to correctly identify the planes when pictures of them were rapidly flashed on a screen (see chapter 3). And Dr. Neal Miller, pioneer in biofeedback training at Rockefeller University in New York, teaches his psychosomatic patients to be supersensitive to body changes, like pulse rate, heart rate, and blood pressure, so that they will learn to control these functions.

So, a good psychotechnique makes us aware of the factors that contribute to or cause our problem, then provides us with substitute behavior to correct it.

2. *A psychotechnique is an antidote to our "guiding fictions."* This is a key element in any valid psychotechnique. A large component of any person's inadequacy, faulty habit, or maladjustment is an exaggerated feeling of hopelessness. It is an ever-present fictitious belief that dampens our confidence and often provokes failure. It is a sweeping generalization we make about ourselves that (often unconsciously) says, "nothing can rescue me from this symptom."

We can illustrate some guiding fictions by placing the words "I don't know" before each of the entries in the table of contents of this book. Thus we would have:

> I don't know . . . how to be more assertive.
> I don't know . . . how to relax.
> I don't know . . . how to overcome depression.

These beliefs keep us entangled in our problem.

But look closely at these guiding fictions. Isn't it true that there are some times when you *can* be more assertive, and that there are some times when you *can* relax, and there are some times when you *can* deal with depression?

If you're honest about it, you could admit that there are times and circumstances under which you can cope with your problems, providing the conditions are just right for you. This proves only one thing, that you have the capacity, however small, to cope, and that this endures as a trainable part of you which can be strengthened.

In brief, a psychotechnique should dispel your guiding fiction —an untested assumption that you are incompetent and one that precipitates further failures.

At times, all of us make mistakes in managing our lives. We form self-defeating psychotechniques. The next chapter shows how this can happen in a variety of ways in day-to-day living.

3

TEN PSYCHOTECHNIQUES—ALL WRONG
or, How We Develop Faulty Psychotechniques

The human psyche is no less than a marvelous and delicately balanced instrument for achieving happiness. We would expect a machine or other instrument to break down or commit errors if we operated it incorrectly. Why, then, should we assume that our mind will perform well if we don't understand it?

During World War II, Samuel Renshaw, a research psychologist at Ohio State University, tested thousands of servicemen and found that they misused their vision, utilizing it to only 20 percent of its full capacity. He designed airplane recognition courses that taught them to identify the silhouettes of airplanes flashed on a screen at very high speeds, like one-tenth or one twenty-fifth of a second. At first the pictures were only formless blurs, but in time the men could identify aircraft at speeds of up to one seventy-fifth of a second. Renshaw brought his subjects up to a level of skill in reproducing visual figures that he considered to be at the genius level. He taught them to increase their visual effectiveness by as much as 500 percent in just a few days of training. Renshaw's work is related to the central thesis of this book: If it is true that our vision can be improved with training, think how much more we could benefit if the human mind, an infinitely more versatile entity than our eyes, were also trained in the proper way!

Every day, millions of people misuse their psyche. They use it much like a violinist who creates noise rather than a brilliant credenza. They form faulty habits of response to stress, which grow stronger each day they are repeated. For our purposes, consider a cluster of habits to be a psychotechnique that can either help or harm us. The position of this book is that *we can learn to build a reliable, effective armory of such techniques to help us over-*

come a variety of day-to-day problems.*

We are indeed creatures of habit, but no one knows exactly how we develop habits or why we select the wrong ones to cope with reality's challenges. Take the case of Mary Olson. Lately she has become worried about her job performance. She has formed the habit of visiting the local cocktail lounge with friends each day after work. This gives her a temporary escape from the pressures of her job. But another person in the same situation might go on a shopping spree to dispel her downcast mood. Still another might develop migraine headaches. These are all attempts to cope with the problem, but most of the coping patterns that we adopt in life are not taught to us—we haphazardly fashion them through our personal experience, and too often they frustrate and disable us. A faulty psychotechnique is a maladjustment. Let's take a look at a few:

Jane is plump at 152 pounds. She is a compulsive eater. When she talks on the phone, she usually nibbles candy or cookies, which are kept in a jar nearby. Often, she does this without even being conscious of it. Jane has formed a faulty psychotechnique. By repeatedly eating and speaking on the phone at the same time, she unwittingly strengthens an association bond between the two activities. Each phone call is a cue to eat and a reinforcement of a habit pattern that will be increasingly more difficult to break with each call. (See chapter 25 for a psychotechnique Jane should use.)

Henry is a high-strung man. He has the irksome habit of snapping at others. For example, one evening he received a phone call from his foreman, who excitedly reprimanded him for sending the wrong shipment to one of their best customers. Henry, a bit of a perfectionist, took this scolding badly. Soon after he hung up, he lashed out at his teenage son and chided the boy for having an untidy room.

Over the years Henry has built up the faulty psychotechnique of releasing anger at those within his immediate range. He has conditioned himself to scapegoat others, and he thereby incurs

---

* About 75 percent of the studies mentioned in the psychological journals deal with human learning. Indeed, learning is such an important aspect of our day-to-day adjustment that we work at it for a large part of every day of our lives. Unfortunately, we also misuse this human function more than any other.

resentment from those who have not hurt him. He hasn't learned the following correct four-step psychotechnique of:

1. Momentarily taking time-out from the situation and staying alone for a few minutes.
2. Thinking about why he is angry.
3. Determining exactly who should be the target of his anger.
4. Expressing his feelings *only* to that person or persons and not to those who happen to be around him.

(See chapter 16 for more information on the psychotechnique that Henry should use.)

Grandmother Moore is sincere and conscientious. She uses a hard line in disciplining her three grandchildren. Her style of keeping them in line is to tell them what they shouldn't do. She begins every admonition with a negative. If a child tracks mud into the house, she says, "Please don't track your muddy feet on the rug." At dinner, if a child eats in huge gulps, she says, "You shouldn't take too much on your fork," and "Don't eat big mouthfuls." When her husband leaves for work, she reminds him, "Please don't leave the front gate open."

What faulty technique is Grandmother Moore using to alter the behavior of others? It may seem like a subtle point, but her mistake is that she uses negative suggestions instead of positive ones. She is not aware that when a command or suggestion is phrased positively, it is learned faster and is better retained. Grandmother Moore would get much more out of her young charges, and her husband too, if she said instead, "Please wipe your feet off before you enter the house," or "Please shut the gate on the way out." (See chapter 41 for the psychotechnique that Grandmother Moore should use.)

Lillian feels like a hopeless insomniac since she lost her job. She is determined to conquer her sleeplessness, so each night she takes warm milk, a hot bath, and promptly gets into bed. Then the problem starts.

For about three hours she just tosses and turns. She tries to relax and let her mind drift, refusing to give in to her insomnia. She forces herself to remain in bed, rationalizing that even though she is awake, she is still resting her body. Finally, after several fitful hours, she falls asleep, exhausted.

What faulty psychotechnique has Lillian developed? Insomniacs often condition themselves to be poor sleepers. By doggedly remaining in bed, Lillian inadvertently reinforces her *place habit* by associating the bed with her nonsleeping state. The more she does this, the harder it will be for her to cure her insomnia. Many insomniacs misuse their beds in the way that Lillian does. They use them for everything else but sleep. They have learned to lounge, read, watch TV, and even eat there. Their bed has not become strongly reinforced in their minds as a place to sleep.

What Lillian needs is to gradually break this chain of association by getting into the bed *only* when she is absolutely ready to use it for sleeping. (See chapter 22 for the psychotechnique that Lillian should use.)

Phil has been a foreman for fifteen years. He is a hardened product of the corporate world who does not coddle his workers. When a subordinate makes an error, Phil's management style is to point it out to him in front of the other people in the unit. "This gives everyone the chance to profit from another's mistake and I don't have to repeat myself with the others," says Phil. He also claims it teaches the others that "they better not make the same error."

Phil is using the wrong psychotechnique in managing his workers. He violates one of the basic rules of discipline psychology, which is that criticism should be made privately. (See chapters 50 and 51 for the psychotechnique that Phil should use.)

Jim Foster is a freelance fiction writer. He is only moderately successful in selling his stories. His usual *modus operandi* is to meet with the editors to discuss an idea, but more often than not he does not receive a commission for a story.

Ann Brinks is a hardworking designer. She went to her boss and asked for a promotion but was refused.

What faulty psychotechniques were both Jim and Ann using? In anything we do, our mental set is an important factor in our success or failure. Both Jim and Ann had developed the faulty pattern of entering an important situation without proper preparation. They lacked the correct mental set. Jim has his story well enough in mind. What he has not done is to rehearse his interview with someone who could play the role of the editor.

With a friend, he should have rehearsed possible rebuttals

from the editor in a role-playing situation. Or he could have memorized definite phrases or terms that might have caught the editor's fancy. In short, he should have gone over his presentation before the interview and improved his chances of success.

Ann, like Jim, did not prepare beforehand. She had an outline of reasons for her request, but didn't spend enough time thinking what her boss's objections might be. In both cases, there was no "psyching up," a proven technique that helps people to prepare psychologically for actual situations. Baseball and football coaches use it before a game, army officers practice it with their soldiers before combat, and sales managers employ it on their salespeople before a big sales campaign. (See chapters 17 and 18 for the psychotechniques that both Jim and Ann should use.)

Sue is a high-school student. Her study pattern is to do her schoolwork after dinner each night. She starts first with history, her most difficult subject; then she moves on to math, social studies, and finally science, her easiest subject. By studying her hardest subject first, Sue is strengthening a faulty psychotechnique. She would get much more out of her studies if she started first with a warm-up period. This means not immediately delving into hard work, but, rather, tackling the simplest subjects first. Somewhere in the middle of the period the most difficult material should be introduced, never at the end when fatigue may be mounting. Another thing that Sue should do if she wishes to maximize her study effectiveness is to hit the books immediately after school rather than let several hours go by. In this way her memory of what took place in class that day is still fresh. (See chapter 49 for the psychotechniques Sue should use.)

Fred is an ambitious second-year medical student. On nights before exams he enjoys studying while lying in bed. Fred could be getting much more out of his studies if he did not use this faulty psychotechnique. He misuses his recall powers because, unknown to him, his posture influences his memory. Many studies have shown that a number of factors are involved in the recall process and one of these is called *postural status,* or *internal mood.* Subjects in an experiment learned certain material either while lying down or standing. Later they were tested. Those who were in the same position for both the learning and the testing had better recall than those who changed their postures. Fred would obtain better grades if he studied while seated, since this will be his position at test time. Studying in bed is not as effective for him as studying at his desk, unless, of course, he can persuade his professor to let him take his exams lying down. (See chapter 49 for the psychotechnique that Fred should use.)

Allen takes office files home each night. He must study them carefully to prepare a presentation for his department manager the next day. But his reports have been only fair, and he can't understand why. His nightly routine is to settle back in his favorite easy chair in the quiet of his den and wade into the reports. Allen doesn't know it but he has a faulty psychotechnique working against him.

His chair is the one he enjoys more than any other in the house. He dozes in it, drinks beer in it, reads the sports page in it. In fact, if he is not in his garden or workshop, chances are Allen can be found resting in his favorite lounger in the den.

He has developed a strong place habit for that chair and his mind has associated it with a variety of activities. He contaminates his mental set when he also tries to study there, because being in that chair generates relaxation and the pleasure of easy thinking. (See chapter 49 for the psychotechnique that Allen should use.)

These are ten examples of maladjustments to life situations caused by the use of wrong psychotechniques. Each person tries to tap his or her resourcefulness but nevertheless meets with frustrating results. In human affairs it's the rule rather than the exception that we limp through life with faulty response patterns. We learn the vast majority of these from others, most notably our family. (Chances are that in a home where parents are maladjusted, children will develop poor psychotechniques.)

So be sufficiently forewarned that a faulty psychotechnique can sneak up on you, even when you have the best of intentions to solve a problem in a rational way.

4

THE CASE FOR PSYCHOTECHNIQUES

All theories of behavior are debatable. Not so with a psycho-technique, which either works or doesn't. Psychologists often expend too much effort debating the theories behind the techniques they use. Such theoretical insights, of course, may help to further our body of psychological knowledge, as Wolpe's work (described in chapter 1) has done. However, a therapist need not know the underlying explanations for a proven psychotechnique in order for it to help his clients.

Arnold Lazarus, professor of psychology at Rutgers University in New Jersey, perhaps the most famous behavior therapist, says:

> Many therapists waste time because they are primarily interested in theorizing and when they do [theorize] they develop vested interest in strengthening and confirming that system's basic theoretical underpinnings. Almost inevitably, one's selectivity of perception comes into play, so that pet theories become blessed with all sorts of confirming "data" and substantiating "evidence." Disregarding the Guru's untestable ideas about how and why his technique proves effective, we would test it out on our clients. If it seemed to work with them, we would note that as an impeccable observation.... Yet, by borrowing and administering this technique we would in no way be subscribing to any of the Guru's unprovable tenets.

Many branches of science proceed in this way. A method comes first, then subsequently a theory that explains it. Electricity, used in countless ways, still lacks a theory that explains it; so it is with many of the psychotechniques given in this book.

14

The Need for a Self-Help Approach

It is estimated that some eighteen million people receive or are in need of mental health services in the United States. Their difficulties range from mild maladjustment to crippling psychosis. Such huge numbers of disabilities make it impossible to provide sufficient trained personnel to meet the demand. Aside from the large numbers of troubled people with serious psychological handicaps, there are millions of others who require assistance with normal, day-to-day activities—the range of problems that mainly concerns us in this book.

Dr. Gerald Rosen, who has probably done more than anyone else to evaluate and compile evidence for and against self-help techniques, believes that they are here to stay. He says, "The development of self-help behavior therapies has tremendous implications for the health professions. What is perhaps most important is that these programs may enable therapists to extend, more efficiently, professional services to a greater number of individuals. Effective programs that can be purchased in book stores and totally self-administered may eliminate the need for many individuals to consult with professionals."

Costs Are Skyrocketing

When there is a limitation on goods and services offered by any profession, it predictably affects consumer costs. For example, fees for psychotherapy in recent years have risen so sharply that they are almost out of sight of the average wage earner who needs those services. It is not uncommon for individual psychotherapy to range from forty to one hundred dollars a session, several times a week. This state of affairs has spurred many insurance carriers, who traditionally have subsidized psychiatrists, to increase their coverage for treatment by psychologists as well.*

So, as we see, a self-help behavior technology is strongly justi-

*Another direct result of high costs and scarcity of professionals is the proliferation of self-help groups, some of dubious validity. They include EST, TM, Transactional Analysis, Yoga, Mind Control, Psychocybernetics, Rolfing, Encounters, Marathons, Confrontations, Zen, Tai Chi, and others. Most are transient, but nevertheless reflect the fact that large numbers of our population seek help in gaining a more stable life style.

fied. Properly executed, it can relieve the burden borne by a limited number of mental health providers, it can reach the masses of people, and it has the advantage of being economically feasible.

This book will reveal dozens of psychotechniques that will teach you, step by step, to take charge of your life and achieve happiness; but it can't be done unless you are in the proper frame of mind. The next chapter will explain what your investment will have to be.

5

HOW TO GET THE MOST FROM THIS BOOK

Your Part in the Process of Change

This book will give you the chance to break out of your mold. But any self-guided system always requires more effort than one that involves the assistance of a professional. There are four conditions that must be met before any psychotechnique will be useful to you. You must have:

1. *Realization* that you *have* a problem.
2. *Desire* to solve that problem.
3. *Commitment* to give up undesirable responses and follow a psychotechnique until the target behavior appears. This requires that you set a goal to be achieved within a reasonable length of time.
4. *Faith* that each psychotechnique has been successfully tested either clinically or experimentally on men and women who have the problem in question.

Self-help books are often long, documented accounts on a subject in which experiments are cited, studies quoted, surveys given, statistics noted, and long case histories recorded. Before you are finally rewarded with a bit of "how-to" advice—a specific principle, technique, or explanation of your problem—there are all these preliminary statements to the main event. We're conditioned to this format when we read such a book.

Here, we ask you to have faith that there is a rationale for each psychotechnique, which means dispensing with any sort of sales talk for a specific psychotechnique. In the final analysis the best way to be sold on anything new is through your own successful experience with it, no matter how slight. So, as you begin a psychotechnique, choose one that is simple, one that you need

17

very much and that will offer the highest probability of success.*

Why Immediate Success Is Crucial

All the psychotechniques in this book have been described within an operant conditioning framework, so that success in any one of them will act as a reinforcer for subsequent new target behavior. This is a principle of learning proposed in 1938 by psychologist Edward Thorndike, called the "law of effect." It states that when a response is followed by satisfaction, it tends to be repeated. So, each degree of success you have with one of the psychotechniques in this book strengthens both the chance that you will use that psychotechnique again and the likelihood that you will learn the new behavior. The thing to keep in mind is that you are after a success experience *as soon as possible* after you start. This will create a positive motivational set and build your confidence in the rationale of this book.

A Caution

The psychotechniques offered here are not intended to rebuild your personality or, in cases of severe disturbances, to be a substitute for psychotherapy. Some symptoms may be resistant to change because of secondary gains that they afford the sufferer. Such is the case with the child who gets attention because of his nightmares or eye twitch, or the person with a fear of trains, which prevents him from traveling to an unpleasant job.

Another thing to bear in mind is that although most of the psychotechniques will be useful to individuals, some procedures will be maximally effective if two people are involved, like a parent and child or a husband and wife. Many studies have proven

*A word about psychotechniques and bibliotherapy: For some four decades, bibliotherapy (a carefully selected variety of books and printed material) has helped busy psychotherapists to help their clients make better adjustments to life problems. In the strictest sense of the term, a printed psychotechnique is a form of bibliotherapy, and, as we hope to show in this book, a collection of such psychotechniques is a valid concept in human growth.

that laymen can be trained to be therapists for their relatives or friends.

Like the Wally Stones and Nancy Millers of the world, most of us fall into a problem, struggle with it, then if we're lucky, hit upon a solution. Such is the human condition—an existence of eternal problem-solving. Yet, even though we are not formally taught to overcome psychological distress, we do haphazardly acquire a repertoire of coping techniques out of our experience, which helps us along through life. Unfortunately, many of these are faulty, as we saw in chapter 3, and may lead to more serious complications later on. For us, a hopeful adventure is offered by the many self-help books that cascade from the presses annually. (In 1976, *Books in Print* listed about seven hundred books of the "how-to" variety.) Each promises the royal route to happiness. Each advises how to get power, overcome insecurity, conquer negative thinking, be persuasive, socially attractive, or grow rich. Many are well written and highly convincing, but too often they are based on conventional notions about human psychology. After an initial burst of enthusiasm, the book is abandoned to a shelf and is forgotten. It has not become an active part of a reader's life.

This book tries to correct this state of affairs by describing psychotechniques that have *proven usefulness*—in education, medicine, psychology and psychiatry, and other fields. It is a book to be consulted over the years as problems arise that block us from happy living.

There are five key chapters in this book, chapters 6 through 10, on relaxation and fear desensitization. You should read them carefully, because they will be used with other psychotechniques in the book.

PART ONE
*For a Better
Personal Life*

6

HOW TO RELAX

Is tension in the mind or in the body? Philosophers have pondered mind-body questions like this in vain. The evidence so far indicates that tension begins with a perception (in the mind), which then affects the body. When we are worried, nervous, fearful, or angry about something, we feel the tension to be in our muscles, not in our mind. This stress can alter almost every process in the human repertoire. It can upset our hormonal balance and increase blood pressure, heart rate, metabolism, sugar consumption, and breathing rhythm.

Research on anxiety shows that it is difficult, if not impossible, to be anxious if our muscles are completely relaxed. This point alone tells the story—namely, that the state of our body influences our emotions and our mental functions as well. This gives us a *key* idea in this book: *Most every human function will improve if we are normally relaxed.*

Although relaxation techniques have existed since ancient times, it wasn't until 1910 that a young medical student, Edmund Jacobson of Chicago, first presented a concise, scientifically tested technique of relaxation. At Harvard University he reported that medical patients could be trained to control their muscles through "progressive relaxation." He taught that muscles have to "unlearn" their habit of being tense. He called this a *nerve rest* method. The logic was as follows: All muscles receive nerves that emanate from the brain and spinal cord, so when these muscles relax, their nerves also relax. This process has a regulating effect on the nervous system itself and, therefore, on our thoughts and feelings, too.

Jacobson saw dramatic relief in scores of physical disorders like high blood pressure, indigestion, heart strain, and colitis. He

23

is still alive today and his method is the first and last word in relaxation techniques.

We present it here with some refinements drawn from other sources.

Psychotechniques for Relaxation*

Step 1. Lie down in a quiet and dimly lit room. Make yourself as comfortable as possible.

Step 2. Allow your eyes to close as you slowly take a deep breath. Hold it for ten seconds. Study the tension this creates in your chest, neck, abdomen, and shoulders. Exhale slowly and relax. Imagine that the tension is leaving your body as you exhale say to yourself, "My breath flows in and out like the tides." Repeat this five or six times, then pause for twenty seconds.

Step 3. Now tense every muscle in your body for ten seconds, then let go and allow relaxation to occur. Observe the difference between your muscles when tensed and when relaxed. This is called the tension-release method. As you repeat this three times, keep your mind completely free. Just let thoughts come and go freely as they will. Don't focus on anything. Keep in mind the image of yourself lying down, relaxing more and more. Tell youself that if you hear sounds they won't disturb you. At this point, you should be somewhat relaxed.

Step 4. Now imagine as vividly as you can a warm, soothing feeling entering your toes. Feel it moving through the bones, muscles, and ligaments of your feet. It will soon make its way through your body to the top of your head. Imagine the feeling penetrating deep into your feet, then passing through your ankles into the calves of your legs. Keep repeating to yourself, "Calm, relax, let go."

Step 5. Imagine the feeling moving up through your ankles into your thighs, relaxing you as it goes, relaxing all parts of your thighs. Next, imagine it moving up through your groin, buttocks,

---

*This is the single most important chapter in this book since muscle tension exists in every problem that we describe. Simply learn to relax and you will derive maximum benefits from the psychotechniques you choose.

This relaxation procedure can be tape recorded word for word by yourself or someone else and played over and over again. Try to use a subdued, monotone voice.

and lower abdomen—relaxing all muscles, tendons, and so on. Remember, there is nothing to think about except to relax. Again, try to get the image of yourself lying there, relaxing, letting go.

Imagine the sensation moving up through your abdomen and lower back. Feel the muscles letting go, deeper and deeper. Feel the tension leaving your body. Imagine your visceral organs relaxing—the liver, kidneys, spleen, intestines, stomach. Next, the feeling moves up into your upper chest and back. Your heart and lungs are working smoothly. You feel calm and serene.

The feeling continues up into your neck and shoulders. Imagine the relaxation going down each arm to the fingertips. Just let go. No tension. Deeper and deeper, relaxed. Next, the feeling continues up, deep into your throat. Feel your tongue and mouth relaxing. Separate your jaws and relax your jaw muscles. Let your mouth hang open somewhat. Tell yourself, "Let go."

Then the feeling moves into your facial muscles. Feel the tension leaving the tiny muscles around your lips, chin, cheeks, nose. Next, the soothing sensation moves into your eyelids, eyeballs, eye muscles, and eyebrows. Feel your eyes letting go, floating freely, without tension. The feeling moves into your forehead and then your scalp, down the back of your head. Keep letting go. Finally, the feeling penetrates deep into your brain. There is a soothing, relaxing peace, with nothing to think about. Your brain is calm and serene. The only image you have is of yourself lying there, completely relaxed.

Now feel your entire body loose and tension-free—every blood vessel, tendon, nerve, ligament, membrane, gland, and muscle—as if you were a rag doll. Enjoy the relaxation, the calm. Pause for about twenty seconds.

Step 6. Now count to yourself from one to ten and suggest that your muscles will let go even further as you approach ten. Remember, *whatever it is that you seem to be doing to relax, continue it far past the point where your body feels relaxed.*

Step 7. Before you get up, you must bring yourself to an alert state of mind. Do the following: Begin counting slowly to twenty and when you reach fifteen, begin counting aloud. Say to yourself that when you reach twenty your eyes will open, you will be alert and refreshed. All parts of your body will be relaxed and normal.

This relaxation process should take about fifteen minutes. Don't rush it. Repeat it at least three times each day. It can even be practiced in a sitting position while traveling on a bus or train. Most people improve dramatically in just a few sessions. In time, you may speed up the process until you achieve complete relaxation in three or four minutes.

7

DEALING WITH FEAR

Poet Ralph Waldo Emerson once remarked that fear always springs from ignorance. Unfortunately, modern psychiatry has only recently begun to replace ignorance with knowledge as an antidote to our fears. In the past, it probed the unconscious in vain for answers to phobias and often wasted the time of the analyst and the money of the analysand. But within the last fifteen years we have discovered that the more we know about how fears are formed and unformed, the better are our chances for conquering them.

We now know that fears often begin as minor disturbances, and if allowed to continue and become reinforced, they develop into full-blown phobias. For years, simple intuitive wisdom advised that minor fears were to be dealt with head-on, when they were first noticed.

In horsemanship, for example, this logic was applied to both the fears of horses and of those who rode them. Riders who fell at the jump, no matter how shaken, were urged to remount quickly and jump again, albeit over a lower hurdle. This bit of folk wisdom was based on solid psychological principles: To remount immediately and jump again did not permit either the horse or rider to incubate and reinforce the fear of jumping.

Research on the subject of dealing with fears boils down to three basic psychotechniques:

1. Image desensitization, in which you imagine scenes that relate to the feared object and then finally face that object in imagination.
2. In-life desensitization, in which you actually move step by step toward the feared object and ultimately confront it.
3. Image/in-life desensitization, which is a combination of both the above.

Image/in-life desensitization is by far the best of the three methods, but sometimes it is not convenient for us to face our feared object in real life. (If you had a fear of spiders, you'd have to hunt down the elusive insect and then confront it, or if you were afraid of thunder, you might have to wait for a storm.) Image desensitization eliminates these obstacles because we can fashion our own scenes with whatever intensity, duration, and complexity we may desire.

In the next three chapters we will present each of these three methods for overcoming fears. We suggest you start with the first one; if it doesn't work for you, go on to the others. But before you begin the psychotechniques themselves you must first plan a strategy:

1. *Study your fear for a week.* Try to understand why and under what circumstances it comes on. Is it around certain people? At certain times of the day? In certain settings?

2. *Try to narrow down your fear as much as possible.* Don't think of it in general terms. For example, what you consider a fear of the outdoors may really be a fear of shopping in department stores. Or what you think is a fear of flying may in reality be a fear of enclosed places, of heights, of loud noises, or of being strapped down. A fear of doctors may be, rather, a fear of blood, pain, authority, or learning that one has a serious disease. One of the main reasons a psychotechnique may fail to cure a fear is that the focus is on the wrong fear. It is essential that you pinpoint your exact fear before you launch a self-desensitization program.

3. *Make a list of your fears from least to most frightening.* It is always better to desensitize simple fears before attempting complex ones. Thus, if you have a fear of airplanes and one of escalators, conquer the escalator fear first, then go on to planes.

4. *Construct a fear hierarchy.* Pick a fear, then jot down on a pad a real situation concerning the fear that causes you the *most* anxiety. With a fear of birds, for example, in a real situation you might be holding a pigeon or having a parakeet land on your shoulder. Next, write down a related situation that causes you the *least* anxiety; for example, seeing a bird high in the sky. Now generate a series of situations that fall between these two extremes, and rate each on a scale from 1 to 10 (1 being zero anxiety and 10 being sheer terror).

5. *If in doubt, rate your anxiety high.* An important point about constructing your fear hierarchy is that, if you're not sure how anxious a situation might make you feel, it is better to rate it higher rather than lower on the scale.

6. *Prepare positive self-talk statements.* We all talk to ourselves. Our thoughts influence our feelings and actions. When we face something we fear, such as making a complaint in a store, we may be victimized by our own inner speech. For example, it has been found that people self-talk at such times and say things like: "I won't be able to convince the manager," "He will surely outtalk me," or "I won't recall all the things I'd like to complain about." It will help you to face your fears if you prepare some positive and supportive self-statements to accompany your fear situations. In the above situation, for example, you might use positive self-talk like: "I will be calm and relaxed," "I will line up all my arguments and firmly present them," "The manager is human, too. He wants my business," "He hears insincere people sometimes, but I'm not one of them. I've got to make him recognize that." Jot down one or two such statements for each fear situation. For example, Mary, who is preparing to conquer her fear of dogs (see the example on page 33), could write: "I see a dog in the distance," "The dog seems neutral," "People near that dog are calm," "Why shouldn't I feel the same?" "I'll keep relaxed as I approach him."

7. *Relax.* Finally, when you go through each situation remember to breathe easily and deeply. Stay relaxed and repeat cue words like "calm," "easy," "peaceful." After you've made these preparations you are ready to try one of the three psychotechniques for overcoming fears.

8

HOW TO DESENSITIZE FEAR USING IMAGES

For years, Lisa feared the water. At beach parties, she sat on the hot sand and watched longingly while others frolicked in the surf. Now swimming delights her and she even takes frequent canoe trips.

Socially, Bob isn't exactly a "shrinking violet," but he did have a problem that bothered him for years. He used to freeze up when he phoned girls for dates. He always felt they would reject him. Now he calls them without hesitation. Last month he made a date (by phone) with a campus beauty for his senior prom.

It wasn't by magic that these persons overcame their particular phobias. It was through image desensitization. This method reprograms negative learning experiences that leave us with a variety of symptoms like anxiety, shyness, and insecurity. It bypasses lengthy psychotherapy and psychoanalysis and its cures last just about as long. One follow-up study of a group of seventy-eight desensitized patients of Dr. Arnold Lazarus, two years after their treatment, showed that 95 percent remained cured of their fears or were greatly improved.

Lisa and Bob overcame their difficulties by consulting a skilled professional. But it's been proven that almost anyone, if given guidance, can desensitize himself to some degree without the aid of a doctor. Here is a two-step technique I call *consolidated desensitization*. (Read it carefully. It will be an important part of other self-help methods in this book.) The technique is a refinement of psychiatrist Dr. Joseph Wolpe's pioneering work in the 1950s, and if you follow it exactly, you will reap benefits from it. Over the past ten years, I have taught it with good results to hundreds of patients.

Many of our fears are based on faulty learning, so it will help first to know a bit about learning theory.

Learning always involves associations. For example, we learn to associate a pencil with writing, soap with washing, smoke with fire, and so forth. A fear is a learned association, too. It is an emotional reaction learned either directly through our own experience or through the behavior of others. If we fear entering an elevator, it means that somehow we've learned to associate elevators with a state of uneasiness (fear). The goal of desensitization is to substitute another bodily feeling for the fear. The one most often chosen by behavior therapists is relaxation. It's called a *reciprocal inhibitor,* because it replaces and inhibits the feeling of fear.

In desensitizing a fear of elevators, we must eventually take repeated rides and, at the same time, be relaxed and not fearful. This in-life desensitization is an excellent method, but is often too time consuming.

Another way to desensitize is with the imagination. A relaxed patient *imagines* a ride in an elevator and the results are satisfactory, though not as good as if he really were there.

So much for theory; now to use image-desensitization on yourself. Here are the two steps to follow:

1. Follow chapter 6 on relaxation and become completely relaxed.

2. Imagine your fear situation.

The thing to keep in mind in this second step is that you must desensitize yourself to the exact phobic stimulus and not just a superficial one. For example, you may fear riding in trains, but what you actually fear is closed places. Or your phobia for swimming may really be a fear of suffocating. Getting to this basic fear is perhaps the hardest part of the whole process. To help you to do this, follow steps 1 through 7, starting on page 28.

Once you have pinpointed your fear, picture yourself gradually approaching your phobic stimulus. Do not picture watching yourself in the scene. Rather, imagine actually *being* there. Don't rush; go very slowly, step by step. For example, if you fear a job interview or asking for a raise, begin by seeing yourself awakening, eating breakfast, preparing to leave your home, then walking to the bus stop, riding on the bus, arriving at the office, and so on.

Imagine the entire sequence of actions that lead up to and finally culminate in the "end point"; that is (using our examples), successfully completing the interview or asking for the raise. Visualize each scene as vividly as possible, through all your senses—hearing, smell, touch, taste, and sight. See yourself composed and confident, giving the right answers to questions. The main thing is to be tension-free throughout the imagery sequences. Bear in mind that tense muscles pave the way for fear, but relaxed muscles are incompatible with it and will not permit it to occur.

Should you suddenly tense up, you must again relax, then backtrack to images that did not cause tension. Follow through until you finally get through the situation to the end point and feel reasonably satisfied with the results. Now you are ready to face your fear situation in real life.

It's best to desensitize your simplest fears first, then go on to stronger ones. For maximum effectiveness, repeat this desensitization exercise as often as possible up to the time when you face your phobic situation. You should gain at least partial relief at first, but as in all new learning, with practice you will improve.

9

HOW TO DESENSITIZE FEAR THROUGH ACTIONS

A second method of desensitizing yourself is to actually face your fear object. If you recall, when you applied image desensitization (chapter 8) using only your imagination, you went from the least upsetting scene to the final scene—the end point (the phobic stimulus itself). All desensitization must take place gradually, and action-desensitization requires the same approach only you are to do it "live." To give you a quick feeling for what you must do, here is an example to follow and apply to yourself:

Mary was a young housewife and a competent mother of two small children. She had a phobia for dogs. Each time she saw one, she trembled and hurried herself and the children away. It had become so bad that the children were now almost as frightened as she was.

Mary's program went as follows: First, she was given this list of situations:

1. Look at a dog for at least one minute from a distance of fifty yards.
2. Look at a dog for at least one minute from a distance of thirty yards.
3. Take one step toward a dog from thirty yards.
4. Take one step toward a dog on a leash from twenty yards.
5. Take two steps toward a dog on a leash from twenty yards.
6. Take five steps toward a dog on a leash from twenty yards.
7. Take one step toward a dog on a leash from fifteen yards.
8. Take three steps toward a dog on a leash from fifteen yards.
9. Take one step toward a leashed dog at ten yards.
10. Take two steps toward a leashed dog at ten yards.

11. After you've spoken to its owner, call the dog by name at ten yards.*

12. Walk to within five yards of a leashed dog.

13. Speak gently to the dog at five yards for a full minute.

14. Bend over and softly speak to the dog at three yards.

15. With the owner's permission, allow the dog to sniff you.

16. Extend your hand and let the dog sniff you.

17. (Target) pet the dog.

Mary was then told the following:

Use the relaxation psychotechnique (chapter 6). When you are relaxed go to a park where people walk their dogs, and enter the first situation. If you feel no appreciable change in your tension level, take a one-minute break, then proceed to step 2. If you get through step 2 without noticing any difference in your tension, go on to step 3, and so on. Work through the list slowly with a few situations each day until you finally accomplish step 17.

Remember, through the entire procedure breathe easily and deeply. Use positive self-talk (see page 29). Should you feel tension building, stop immediately and go back to the previous situation in which you were relatively tension-free, or return tomorrow and resume from this point.

Each day, prepare yourself by becoming completely relaxed before you go to the park.

Now with the example of Mary in mind, follow these steps in using the action desensitization psychotechnique for yourself. In brief:

1. Make a list of situations related to your fear. This was step 4 in chapter 7.

2. As Mary did, try situation 1. If you feel tension as you proceed through your list, go back and face a less threatening situation and try that.

3. If you find no rise in your tension level for a situation, go onto the next one.

4. Take a few situations each day, gradually working up through the last situation (your end point, or target).

---

*For steps 11 through 17, Mary was told to explain to an acquaintance who had a friendly dog what she was doing and to ask his help.

5. Remember to keep the situations simple and move toward your end point in small steps.*

Here are some sample in-life hierarchies to use or to help you construct your own.‡

Fear Situation Hierarchy for a Fear of Heights

1. Stand on a chair.
2. Stand at the top of a short flight of stairs for one minute.
3. Stand at the top of a long flight of stairs for one minute.
4. Look out a second-story window for half a minute.
5. Look out a second-story window for two minutes.
6. Look out a third-floor window for half a minute.
7. Look out a sixth-floor window for one minute.
8. Look out a tenth-floor window for two minutes.
9. Look out a fifteenth-floor window for two minutes.
10. Look out an eighteenth-floor window for three minutes.
11. (Target) take the elevator to the top of a high building (twenty to thirty stories) and look out a window for a full five minutes.

Fear Situation Hierarchy for Driving a Car

1. Sit in the back seat of a car, motor off, for five minutes.
2. Sit in the passenger seat of a car, motor off, for five minutes.
3. Sit in the driver's seat of a car, motor off, for five minutes.
4. Start the motor, then after ten seconds turn it off.
5. Run the motor for a full minute.
6. Run the motor for a full five minutes.

---

*We are more likely to succeed if we take a small step rather than a giant one. It is theoretically possible to diminish the size of each step to such a small increment that it becomes virtually "painless" to take that step. By doing so we increase our confidence in accomplishing our goal.

‡Rates of desensitization differ from one person to another, so that several steps in any hierarchy may be skipped if you feel strong enough to do so. On the other hand, additional steps may be interspersed between the ones you have listed to make an even more gradual approach to the end point (target behavior).

7. Put the car in gear and move only a few feet forward, then turn the engine off.

8. Move the car two full car lengths, then stop and apply the hand brake; idle the car for a full five minutes.

9. Move the car a quarter block, then idle the engine for five minutes.

10. Move the car a half block, then park.

11. Circle the block once, then park.

12. Circle the block for a full ten minutes.

13. Drive somewhere and back for a full fifteen minutes.

14. (Target) Drive to a shopping area not more than fifteen minutes away. Shop. Return home.

Note: when you begin to actually move the car, do so in light traffic. Each of these steps can be carried out with a friend in the car, with the exception of step 14, which must be done alone.

10

HOW TO DESENSITIZE FEAR USING
IMAGES AND ACTIONS

To demonstrate this third basic psychotechnique we will use the fear of flying. It is one of the most common fears and afflicts some ten to twenty million Americans.

Psychotechniques for Overcoming a Fear of Flying

Step 1. Relax completely (use chapter 6).

Step 2. While relaxed, look through books and pamphlets that contain airplane pictures and stories.* If you become tense or afraid, set the material aside until you are once again relaxed. Then resume.

Step 3. Avoid conversation about flying with people who still fear airplanes.

Step 4. Talk with people who have conquered their fear of flying. Try to learn as much as possible about the things that seemed to help them.

Step 5. If you have other, simpler fears, such as fears of elevators, bridges, tunnels, try to conquer or reduce them first. They usually are related to your main problem.

Step 6. Plan a short visit to a high building. But before you leave, review chapter 8 on image desensitization. This means relaxing and then imagining all the scenes that you would go through to reach the end point of looking out an upper-story window. Your scenes might go like this: leaving your home, rid-

*Some of these can be obtained free by writing to the consumer relations department of various airlines. Request any booklets they may have on overcoming flight anxiety and on safety features of airplanes. Read accident statistics that compare land, air, and sea travel (you will learn that mile for mile, air travel is by far the safest way to go).

ing a car, bus, or train to the high building; seeing the building from afar, entering, walking toward the elevator, and so on. In your last scene you should be looking out of an upper-story window of the building.

If all goes well with the imagery, then actually visit a tall building. Imagine that this is how it might be from up in an airplane. You'll probably feel some degree of tension, so don't try to brainwash yourself into not admitting your fear. Relax as much as possible. Focus on your muscles and try to strive for the feeling of letting go.

Step 7. If you've succeeded so far, you are now ready for a visit to an airport, preferably with a companion. An hour or so before you leave, go through the imagery desensitization again. Your imagery should consist of scenes that gradually lead up to your arrival at the airport. Vividly imagine the sights, sounds, and smells you'll encounter when you are there.

Step 8. Plan an enjoyable experience at the airport. Calmly soak up the atmosphere. Walk around, look at the planes, converse with airline personnel, have lunch or a soda there, or make a phone call to a friend. Make it a brief visit. If your anxiety becomes intolerable, leave promptly, but repeat this step another day.

Step 9. If your eventual goal is to take a long plane flight, at this point don't plunge right into a transatlantic hop. Instead, take a short trip, again preferably with someone you know. A few hours before you leave, once again go through image desensitization, and for your imagery scenes, see yourself going through the entire process of leaving and returning. During the trip, which ideally should last one hour or less, focus on your muscles and relax. Eat and drink lightly before and during the flight.

Step 10. If you begin to tense up when you're in the air, *don't* look out the window. Focus on the inside of the plane. Remember to relax your muscles.

Most of us learn better if we receive rewards along the way. So after you succeed in each step, give yourself something—a movie, a small gift, dinner out, or whatever pleases you. The most important point in self-desensitization is to substitute relaxation for anxiety. This deconditioning is always done gradually. In brief:

1. First pick your end point (fear target).

2. Plan ahead of time how to approach your feared object in a step-by-step fashion, using pictures, talks with friends, visits to the vicinity of the fear situation, and so forth.

3. Before you enter a life situation, take a few minutes to rehearse it by using imagination, as discussed in chapter 8.

4. Remember, take gradual steps toward the end point. No step can be too little. Don't worry if you feel some tension.

5. If you feel anxiety, stop immediately and pick up at that point on another day.

Most people who follow these psychotechniques will achieve some degree of success. By the way, if you fear flying and if you felt comfortable and at ease while going through this chapter, you've already started the process of desensitization.

So far we've been talking about psychotechniques that prepare you to meet the fear situation. But, you might ask, what do I do if I suddenly find myself confronted by the feared object or situation? Here are six psychotechniques you can use. They were devised by Dr. Manuel Zane of the White Plains Hospital in New York, who has used them for many years with success. He calls his method *contextual therapy.*

Step 1. *Expect and allow your fear to come.* Your real fear experiences, and even more so the ones you've imagined, have made you extraordinarily sensitive to the phobic situation, so automatically you must react with fear to even the slightest contact. If you expect that fear will come, you are much less likely to become seriously upset when it appears.

If you can allow your fear to come, you can learn ways to deal with it. If you fight the fear, then you become sensitized, your fear is more likely to spiral, and your phobia gets worse.

So reset your goal: Instead of trying to block the fear, resolve to try to deal with it. As you learn to stay in the phobic situation, you'll discover new points of security. These will reduce your sensitivity.

Step 2. *When fear comes, stop, wait, let it be.* Sometimes you only feel uneasy in the phobic situation. At other times you may feel a sudden jolt of fear.

Regardless of the intensity of the feeling, you will manage

better if you can learn to wait. When you get the feeling, remind yourself that you've just had your automatic reaction of fear and that nothing terrible has actually happened. You dread what you imagine *might* happen in the future. If you can just wait, the fear will pass.

Usually, even the slightest anxiety acts as a signal for your body and mind to start racing and reacting to the limitless danger you anticipate.

Try to ignore the signal and concentrate on just waiting. When you learn to do this, you will be able to change your thinking and the spiraling process will stop. It may sound impossible now, but in time, with practice, you will find that it works.

Step 3. *Label your fear from zero to ten. Be aware that the level changes.* You will be less overwhelmed and in better control if you learn to recognize the levels of the fear you're experiencing. You can do this by using a scale from zero to ten. Zero means you feel no fear. Ten means your fear is so intense that it's hardly bearable. As you estimate your fear level, you will find that it usually goes up and down, up and down, in relation to what you are thinking and doing. As you observe what is happening, you automatically will stop thinking and imagining the worst and your spiraling will stop. You also will feel less afraid of your own fear and less alone with your inner experience.

Step 4. *Focus on the present and do familiar tasks.* In the phobic situation, try to focus on real things in the present that are comforting. You'll have to experiment to see what works best for you. Look around you; consider the details of faces, clothes, furnishings, or the landscape that you see. Feel the textures of surfaces near you. Listen and try to comprehend what you hear. Cook, clean, work, read, write, sing, hum, count, talk, eat, walk. Do anything that you find will keep you connected to the real world—whatever is comforting and prevents you from being pulled into the world of unrealistic phobic thoughts and imagery that is terrifying.

Move slowly and deliberately or, if you wish, quickly and purposefully. Take a deep breath and let it out slowly to a count of five. Practice tightening, then relaxing, different parts of your body. Talk to someone. Talk to yourself. While you are involved in doing such familiar, manageable things, your fear may rise but it cannot spiral. Spiraling fear occurs and speeds up as your attention and involvement shifts more and more from the real world into the private world created by your unrealistic thoughts and imagery. Then what's in your mind feels more real and affects you more strongly than the reality. To reiterate: Your fear will not spiral if you do familiar, manageable things in the present.

Instead of believing only that getting home or running out will help you, learn that your recovery from panic and fear can come through simple, familiar acts right where you are.

An activity that puts you back in touch with what you know can restore your ability to rely on your body and your mind.

Step 5. *Do things* while *you are feeling fear.* It is a very real accomplishment to be able to perform tasks while you are feeling fear. As you become more comfortable with the feelings of fear, you will be controlling your automatic reactions to them and reducing your phobic sensitivity. As you learn to function in the presence of fear, you learn by your own experience that these feelings do not have to lead to the terrifying, spiraling state. You begin to engage in activities that seemed impossible before.

And finally, step 6, *expect and allow your fear to reappear.* If you work at this program, you will probably begin to see results. Enjoy your successes, but try not to become overconfident or feel that you have it licked, because setbacks are inevitable with progress. If you are not prepared for the setbacks, they can leave you upset, demoralized, and depressed. You must gain enough good experiences, through practice, to sustain you when things get difficult.

The path may be rocky but there is a way.

11

HOW TO RELAX THROUGH MEDITATION

We're all victims of stress. The harried housewife, the pressured student, or the ambitious salesman knows that the burden of everyday responsibility can drain our vitality for happy living. All too often, when stress hits we don't know how to handle it. We fail at work, get into family fights, and fall behind at school. Or we handle the pressure by leaning on crutches such as overeating or cigarettes, alcohol, and other drugs, to bring us peace of mind.

But a different way to help gain a measure of control over our mental state is with meditation, a technique that can be learned in a few minutes. It has brought peace to thousands under stress and it has given relief to those with mental and physical problems like migraine headaches, tension states, anxiety, low back pain, arthritis, heart irregularities, asthma—all conditions that call for sensible living and a minimum of excitement.

Meditation has been especially successful for people suffering from high blood pressure. Dr. Herbert Benson of the Harvard Medical School taught a group of thirty-six volunteers to meditate. After several weeks, their blood pressure dropped from 146/93.5 to 137/88.9. This means that they went from a borderline high measurement down to the normal range. When several subjects stopped meditating, their blood pressure shot up again within a month to their previously high levels.

Meditation is not something mystical, even if for many Americans it conjures up visions of a sacred Far Eastern philosophy, communing with the universe, and thinking profound cosmic thoughts.

The recent popularity of Transcendental Meditation might have added to the muddle. It holds, for example, that one should not divulge one's mantra (a word repeated during meditation exercises) to anyone, lest it lose its "power." It holds that the one mantra, *Om* is supposed to be the supreme mystical syllable, whatever that means. Don't let any of this confuse you. The term *meditation* itself is a confusing misnomer. By definition, the word means "a turning or revolving of a subject in the mind; a continuous thought; contemplation."* But these definitions are the opposite of what the process really is; namely, a technique for keeping the mind entirely thought-free.

Until ten years ago, meditation was relatively ignored by mental health workers, but today many clinicians are teaching it to their clients. You can learn to use it, too, by following these simple instructions.

Psychotechnique of Meditation

1. Sit in a comfortable chair in a quiet room where you will not be disturbed. Use the instructions in chapter 6 to help you relax.

2. After you are relaxed, and with your eyes closed, begin to take slow, deep breaths through your nose, filling your lungs entirely. Each time you exhale completely, repeat a pacifier word to yourself. Dr. Benson uses the word *one,* but I have found it more effective to use a pacifier that is more meaningfully related to what you are trying to do to your mind. Good pacifier words are: *blank, calm, open, peace,* and *clear.* When you say your pacifier, it will be especially helpful to visualize the word itself dropping like a leaf through your entire body all the way down to your toes.

3. Continue to inhale deeply and slowly. Then exhale and simultaneously repeat your pacifier to yourself. The object is not to allow any ideas to form in your mind. Do not work mentally at anything whatever. Just let your mind unwind and *let thoughts and images come and go like lazy rudderless sailboats in a silent breeze. If thoughts beckon and try to form, don't cooperate!*

Continue this type of breathing for fifteen minutes. When you finish, sit quietly for a few moments and then slowly open your eyes. That's it. Nothing else is required.

*Funk and Wagnalls Dictionary, 1963 international ed.

If you look at yourself in a mirror, you won't see anything visibly changed. Don't be dismayed. You can be fairly sure that measurable changes are occurring inside your body, in your internal organs, which are having beneficial effects on you.

After meditating, most people feel peacefully slowed down and enjoy an unmatched tranquility. Many use it to get back to sleep after they've awakened during the night. Repeat the meditation exercise three times daily.

Some Pointers

1. A favorite time and place to meditate is on the way home on a bus or train.

2. Don't meditate after you eat.

3. Try to be consistent about the time and place for your meditation.

4. Don't give yourself suggestions of ideas, attitudes, or feelings while meditating.

5. After a few sessions, you may wish to take your pulse and heart rate before you meditate. Afterwards, take them again. Record these changes on a graph each day to chart your progress. *Don't* expect miracles. *Do* expect steady progress in achieving mental relaxation with each session.

12

HOW TO UNWIND THROUGH IMAGERY

There is another method, aside from meditation, that can help you to unwind from the rigors of everyday stress. It involves imagery. Here are two imagery exercises composed by psychiatrist Richard Shames and psychologist Chuck Sterin of the Holistic Health and Nutrition Institute of Mill Valley, California. The exercises have been used successfully with hypnotic subjects and are so beautiful that I include them here. Use them after you have become relaxed in order to implant wholesome thoughts and feelings in your mind. Hypnosis is not necessary.

The Rose Process

Imagine a rose. You see before you a perfect flower, a thing of great beauty with a delicate fragrance. For a while you simply enjoy its utter perfection. Then you imagine the flower having a special magnetic quality. It begins to gather to itself all the negativity, all the problems and difficulties that have been intruding on your consciousness. You feel yourself becoming cleansed and purified as the rose continues to take into itself all your bad feelings. At this point you can imagine one of two things: Either the rose remains unsullied, absorbing and transforming the negativity into its own purity, or, instead, it finally explodes and all the tribulations disappear in the explosion. Imagine whichever feels more comfortable to you.

The Water-Level Process

Imagine a series of scattered streams tumbling down a hillside. This might include a lofty waterfall and some churning, agitated cataracts. You follow the scattered, agitated energy of the water until it finally empties into a supremely quiet, tranquil pool or lake. The water has reached its level and now has no more need to rush and roar about. You remind yourself, while contemplating the tranquility of the deep pool, that all of us sometimes go along like the water, passing through periods of seething, stormy discontent. And then you see those periods merging into the peacefulness of the undisturbed pool. You are moving toward rest, toward inner peace. Or, you can see the problems in your life as ripples on the surface of the pool. Get in touch with just how deep the pool is, and what a large part of it remains undisturbed by the surface agitation.

13

HOW TO STRENGTHEN YOUR MEMORY

Memory is the butt of many jokes. There was the husband who claimed his wife had the world's worst memory because she remembered everything. Or the man who knew he couldn't remember three things: names, faces, and the third one he never could recall. Also, it has been said that people tie knots in strings around their fingers to remember and nooses around their necks to forget. But despite the joke, you'd best take your memory seriously, for it could mean the difference between success and failure in all phases of your life.

Our human memory is one of our most precious possessions, but are we using it to full capacity to bring about happiness? It is estimated that about 75 percent of all experiments in psychology involve learning and memory, and out of a vast amount of research come techniques that can be applied to using these abilities more effectively.

French philosopher-scientist René Descartes once likened the human mind to a room. If it is in disarray, chances are we will have difficulty remembering well; but if it is in good order, we'll recollect things more easily. It is a fallacy to believe that memory is like a muscle that can be strengthened with exercise. This was once a well-respected viewpoint, and psychologist William James set out to test it. He spent twenty minutes each day for thirty-eight days in rigorous memorizing drills, taking what he believed were "memory exercises." At the end of this time, he concluded that his memory was even poorer than it was before he started. Many other studies have shown that mental exercise does *not* improve memory.

What of the numerous memory systems that are for sale to us through courses and books? Not all are frauds. Many are genuine aids to our memory functions, but they do not increase our recall capacity itself. Instead, they only teach us methods for best using what we have. The fact is that we cannot improve memory. Rather, we can *learn* something better than we did in the past, and thereby increase the probability that we'll remember more of it.

Most of the time when our memory fails it means we have interfered with it in some way. Our brain can literally become clouded by information. We can actually decrease our memory from one situation to another if we are not careful. Take the example of Jim. He is an accountant in an insurance company. He receives highly detailed work assignments at meetings several times each week. Immediately after each meeting he goes to lunch with his friends. This reduces his capacity to recall much of what he learned, through a process known as *retroactive inhibition*. This means that new learning (what he hears his friends say) interferes with his past learning (the work data).

Another way we inhibit or interfere with our previous learning is by going from one task to a similar one, such as from a Spanish class to an Italian class. This is an example of *proactive inhibition,* in which previously learned material interferes with that which is learned subsequently.

Still another memory interference occurs by going from a speedy task suddenly to one that requires a very slow pace, without the benefit of a middle period in which to gradually slow down.

We forget about 70 percent of what we learn just a few hours after we've learned it. So the curve of forgetting has a sharp decline immediately after the learning session. This means: Do not interfere with your new learning immediately after your study session by making some of the above mistakes.

Psychotechniques to Improve Your Memory

Mnemonics. These are memory devices or systems that help us to remember. Until thirty or forty years ago, they were looked down upon by educators and psychologists. But since then they have proven worthwhile. Whether you know it or not, you probably use dozens of them in your daily living. One of the more common ones reminds us in which direction to set our clocks for either daylight or standard time. It is "spring ahead, and fall behind." Another, which every high-school student learns, is ROY G BIV. It comprises the first letter of each word for the colors in the spectrum (red, orange, yellow, green, blue, indigo, violet). The PQRST method for studying under pressure (chapter 48) is a mnemonic.

Other mnemonics are more elaborate, like the phrase, "King Philip came over from Germany stoned," to help students of zoology recall the classification of organisms (kingdom, phylum, class, order, genus, and species). Or, "My very educated mother just saved us nine pizzas," to help us recall planets in their order (Mercury, Venus, Earth, Mars, Jupiter, Saturn, Uranus, Neptune, and Pluto).

Form mnemonics whenever you can, about most anything. They are tricks to help you remember facts that might otherwise go unremembered.

I have used the following mnemonic device to help me easily recall a person's face. I study the face very carefully, then I force myself to make an association with a face I already know, even if there is only a remote resemblance. I jot down a note, like "Sandy Smith reminds me of Aunt Rose, only with blue eyes instead of brown, and a bit shorter." When I try to recall the face, even months later, I concentrate on an image of my look-alike (Aunt Rose in this case), and most of the time the image of the person pops into my mind. Some people carry a timer or even a large object like a spoon or wad of paper in their pocket to remind them to stir the stew on the kitchen stove every twenty minutes, make that important phone call at a certain time, take a pill, or put another dime in the parking meter. And every repairman knows that he can test all the keys of a typewriter with "The quick brown fox jumps over a lazy dog," since this sentence contains every letter.

When Ken wants to cool off a beer in a hurry, he puts it into the freezer, then he places an object (a broom, pillow, or newspaper) right on the kitchen floor or on the table to remind him to take the beer out later.

There are countless mnemonics we can invent. Did you ever wake up in the middle of the night to recall something you absolutely had to do next day, like a letter you had to write? If you were too sleepy to turn on the light and jot down the chore, perhaps you simply reversed a button on your pajamas to bring the chore to mind in the morning. A variation is to reach down and toss a shoe or slipper a few feet from the bed. It will also help you recall the chore next morning if you form a strong image of yourself doing the task in question as you touch the button or toss the slipper.

Mnemonics are strongly aided by visualization, so whenever you can, try to form an image of what you wish to recall.

Dr. Robert Sommers, professor of psychology at the University of California at Davis, praises Harry Lorayne's notion of "picturable equivalents." Although Lorayne is a layman with no formal research background in memory, his system does work. One of his central notions is to transform ideas, names, numbers, and so forth into "picturable equivalents," and then link them together into what he calls "ridiculous associations". When you are introduced to someone, immediately try to look for a picturable equivalent; thus, "Mr. Paulson" is seen as a bearded religious figure of the first century, wearing a long robe and standing next to a boy (St. Paul and "son").

Many mnemonists believe that all thinking is based on visualization. Aristotle, centuries ago, was one of the first to say that all ideas involve mental pictures or images.

Some Basic Rules for Improving Your Memory

1. To remember something, the first thing to do is to pay strict attention to it. Tell yourself, "If I focus on this material I reduce the chance of forgetting it later." Keep your eyes and ears alert and sharply focused. Pretend that the material exists only for you, that it is the only thing within your field of awareness and nothing else matters. Think of yourself as a picture of concentration and absorption in your task. If you perceive yourself this way, it will help you to actually zero in on your target.

2. *Have the right mental set.* Tell yourself that you wish to *remember* what you are paying attention to. A good way to do this is to set a meaningful goal for yourself. See yourself in an actual situation using the new learning. Try to regard what you

learn as helpful or useful to you or to someone you love in some way in the future. For example, information on nutrition, child care, or recreation may be seen as useful later on in your life. The mere attempt to be strongly intent on remembering something will definitely help you to retain what you learn.

This mental set will improve your performance in other areas as well, such as being a better conversationalist, being patient, or being more accurate. In one study, students were told to read as fast as they could yet still understand what they read, and it was found they increased their reading speed by an average of 70 percent, with their comprehension remaining constant. A positive mental set can benefit almost any activity and this rule applies to any problem discussed in this book.

3. React actively to whatever it is you are trying to remember. Examine, listen closely, question, challenge, think about it, make connections with other things you know. See tie-ins with the familiar. Keep in mind that curiosity kills only cats. If you make remembering an active process it will help you enormously when you study something.

The mind does not wait passively to absorb knowledge as dry earth waits to receive water. Rather, knowledge must be kicked around like a football—pursued, and finally caught and embraced before it is truly understood.

4. Review or repeat what you have learned to keep it from going stale.* One of the best ways to do this is by active recitation, a proven method for remembering. It involves the "80–20" rule. If you have four hours to memorize something, you will remember it better if you spend three hours (80 percent) reciting the material aloud to yourself or to someone, and only one hour (20 percent) studying or reviewing the material by yourself, rather than simply by studying it for the four hours. One reason recitation is a better method than studying or reviewing in itself is that we remember more when we are actively learning.

Repetition is a rule in all learning. When Albert Schweitzer went to Lambaréné, Africa, to set up his tiny medical unit, he was concerned that the Congolese would not properly take the medicine he administered, because they could not read. So he would

*Asterisked rules have been suggested by psychologists Donald and Eleanor Laird of Colgate University.

carefully explain how to take a drug; than a patient, before he left the hut, was asked to repeat the instructions ten times. Not only was Schweitzer impressing them with the instructions by having his patients repeat them ten times, but they learned the instructions because they were actively involved in the learning process (step 3 above).

5. Focus on the *meanings* of the things you wish to remember.* It is said that scientist Charles Kettering had such poor eyes that he got through college by asking other students to read to him. He later said that this method was fortunate for him; since he could not refer back to his books or reading notes, he had to concentrate hard on the meanings of what he heard his roommates read to him. Thomas Edison was the same type of learner. Having had only three months of formal schooling, he had to read with a strong mental set of extracting meaning from everything he examined.

6. Write it down. If something is worth remembering, it is worth writing down. Don't consider this a chore only for school children. When you write something, you reinforce the memory of it by bringing into play another sense modality, your kinesthetic muscle sense, and thus you strengthen the point in your mind.

7. Visualize what you would recall. Do this as often as you can. As with writing, mental images give you the opportunity to employ another sense modality for imprinting the information on your memory.

8. Group or pattern your ideas into meaningful clusters. The mind recalls a pattern better than it does an assortment of isolated elements. Thus, it is easier for you to remember your social security number as 109–16–4132 than as 109164132. The telephone company has used patterning for years. It "dents" its numbers (e.g., 757–1234) for easier recall and aural recognition.

When you shop, it is easier to recall items to be bought if you already know exactly how many there will be. Also, you will remember them better if they are grouped by the same letters: celery, corn, cabbage, carrots; broccoli, bread, beans, butter, and so forth. Students of British colonial history recall the Bahamas, Barbados, and Bermuda as having the same type of government.

9. Always read with a red pencil in hand, in order to increase

your recall. Make notes in the book itself as you go along. If what you read ties in with other facts you already know, remind yourself of this by writing it down in the margins of the page.

Underline freely and don't be afriad to write down a question if you think the author is wrong, misses a point, doesn't seem to know something, or has left out some important detail in the discussion. Don't be passive. React to what you read!

10. *Part* learning is usually better than *whole* learning. If you are trying to remember a large amount, reduce it to small units and then focus on them one at a time. For example, if you must memorize a poem, first learn it stanza by stanza; then it will all flow together when you bring it to mind. Do the same with long chapters in history, English, and science.

11. You give yourself the best chance of remembering something if you avoid any acitvity immediately after new learning. This means no newspapers, TV, movies, or conversation. Ideally, you will retain more if you sleep immediately after you learn something. If you can't sleep, your mind should just rest calmly after a learning session. This rule seems to be true: *Study before bed and perform on arising*.

12. Moderate amounts of coffee, tea, and cola drinks do improve memory (and for that matter, general brain performance) to some slight degree.

13. Never try to memorize something if you are sick, distraught, frightened, or nervous. Emotions affect our recall ability. It has been shown, for example, that even humiliating experiences will interfere with our memory.

14. It pays to "overlearn." If you have ever tried to memorize something by reading it over and over again until you couldn't stand to look at it once more, you probably were engaging in overlearning. Although you may become stiffly bored with seeing the same material, there's plenty of evidence that overlearning will increase your recollection.

You should utilize overlearning to improve your memory, especially at those times when you might be exceptionally vulnerable to forgetting. Drs. Donald and Eleanor Laird note that we are most apt to forget on occasions that involve:

Names of things as well as of people

Numbers and dates
Unpleasant things
What is learned barely enough to remember it
Facts at odds with our beliefs and prejudices
What we learn by cramming
Our failures
What we pick up incidentally without trying to remember it
(incidental learning)
Material we don't understand
What we learn when embarrassed, frustrated, in poor health,
or fatigued

So when you must memorize something that fits into any of
these categories, spend more time with it than would normally be
necessary for you to learn it

Psychotechniques to Improve Your Social Memory

A memory block in a social setting can be especially frustrating and embarrassing. Although forgetting a name or not recog-
nizing a face is a commonplace occurrence, we still become embarrassed in such situations. Here are some techniques to help
when you are in a social context:

1. When introduced to someone, make sure that you've
heard his name correctly. If you have doubts about it, ask that
it be repeated. Most people use only their eyes and no other
senses to help them remember names. Don't make this mistake.
Repeat the name in your very next breath back to the person and
use it when you can in conversation. It will flatter your new
friend and give you a *motion-hook* association, as well as aural
and visual *hooks* of the name. (A motion hook involves the motion of your lips, tongue, vocal chords, etc.) A study by Dr.
Harold E. Burtt showed that when students immediately repeated the name of someone they met, they recalled the name 34
percent better than if they had not. So say more than "Pleased to
meet you" when you're introduced; say instead, "Nice to meet
you, Mr. Smith," or "Glad to know you, Sally Jones."

2. If it is important enough, write out the name as soon as
possible. This will give you an additional visual hook of the

name, as well as another motion hook (writing).

3. Associate the person with the situation or place where you first met him. Get a picture in your mind of the person who introduced you, the building you were in, the occasion (a classroom, party, meeting).

Later, if you have trouble recalling the person or his name, try to associate "around" the name or face by recalling the place, occasion, or introducer. Often, just reviving these surrounding memories and images will be enough to have the person's face or name pop into your mind.

4. Come to your senses. Memory always works better if we bring as many of our senses into the learning process as possible. Thus, if you see a sign that reads, "Greenville, Pop. 6,743," you will increase your chances of recalling it if you repeat aloud, "Greenville, population 6,743." The more senses you can bring into play, the better. For example, you might look around for a green lawn as you utter your statement.

5. When introduced to someone, use imagery whenever you can to impress his name and face on your memory. If you've met a man who says he is an accountant, that may not be enough to distinguish him in your mind. But if he adds that he works for a pharmaceutical company, try to get an unusual image of him. For example, see him seated before an enormous mountain of pills, counting each one and putting it into a bottle. The more unusual the image, the more likely it will be recalled later.

6. Look for the novel or the unusual. Notice if he's fat, tall, short, thin, loud, glum. Make a mental note of it. If he has a moustache, when you get that image of him counting pills, you might also see him twirling his moustache for each tablet he counts. Or maybe he has mentioned that he always takes the "A" train to work. Try to imagine him on the "A" train, counting vitamin A tablets and putting them into bottles. The more striking and ridiculous the image, the better. Try to make your mind's eye see something as vividly as your real eye would.

7. Make plenty of associations—the wilder the better. In advertising, the first step in a sales campaign is to capture a consumer's attention. This is often done by including an unusual or strange picture or caption in the ad. You must call your mind's attention to what you want to recall in much the same way. After

all, many other facts are jammed into the brain, which are competing for its attention.

The Mental-Walk Technique

If you believe that you are a good visualizer, then this technique will help you to remember a long list of items.

The idea is to close your eyes and picture each of these ideas, events, people, and so forth placed at various points along a route with which you are familiar.

Let's suppose you wish to remember the story that we gave in the prologue of this book about the man eating junket.

You would visualize all the key elements in the story in sequence along a familiar path—one that you have traveled and know well.

Thus, using our story on page xv, you first see a man sitting down, eating junket near your front gate. Then, as you proceed down the street, near the house with the blue shutters, you see gathered a vast number of people with curious looks on their faces (all the people of the world). Next, under the old elm tree, you see "a year-old lion blowing out the candle on his birthday cake," then as you walk a little farther to the drugstore, you see in the windows "a walrus balancing an apple on his back." Next, on the post office steps, you see "a kangaroo jumping over a glass of orange juice." As you move on, you notice outside the school building "a rabbit wondering if a bunch of grapes is tied to its tail." Finally, in a large open area familiar to you (a playground or a town square), you see the junket man again, surrounded by all the people of the world, and he tells them he is, after all, thinking about eating junket.

The effectiveness of the mental-walk technique in improving memory has been proven in careful experiments by a foremost researcher of memory processes, Dr. Gordon Bower, and in studies by anthropologist K. Lynch of MIT.

FIGURE 1

In a mental walk, place items to be learned
in sequence along a familiar route.

Adapted from: Robert Sommer, *The Mind's Eye* (New York: Dell, 1978), p. 122.

Imagery Is a Highly Useful Memory Aid

Here are several tips that will help you to improve your imagery.

1. If you are relaxed, your mental images will be stimulated more readily.
2. Breathe in a regular, normal, and smooth pattern. Poor imagery is associated with irregular breathing.

3. Your imagery will be better if you lie down rather than sit or stand.

4. It has been shown that early memories and their images are recalled better when we are lying down. Be warned, however, that visualization is not a passive process. Don't grow languid about this process because you are reclining; rather, you should work just as hard at visualizing if you lie down as if you were standing or sitting.

HOW TO MANAGE YOUR TIME

Whether we are barons or beggars, time will always prevail as our common enemy. But that's where the similarity ends, for each of us has a rhythm of living that is unique. When there is pressure to perform beyond this pace, we grow nervous and tense and wind up having friction with those who would have us change our tempo.

Psychologists were the first time-efficiency experts in industry, and here are a number of tested strategies they offer for getting more out of those precious minutes, hours, and days which seem to fly by.

Psychotechniques for Managing Your Time

Before you begin your time-management program, *build "time awareness"* by doing the following exercise: Hold a clock with a second hand in front of you. Watch it for a full minute. It moves without hesitation. Think about that irretrievable minute. It is lost and will never return. Let this exercise impress upon you the value of your possession. Vow never again to use time carelessly.

The Ten Golden Keys of Time Management

1. *Set priorities.* There's a famous story about Babe Hermann of the Brooklyn Dodgers. One day while chasing a fly ball he suddenly stopped to retrieve his cap, which had blown off. The ball promptly fell into the outfield for a hit. When you must accomplish a number of things, think about them carefully; then do them in order of importance. Concentrate *only* on the high priorities and then move on to the others. Your ability to focus

your efforts will determine if you'll succeed. Columnist Sydney Harris summed it up: "Winners focus, losers spray."

2. *The "Do List."* After you've ranked your goals, relieve yourself of the burden of remembering them by using a Do List. Most "doers" use one. Anything that is worth doing should go on a Do List. It might seem odd, for example, to see "Get to know the new neighbor," or "Begin a low-fat diet" on the same list with "Buy bread." But the point is that the list is reminding you to *do* something, which can also mean starting a process. "Get to know the new neighbor" could mean merely to take the first little step in that direction, not necessarily to do the whole task at that time.

3. *Plan, plan, plan.* You wouldn't start a car trip to an unfamiliar place without a road map; then why plunge right into a day or week without a plan of some kind?

Every Friday afternoon at work, or Sunday evening at home, plan the week ahead. Assign priorities to activities, compose a Do List, clear your desk, and so forth. Each morning or evening, look at the day ahead. Budget your time for each task. Remember: the more things you have on your mind, the more you must plan.

When you're very busy your anxiety is likely to run high, and that's the time when you especially need planning to help minimize possible errors in judgment. Even when planning smaller tasks, always keep the larger, overall goal in mind.

4. *Delegate.* Whether you're a housewife or an office worker, ask or train others to do tasks that are rightfully theirs. This is a key to freeing you of details. But it takes some ingenuity on your part.

You must be willing to (a) take time to fully explain what must be done; (b) train them to do the job well; (c) permit them to make some errors while they are learning; and (d) check over their work later.

Effective delegating is the way all stable corporations succeed, and if you do it, it will save you considerable time. Also, put aside some money to delegate work to specialists whenever you can. (For example, pay an expert to compute your taxes at tax time.) What an expert can do in minutes may take you hours to accomplish.

5. *Use time blocks when you can.* Carve out an extended span of time to do a particularly special job. When you work in small time-packages, you'll spend many minutes warming up to the subject. If you should be interrupted, you'll waste time getting back your train of thought on a problem that had become clear in your mind.

6. *Curb interruptions.* Victor Hugo wrote: "When the disposal of time is surrendered to the chance of incidents, chaos will reign." Deal with interruptions by rescheduling them if possible. Try to keep your territory under control at all times. At work, keep your door closed part of each day, and if this isn't possible, keep it only partly open all of the day. Avoid eye contact with those who pass by. If someone phones or drops in and asks "Got a moment?" don't answer "Sure, what is it?" Say instead, "It depends," then decide whether the matter deserves your immediate attention or should be rescheduled.

7. *Use a quiet time every day: many executives do.* Put aside a period at work or at home when you will be absolutely alone. Close your door, take your phone off the hook and make yourself as relaxed and comfortable as possible. This is an opportunity for you to do your best thinking, a chance to tackle questions that require your most serious planning. During this time, *don't* dive headlong into your task; rather, put your feet up on the desk, keep your mind calm and free-associate for a while about things on your mind. Jot down notes on thoughts as they come. Make it a habit to do this for part of each day, for a minimum of twenty minutes.

8. *Learn to say no.* Self-discipline is a golden key to good time-management. Time often slips away from us because we defer to those who interrupt us. Recognize this tendency as a weakness and don't allow your work to be sidetracked by the idle intrusions of others.

Sometimes we ourselves unwittingly invite interruptions. Ask yourself:

Do I fall into these time traps because I need their approval?

Do I give them my time with a string attached so that later I'll get a favor from them?

Do I fear they'll be hurt or angry if I politely but firmly say no?

Don't be a crowd pleaser.

9. *Keep records.* This is a proven method that timesavers use. Always carry a small day-by-day memo book inside your pocket or purse. Record in it anything that's worth remembering: phone numbers, addresses, expenses, names of people, places you went, what people said, prices in various stores for the same item, dates of upcoming events, and so forth. Think of your daily log as your memory extension, rather than as your record book. Anything, no matter how simple, can be included in it.

When the book fills up, save it as a valuable reference document for years to come. You'll never have to worry about not recalling "what's his name" or when you last spoke to him.

10. *Divide and conquer.* Learn to break down large tasks into manageable units. Do this especially if the job is unpleasant or difficult. Each step you achieve acts as a reward, a satisfaction to you, and keeps you going toward the main goal. Dr. Robert Riley, director of planning at the University of Cincinnati, reminds students, businesspeople and housewives to break large jobs into smaller jobs by saying, "Remember, you can eat an elephant if you do it one bite at a time."

Other Useful Psychotechniques for Managing Your Time

1. *Fight perfectionism.* Break your compulsion for doing everything perfectly. It may be true that Michaelangelo once said, "Trifles make perfections, and perfections are not trifles," but then again we aren't all Michaelangelos.

Be realistic. Don't get bogged down in details. If you tend to be a perfectionist, do the job first, then go back later to refine it —if you have time.

2. *Save energy.* Don't waste your strength on trivial things until you first do the important ones. Try to be as fresh as possible when you hit top-priority jobs.

3. *Get help.* No one knows better how you mismanage your time than those who live or work with you. Enlist their help. Ask them how they think you waste time or energy. They might further cooperate by reminding you when you are not aware of it that you are wasting time.

Don't be too proud to ask others to recommend timesaver

tips they use, especially those people whom you admire for their efficiency. One housewife asked a friend about shopping and received a tip that helped her save time. She prepared a shopping list according to the floor plan of the supermarket to avoid the frustration of criss-crossing the store while shopping.

4. *Don't be an adrenalin junkie.* Some people haven't learned the lesson that fighting time is like trying to fight the ocean. They've developed the self-defeating habit of living from deadline to deadline. They need a crisis to move them to action. Give yourself plenty of time to complete a job. If you can't, then reschedule it. It's a fact that rapid, pressured work produces many mistakes in judgment, some of which may be very costly.

5. *Create time awareness.* At the office if you have to meet with groups for brief periods fairly often, don't do it sitting down. If possible, use stand-up meetings instead. During most conferences, too much time is spent on trivia. If yours have a habit of running over, it's probably *you* who have fostered this habit of "trivializing" in others, and it's up to you to break it.

Create time awareness in them by what you say and do. Douglas Southall Freeman, brilliant editor of the *Richmond News Leader,* has a sign tacked over the clock that faces visitors who come to his office. It reads: "Time alone is irreplaceable: don't waste it." You might even improve on Freeman's reminder by making yours a "minutes remaining" clock.

6. *Avoid the "cluttered desk syndrome."* It will take you more minutes to locate an item on an over-crowded desk and this time adds up. Studies have shown that a littered desk is a distraction and a time waster, and produces errors in work performance.

7. *Handling the paper blitz.* Probably our most significant time loss involves reading through the deluge of newspapers, magazines, reports, letters, junk mail, and bulletins that hits us daily. Try to handle each piece of paper only once whenever possible.

The best way to deal with your mail is to place it on a pile in front of you and read each piece carefully. Then take one of three possible actions:

a. Answer it (if feasible, reply to a letter by writing on the letter itself).

    b. Put it in a "do later" file.
    c. Discard it.

Always file important papers as soon as they come in to avoid a pileup.

For Procrastinators

    8. *Chaining.* If you're a procrastinator who is running out of time on a certain job, make the task easier by using a time-tested technique from learning psychology called *chaining.* Suppose you've delayed washing the car. Get the process going with a "leading task." Take a very simple step toward the goal. It should not require any planning and should be quick and easy. It might mean simply taking the car out of the garage, or getting the hose out, or fetching the soap and bucket. Other examples of leading tasks are rolling a piece of paper into your typewriter to lead you to writing that letter or buying a paint brush to lead you to signing up for that art course.

    A leading task is often just enough momentum for overcoming resistance and sustaining motivation to complete a job that has been kept too long on the shelf.

    9. *Making your mood work for you.* Sometimes it's our mood that stops us from getting things done. If you're not feeling up to a particular assignment, ask yourself: "Is there *anything,* no matter how small, that I am willing to do in my present mood?" Then if you get an idea, do it as soon as you can. In this way you are making your mood work for and not against you.

    10. *Self-imposed deadline.* If you can honestly admit that you are procrastinating about doing something you dislike or suspect will be unpleasant, lay down a deadline for yourself. Often a self-imposed deadline is enough to create action. Of course it's even better to tell other people about your deadline. Although we often break commitments to ourselves, we're not so likely to do so with others.

    11. *Use imagery.* When you know that you're foot-dragging about doing something, and everything you've tried has failed to break the deadlock, try using imagery to move you off dead center. Lie down and imagine yourself actually taking the first steps to doing the chore. See yourself as vividly as possible, going

through the motions confidently and without hesitation. Visualize yourself succeeding and feeling good about it. All through the imagery remain as relaxed as possible.

The rationale for using imagery before beginning something rests on the theory of *ideo-motor action,* which states that when we imagine an action, we start a process of activity going in our muscles and glands, which is the same process we would start if we actually performed the action. We explained this in some detail on page 31.

12. *Search for timesavers.* Keep searching for new ways to save your time and conserve your energy. Alan Lakein, world renowned time-management consultant advises people to ask themselves frequently, "What is the best use of my time right now?"

A final note: Time managers don't advocate that we become obsessed with every minute of our lives. Rather, they teach that there is a time to relax, engage in leisure activity, and be unaware of time's passage. This is not time wasted; it is indeed necessary. Nor do they advocate that we become a time-concious personality, who lives by the tyranny of "the should" (i.e., I should make every moment useful; I should be doing this or that). These are so-called Sunday neurotics who suffer from leisure phobia and live through veritable agony each weekend until they return to work Monday morning. Time managers tell us, rather, that if we learn to use time sensibly we'll have greater leisure to enjoy as we wish.

PART TWO
Dealing with People

15

HOW TO WIN AN ARGUMENT

Alfred Adler, the psychoanalyst, taught that man's lifelong struggle will always be to overcome his feelings of inferiority. He argued that power over others, whether subtle or obvious, is the inner ambition of all socialized people.

To whatever extent these notions are true, we do indeed clash with each other, either muscle against muscle or in the civilized combat of argument; and more likely than not, neither side changes its opinion. Dale Carnegie has wisely advised that the way to get the best of an argument is to avoid it.

But sometimes a conflict is unavoidable and we must engage in the art of verbal self-defense. If we don't know the rules, we're going to be hurt.

Here are some strategies from experts to help you win in a confrontation:

Psychotechniques for Winning an Argument

1. *Draw out your opponent.** It is to your advantage to let him state his case first. Ask specific questions to learn his opinions on the issues under debate. Express interest and get as much detail as possible. Repeat his ideas back to him so that he is sure you understand them.

The reasoning behind this drawing out technique is that most people have not clearly thought through their positions. Often, just by explaining their stand, you will change their mind. Anoth-

*This technique is adapted from Dr. Jack Wiggins, *"How to Argue Successfully"* (Berea, Ohio: Personal Growth Press, 1971).

er reason for drawing out an opponent is to know what you will be up against later.

2. *Be calm.* When it is your turn to speak, start slowly. Begin with clear, simple statements that you feel he will agree with. Avoid making extreme statements or claims. Don't rush. If it upsets you to make eye contact, look away from him and state your case.

3. *Attack generalizations.** When your opponent starts to generalize by saying "all" when "some" is nearer the truth, neutralize his claims by showing exceptions. For example, if he says all single people are unreliable, say "such as Speaker of the House Sam Rayburn or the Pope?"

4. *Blast "labelizing" and "jargonese."** Don't permit him to use labels or technical jargon. When he does, force him to define the terms. Many people only half comprehend the terms they use and can seldom express verbally what they mean by them. Lawyers take advantage of this weakness and ask witnesses to define the terms they use. Asking for definitions will give you more time to think out better answers to his argument.

If he uses labels, you might ask, "What do you mean by Marxism (or free enterprise or socialism, etc.)?" Be especially on guard for emotional words against religious and ethnic groups.

If he jumps to a biased conclusion, remind him of the story about George M. Cohan, who was refused a room reservation by a hotel clerk who said, "I'm sorry, we don't accept people of your faith." To which the famous songwriter replied, "You thought I was Jewish and I thought you were a good American. We were both wrong."

5. *Keep your temper.** If your opponent gets angry, let his rage get hotter. It will distort his thinking and weaken his argument. Don't insult, even if he insults you. This is especially important if you're in front of others. If you're calm, you'll gain the support of the group, and this, in turn, will unnerve him. To remind you to keep your cool, remember the phrase, "A man is like a piece of steel; when he loses his temper he is worthless."

6. *Point out his broken-record blitz.* Tell him he's repeating himself and that chanting something doesn't make it any truer.

---

*Asterisked points are adapted from Dr. Ray Montsalvatge, *"Twenty-five Ways to Win an Argument,"* Manage* (American Management Association, 1962).

Restate his comment and remind him that Nazi propaganda minister Joseph Goebbels used to say that if you repeat a lie often enough, people will believe it as the truth.

7. *Use squelches.** A "last-word squelch" is often the mortal wound that clinches an argument. If you see an opportunity for a squelch, use it; but don't use it to dishonor, demean, or ridicule your opponent unfairly. A perfect squelch requires practice. It needs a minimum of words and precise timing. It must be in good taste yet have enough edge on it to disarm him and leave him momentarily without a comeback.

Some memorable squelches include that of the driver of a small car who was almost hit by a bus. When the bus driver yelled that he could hardly see her car, the near-victim, in easy hearing of all the bus passengers, replied, "Oh, I'm so sorry. I'll bet you have an even harder time seeing children."

Another took place when Alfred Smith was campaigning for governor of New York state. A heckler shouted, "Go ahead, Al, tell 'em all you know. It won't take long." Smith shot back, "I'll tell 'em what we both know. It won't take much longer."

8. *Stamp out trite statements.** Be on the alert for pat, overworked, unproven statements. Try to have ready answers. If he says that his is the exception which proves the rule, point out that rules can't be proved that way. When he says, "You can't change human nature," remind him that you and a cannibal are both human but your menu is a bit different. If he stops you with, "If I do it for you, I'll have to do it for everyone else," ask him if everybody else is asking him. If he insists that the majority is always right, refresh his memory by saying that the only one who votes against the lynch mob is the victim.

9. *Suspect statistics.** Don't swallow statistics without a fight. When he throws figures around, ask him: (1) Where were they published? (2) When were they compiled? (3) What authority gathered them? Remind him of the man who drowned in a river the depth of which averaged only sixteen inches each year, or about the people during World War II who were said to be tricked when they bought a blend of meat that was 50 percent horse meat and 50 percent rabbit—one horse to one rabbit. Agree that his figures may be accurate, but don't accept them without a fight.

10. *Shoot down poor examples.** When he tries to make a point by giving a poor example, hit him with criticism. Remind him about the staid schoolteacher who wanted to impress on children the evils of alcohol. She dropped a worm into a glass of whiskey, and when it curled up and died, a student bellowed that the point of the example was, if you drank whiskey you'd never have worms.

11. *Save your ammunition.* Don't offer any answers or explanations before they are requested or actually needed. If you sell your point of view too hard, with a lot of documentation, it may create the impression that you are defensive or insecure about your position. This can change or color the attitudes of your opponent and will also influence the reactions of observers.

(Another point: If you go into an argument with the conviction that your opponent is bullheaded and won't buy your ideas, chances are he will sense your attitude and realize he's being treated differently than he's been used to. He may then indeed become a bullhead, the very thing you dreaded and tried to avoid.)

12. *Let him save face.* If the points you've made have hit their mark, and he seems to be reeling from the impact, remember to give him a way out. Don't make it hard for him to back off and save face.

Remember, however, that some people out of stubborn pride remain a slave to their original position, even after they've been proven wrong. If this happens, then let it be.

13. *Don't be a "subversive half-listener."* Professor Ralph Nichols of the University of Minnesota reminds us that when most listeners are aroused, they become preoccupied simultaneously with three undercover plans of attack: They begin to calculate what hurt is being done to their egos; they plot an embarrassing question to hurl at their adversary; and they enjoy the fantasy of posing a put-down rebuttal and vanquishing him. If you have all this in your mind, chances are you're not going to be sharply attuned to flaws and illogical reasoning that your opponent may subsequently give. Be on guard against these fantasy tendencies in yourself. Pay strict attention to what the other person is saying.

No one can say precisely when a discussion ends and an argument begins. It's not the content of what is being said that determines where to draw the line between the two, but, rather, the amount of heat generated between the participants.

Use these strategies any time you try to convince someone of your point of view, but always remember to tone them down or step them up according to the amount of opposition you encounter.

Special Points about Debating

There may be a time when you will have to face adversaries formally on a speaker's platform. Here are two points to keep in mind:

1. If there is an immediate presentation of two points of view, then you should try to present yours *first*.

2. If there will be a recess between the two presentations, then you should try to make your presentation *last*.

16

HOW TO HANDLE YOUR ANGER

It has been said that anger makes dull men witty but it keeps them poor. This statement by philosopher Frances Bacon may be true, but it is far too narrow an explanation for the raw emotion that every human being experiences occasionally, from the moment of birth until the day he dies.

On the one hand, anger is the root cause of wars, the disrupter of human kindness, and the toxin that poisons our love relationships: on the other, it gives us the energy to battle for a cause, to defend ourselves, and to protect those we cherish.

With economic frustration, racial tensions, and terrorism on the rise, anger seems to be an increasingly popular mode for coping with life stress. Yet social scientists have neglected anger as a topic of investigation. Rather, much attention is paid to reactions like aggression and violence.

Psychologist A. Rothenberg, an expert on anger, has said, "We interpret the presence of anger, we confront anger, we draw anger, we tranquilize anger and we help the working through of anger. Yet not a single modern psychiatric or psychological volume deals with this topic and an extensive search of periodical literature reveals only a sprinkling of experimental articles and fewer theoretical ones."

Not only is there a scarcity of research on the subject, but it is even less possible to find any specific psychotechnique that can help one overcome a problem of anger.

If you have trouble with your temper and want to learn to regulate your anger, you will have an easier time of it if you understand something about this emotion and how it operates.

These are some characteristics of anger:

1. Anger can be a subjective reaction to threat. The first step in generating anger is an appraisal of the situation (usually a split-

second process). Threat, like beauty, is in the eyes of the beholder. Our interpretation of a situation depends on our previous experience with it and what meanings we attach to it.

What one person feels as strong frustration another may find a tolerable annoyance. The Greek Stoic philosopher Epictetus said, "Men are not troubled by things themselves but by their thoughts about them."

2. Anger is paradoxical. Anger has a double function: on the one hand, it gives us immediate tension release and is thereby satisfying; on the other, it can both destroy others and create within us an outpouring of chemical substances that could harm us over the long run.

3. Anger is an energizer. Anger mobilizes our strength in a time of stress. The Chinese word for anger is *sheng ch'i,* which means "to generate energy." Often, if we didn't feel anger we would be unable to fulfill our duties and responsibilities.

4. Anger creates the feeling of power. Those involved in physical battle (fighters, athletes, soldiers) are better motivated if they can feel anger toward their adversaries. During war, soldiers are taught a battle cry, which enlivens their spirits and focuses their efforts on destroying the enemy.

5. Anger is expressed in two main ways: (1) intellectually, through a nonphysical reaction in which we use reason and judgment to manipulate or overcome our foes, and (2) emotionally, through a response that is faster and more direct but which may produce counter anger, adding to our difficulties. In most situations we use a combination of both these coping reactions.

6. Anger blocks learning. There is solid evidence that strong emotions like anger are naturally antagonistic to adaptive learning. They disturb our perceptions and disrupt memory, reasoning, judgment, and many other mental faculties. An oriental proverb advises us never to answer a letter while we are angry. Strong anger may weaken our chance of learning to deal constructively with the same frustrating situation when it occurs in the future.

7. Anger can cause regression. Many people when angry tend to show primitive reactions like going into a rage, creating a disturbance, making a fuss, raising their voice, throwing something, or sulking. These are adult equivalents of childish temper tan-

trums—carry-over tactics from earlier years.

8. Anger can be self-destructive. Some personalities (intrapunitive types) may turn their anger inward in a "hate campaign" against themselves. This usually results in symptoms like migraine headaches, peptic ulcers, high blood pressure, or constipation, as well as feelings of depression and personal inadequacy.

9. Anger is a problem when (a) it arises easily and too frequently as a reaction to a variety of situations; (b) it is too intense, that is, we overreact to minor frustrations and disturbances; (c) it lasts too long; (d) it leads to destructiveness; (e) it weakens healthy interpersonal relationships; and (f) it leads to any of the symptoms in point 8 above.

Psychotechniques for Handling Anger

A number of psychotechniques are available for controlling or releasing angry feelings. Use any that seem to be especially helpful to you, and remember, the more frequently you practice each of them, the more efficient you become in dealing with your anger.

1. Before using any of the psychotechniques, study your anger by keeping a diary of incidents that cause it. This is an important and useful way to become educated about its patterns.

With the diary, you can pick up clues about whether your anger was due to fatigue, illness, or pressures and whether it was appropriate. It will also help you to know if it was you or the other person who was at fault.

There are five things to include in your diary:

a. Identify the person or persons who triggered your anger.

b. Determine whether yours was justified or unjustified anger. Be honest.

c. Note the frequency of the anger experiences.

d. Record the degree of your anger reaction (was it mild, moderate, or strong).

e. How well did you handle it?

Each week review the diary and try to learn something about

your anger from it. If possible, talk over the entries with someone who can be objective with you.*

2. *Reverse role-play*. With the aid of a partner, try to role-play the part of the person who made you angry, while your partner plays your role. Do this sincerely for about ten minutes: be honest in your reactions and arguments.

3. *Relaxation*. Use the relaxation psychotechnique in chapter 6 and keep as relaxed as possible during the course of the day. The more you maintain a low tension level, the less likely you are to blow up. Try to relax especially when you are in a potentially "hot" situation. Gain skill in becoming relaxed quickly in case you should need to enter a difficult situation.

4. *Physical activity*. This will help you to discharge emotions that build up within you, and the more strenuous the exercise the better. Washing the car, chopping wood, housework, jogging, and swimming are excellent for releasing physical tension.

5. *Ventilation*. Talking out your feelings with someone you trust, and who will be neutral, is a good way to drain off your anger. It is a psychotechnique universally used by psychotherapists.

6. *Creative activity*. This has proven useful in diverting angry feelings. Painting, writing a letter, or working at a hobby are the more common methods used. Try to utilize these diversions as much as possible.

7. *Imaginary letter-writing*. Some counselors have worked out a psychotechnique in which their clients express in writing all the things they wish to declare to the person or persons who have made them angry. If you use this method you can even show this letter to someone close to you and get his reaction. But the important point here is *not* to mail the letter, but instead to put it aside for several days and then reread it. Usually the second time you read it you can easily recognize your own emotional exaggerations and thus, feel more stability.

8. *Time-out*. Sometimes there is nothing left to do in a frustrating moment other than to withdraw, lest your emotions go out of control. When you feel this to be the case, it is time to just leave the scene and go to some neutral place while tempers cool.

* This diary method was developed by Professor Raymond Novaco of the University of California at Irvine.

This does *not* mean that you have given up the argument, but rather that you will return again at another time to resolve it, when you can be more objective with your adversary. Some psychologists have found that time-out is even more effective if you engage in deep muscle relaxation simultaneously.

9. *Squelch rehearsal.* Often, people who readily show anger are the ones who have trouble expressing their emotions verbally. Many are inarticulate and resort quickly to pushing, shoving, punching, to solve their differences with others. It has been found that if one learns a repertoire of short snappy retorts to be used in annoying situations, these can frequently short-circuit the build-up of anger. This psychotechnique involves creating and practicing pat phrases to use when you find yourself in a tight spot. Here is an example: A person cuts into line ahead of you. Your remarks might go as follows (starting off tactfully):

"Please don't cut into the line. I have been here before you and don't want any more inconveniences. There is a line here and we are all waiting for the same thing."

"Pardon me, but the end of the line is back there; that's where we all started."

"Please don't crash the line. I know you wouldn't like it if someone did it to you."

"The back of the line is there. We are all waiting our turn. Why should you be something special."

"Excuse me but all of us here mind that you are getting ahead of us."

"Don't cut in."

This psychotechnique is something like scriptwriting, which is discussed in chapter 18, for in a sense you prethink just what you will say in a given circumstance. Now pick five such situations and prepare at least five ready-made retorts for each.

10. *Analyze your inner speech.* The next time you become angry, try to be aware of just what it is you are telling yourself. If you listen with the "third ear," you will soon be aware that there are actual phrases which run through your mind all the time you are upset, and that these coerce you into feeling angry. For example, Bob, who is ignored by a waiter, might actually subvocalize to himself: "He makes me feel like a second-class customer; he

looks down on me; I feel stupid; I must look inadequate to the other patrons; they must see me as a jerk. I am better than he is; he is a lowly waiter and my job is far more important than his; how dare he!" All these inner utterances will shape the outcome of Bob's behavior. (It is not difficult to imagine what his reaction will be when he finally comes face to face with the waiter who has avoided him.)

If you were Bob, you could discover how to control your reactions. The answer is to make a concious effort to be aware of your inner dialogue. Try to eliminate, correct, and soften these self-statements. Be aware that they are inflaming your anger all the more and blocking your judgment.*

11. *Self-desensitization.* This is another psychotechnique for strengthening your control over anger. Follow the desensitization steps in chapter 8, and for the imagery visualize the anger situation, but at the same time remain relaxed. See the entire episode from start to finish. If you become tense you must go back into the imagery sequence and start again.

Another self-desensitization technique is to use a number of anger scenes graded from weakest to strongest. Write out ten of these scenes; then with your eyes closed imagine each of them beginning with the mildest. As soon as you are aware of an angry feeling, shift your attention to your muscles and begin to relax. After the anger has subsided go on to the next scene. When you feel anger again, interrupt the scene by relaxing. Do this for all ten scenes.

By continually interrupting the angry feeling with relaxation you are desensitizing yourself to your anger and building your tolerance for frustration.

12. *Decentration.* Anger often involves tunnel vision. When someone crosses us we remain locked in an angry mood because of the obsessional qualities of the process. Usually, we become so entirely focused on the hurt, pain, or threat to our well-being that we tend to shut out any good thoughts concerning the object of our anger. An example: Steven and Fred are good neighbors.

---

* Psychologist Albert Ellis considers "virtually all anger at a person inappropriate." He says that we talk ourselves in and out of anger by "awfulizing" over something that doesn't deserve so much concern. In his rational emotive therapy he has stressed that a person can be rewarded or punished by his own thinking.

One day Fred returns home after an irritating day at the office and learns that Steven's son has carelessly spilled paint on his driveway. He sharply scolds the boy, who runs home crying. When Steve learns of the incident he becomes angry with Fred. He avoids meeting him. He holds his anger in, and after a few days it becomes a grudge. Now when Steven thinks of Fred he has angry, critical, and derisive thoughts about him. Steven has locked himself into tunnel vision (as Fred may also have done). He momentarily forgets Fred's good qualities, which made the relationship worthwhile only a short time ago. But Steven somehow hopes the freeze between them will thaw out. Decentration might help here. It is a valuable tool for altering moods and has aided those who follow its instructions implicitly. The strategy involves a self-control method in which a person with aggressive feelings learns to focus on aspects of the anger situation other than those which upset him, as well as on the positive qualities of the person or persons involved. It was formulated by a group of Belgian psychologists, who wished to devise a way for people disturbed by hostile feelings to free themselves for more positive thoughts.

The psychologists showed a violent movie to forty-eight soldiers. It gave rise to strong feelings of resentment, bitterness, and aggression among the men. After the film, no attempt was made to talk them out of their feelings, but instead their attention was diverted to positive values of the film. The soldiers were instructed to dwell on, discuss, and write about the film's aesthetic qualities. After this decentration the group's aggressive feelings about the film were considerably reduced. The researchers had given the viewers another frame of reference by which to evaluate what they saw.

The Psychotechnique of Decentration.*

If you are clinging to a feeling of anger toward someone (call

*I have taught this strategy to diffuse angry feelings. One of the things I ask clients to do in step 2 is to think of being at the target's funeral. Ask yourself what would be some of the things you would say to his or her spouse? Do you think you would be a bit more tolerant of his values or points of view. Would your irritation take on a different perspective?

him *the target*) and you are fairly certain that you must resolve the conflict between you someday, then this method, followed step by step, will help you to prepare for the confrontation.

1. First, get completely relaxed using the psychotechnique outlined in chapter 6. Don't necessarily try to talk yourself out of your angry feelings; just follow the directions with objectivity.

2. Next, list on a sheet of paper ten qualities of the target for which you and others might praise him. Try to be honest, even if it hurts. For example, you might write: (a) he is a good provider for his family, (b) he is a fine cook, (c) he keeps a neat house, (d) he is fun to be with, (e) he has a marvelous sense of humor.

3. Discuss this list with someone. Say: "I'm pretty angry about Jim Smith and I don't think it makes much sense to continue this way. I am going to try to learn a technique that can help me handle angry feelings constructively and I would like your help. Please be objective and discuss this list of traits with me. It will give me a better guide to dealing with Jim when I finally do meet with him face to face. Mind you, I am no admitting by all this that I think he is right or I am wrong. Here is the first trait . . ."

4. After you have done this, put your list aside for a few days, then review it and meditate on it for five or ten minutes.

5. Bear in mind that if some day you do not finally face your target, your angry feelings will continue no matter what you do. So for this step write out a short script on what you might say for openers when you meet your target and then what you will discuss with him to clear the air between you.

Managing emotions is a reeducation process. If we remind ourselves from time to time that nursing a grudge can do us serious physiological harm we might be less apt to allow ourselves this luxury.

A final note: Not all anger is bad. As we have indicated, we often need it to energize us, to impel us to do the things we might not otherwise do. Aristotle centuries ago pointed out this selective manner in which anger should be employed. He said: "Anybody can be angry, that is easy; but to be angry with the right person and to the right degree and at the right time and for the right purpose and in the right way, that is not within everybody's power and is not easy."

17

HOW TO BE MORE PERSUASIVE

There is a cartoon that shows a frustrated math teacher explaining division to an apathetic nine-year-old. The child stares at her and demands: "Don't tell me, sell me!"

This bit of humor typifies our attitude about communication. We react better if it touches a responsive chord in us.

Television, probably more than any other medium, has made us sales-conscious. We are continually assailed with suggestions for everything from "don't be a litterbug" to "support your local Red Cross."

Selling ideas or, more accurately, persuading others to believe in them, is an American way of life. Like the nine-year-old child, we have built-in expectations about being persuaded to do the things we do.

If *you* must build your case in another person's mind, on the job, or in school, you can do it more effectively by using the following strategies.

Psychotechniques to Help You Be a Mind-Changer of Others

1. When you face your target, don't begin to convince him immediately. First, exchange the usual pleasantries and be as naturally congenial as possible. Let him take the lead and keep up the small talk as long as he wishes. When you get a signal (and this can be a pause or a break in the conversation of some kind), he's at last ready to hear your message. Now start your presentation.

2. State clearly and honestly your overall objectives; that is,

the reason you are there talking with him.* Try to motivate your prospect by hitting his "hot button." For example, if you are a salesman selling a new floor wax to a store owner or a housewife, focus on your product's benefits—how it will save money, time, trouble. Or if you're a mother who tries to convince your eight-year-old to share toys with a needy friend, you might point out that if she does so, you'll be pleased with her kindness. Also, she will build a friendship and probably be invited to the other child's home more often, be lent toys in return, and so forth. Always stress the benefits of your proposal. Don't overbuild your case or ask too many questions of your prospect. Questions raise anxiety and make people defensive.

3. Socrates, perhaps the greatest of all persuaders, used to lead opponents to agree with points all through his argument. By winning one admission of agreement after another he paved the way for final acceptance of his main idea.

So don't create differences between you, especially at the beginning of your conversation. Rather, prime your target to say yes to the things you mention. Using our example, the salesman might ask a few simple questions, such as "Would you like to save money on your wax bills?" or "Would you like the wax to last longer?" "Shine better?" "Be slip-proof?" Say whatever you believe will be met with assent in order to build a mental set that leads to the big yes later on.

4. Draw out your prospect. The moment you tell him of your objective, he will begin to have various associations. His mind won't remain empty, like a recording machine, waiting for your next idea to hit it. His accumulated thoughts will draw his attention away from your next idea. Therefore, ask a question that requires an explanation and keeps him involved with you. For example: "What do you think of . . .?" or "How do you feel about . . .?" Avoid questions that lead to yes or no answers, such as "Do you agree with . . .?" or "Do you like . . .?" In our example the housewife might be asked what are some good and bad points about the wax she is now using, where does she buy it, how often does she apply it.

---

*Asterisked points are adapted from Dr. Jesse Nirenberg, *Breaking Through to Each Other* (Harper & Row, 1976), and "How to Get Through to Your Customers AND Your Boss," *Industrial Marketing,* June 1976, pp. 122–126.

Drawing out serves three important functions: (a) it clears the person's mind of distracting thoughts; (b) it tips you off about any questions or doubts he has; and (c) it rouses him from his inertia and primes his thinking. This puts him into a mobile state so that he can move forward with you more easily.

5. Don't fight. Years ago, the *Boston Transcript* printed this poem:

> Here lies the body of William Jay
> Who died maintaining the right of way.
> He was right, dead right, as he sped along,
> But he's just as dead as if he were wrong.

This nugget of wisdom applies to the art of persuasion. Don't argue, even if you could easily defeat your prospect. You might win the battle but lose the war. Let him know that you understand by rephrasing his point of view in your own words, then go on to give your counterexamples. In our example, suppose a housewife says: "That last product you sold me arrived a week late. How do you expect me to take another order from you?"

Assuming you know all the facts of the situation, you should reply, "I certainly know how annoyed you must feel about it, but things like this happen even in the best of companies. I'll personally see that it won't occur again."

Expressing your understanding of the other person's position makes him feel that you are willing to be objective, fair, and therefore honest.

Don't crowd him with ideas.* If you have a number of points to cover, keep this important idea in mind: When a person tries to learn a series of facts, each one in the series tends to make him forget the previous ones. So present your ideas one at a time; and even if you have only one or two things to mention, the more complicated they are, the more time he'll need to grasp them. No matter how simple your thoughts are, *don't* present more than *three* at a time.

7. Qualify.* When you meet resistance, it becomes necessary to compare his arguments with yours. The way to do this is to find a common denominator, such as money, time, and effort. Show him that if he does it your way, he will save on one of these factors. Whenever possible, give numerical values to your argu-

ments. If you don't know exact amounts, then give estimates. An even better tactic is to first get *him* to make the estimates; then come up with the exact figures involved yourself.

Supporting your argument with numbers helps to cut down on emotional distortions. Without them, your target will feel that his arguments are just as valid as yours. After you quantify, let him compare for himself the value of his objections and of your position, then ask him to decide.

8. Stay human. Always keep a tone of good feeling throughout the conversation. There's much truth to the saying that honey catches more bees than gall. Don't talk down to your prospect or insult his intelligence. Above all, don't show contempt for any of his rebuttals, even though you might feel it. Keep in mind what G. K. Chesterton once told his son, "Men must be taught as if you taught them not and things unknown proposed as things forgot."

Without sounding repetitious, look for opportunities to emphasize those points on which you both agree. Think of your listener as an ally rather than as an enemy to be trapped or defeated.

9. Let him express himself.* Let your target discuss what to you might appear to be irrelevancies, but which to him are pet peeves or burning issues. When he brings them up, it means he wants to talk about them. Let him fulfill this need within reasonable time limits. Express regret for his difficulties, appreciation for what he gives you, gladness for anything he gains, and any other feelings you have of genuine responsiveness to what he says.

Persuasion is not an exercise in logic. It is a gentle art that taps emotions and sentiments. Be aware of the subtle undercurrents that operate between you and your target and you will become a better persuader. Be guided by what Theodore Parker once said: "Thought convinces; feeling persuades."

18

HOW TO RESOLVE CONFLICTS

"Conflict is the gadfly of thought . . . it stirs us to observation . . . it shocks us out of sheeplike passivity . . . and sets us at noting and contriving." This quote by philosopher John Dewey reflects the reaction of some people who are faced with a conflict; namely, that it acts as an energizer and a stimulus to action. But for the majority of us, conflict means only one thing, stress. And all too often our reaction to stress is one of immobility. We freeze and are unable to carry on.

Chris Argyris, the management psychologist, has worked with thousands of business executives who can't solve problems. They have been repeatedly faced with conflict crises in which they lose their problem-solving versatility. In sensitivity training, which Dr. Argyris originated, his goal is to unfreeze these people and restore their ability to solve conflicts.

If you are ensnared in a conflict with someone, you needn't feel there is no way out. There is a psychotechnique that may help you at least to initiate a solution to your problem. It is called scriptwriting and it was conceived by psychologists Gordon and Sharon Bower of Stanford University. They consider it a negotiating technique that helps conflicting parties arrive at an agreement.

This psychotechnique is not guaranteed to solve your difficulty, but it is a blueprint to follow. It will make your job a lot easier when you take the first steps to resolve your problem. It requires you to take the initiative and is a proven assertiveness training exercise.

Scriptwriting—A Psychotechnique for Dealing with Conflicts

This is a four-step process in which you describe, express,

specify, and then set consequences. The abbreviation DESC stands for each of these four terms.

First answer the following questions about your conflict:

1. Describe: What unwanted behavior has my downer shown? (A downer is a person with whom you are in conflict.)

2. Express: How can I tell him or her how I feel about this?

3. Specify: What behavior might we mutually agree on to change in ourselves to resolve our conflict?

4. Consequences: What rewarding consequences can I provide to my downer for sticking to our agreement?

Now begin to actually write your script.

Step 1. *Describe.* Begin to write your script by describing to your downer the exact behavior you find bothersome. Be as objective and specific as possible, for example, "You seem to be giving me hostile glances lately," or, "The other night you criticized me again in public about my driving." Don't psychoanalyze him. Instead, use simple, concrete terms to describe his behavior. Don't accuse him of bad faith or ulterior motives.

Step 2. *Express.* Write what you *feel* about his offensive behavior. Select the exact words that describe or reflect the way you honestly feel. For example, "When you give me those glances, I feel upset and puzzled about where our friendship stands," or, "I feel belittled when you dwell on my driving habits when others are around." Avoid hurting your downer or provoking guilt feelings.

Step 3. *Specify.* After you describe your downer's behavior and express your feelings about it, ask *explicitly* for a behavior change. For example, "I'd like you to tell me directly when I have said or done anything that annoys you," or, "I would like you to stop criticizing me in public."

Requests are most likely to be accepted and adhered to if you give only a few at a time. Best results happen with only one request. Remember, the request must be reasonable. Be aware that there is your end of the contract to fulfill also; that's the next step.

Step 4. *Consequences.* Here, write out the payoff or penalties to both parties if they keep or break the contract. Spell out the reward that the downer is to receive if he changes his behavior. For example, "If you will level with me when you feel annoyed with me, I will try hard not to do it again," or, "If you stop criticizing me in public, I will try to be extra careful when I drive."

If the consequence is a punishment, you might say, "If you keep snubbing me, I guess I will just have to react in kind toward you," or, "If you don't stop criticizing me in public, I'll have to defend myself against you by criticizing your bad habits, too."

The Bowers suggest emphasizing positive consequences and soft-pedaling punishing consequences.

If you have never taken the time to plan a confrontation you will readily see the benefits of scriptwriting: (a) It forces you to clarify the situation and define your needs. You get a chance to think objectively about your actions; (b) it gives you a small concrete task as a starting point toward assertion; (c) it gives you confidence in handling the next confrontation assertively because you know what your "considered proposals" are going to be. You avoid stupid, thoughtless outbursts you will later regret; and (d) it gives you the chance to plan out the right words with just the right balance to express exactly what you want. You also have a written record to review instead of relying on your memory.

Here are some sample DESC scripts, which the authors give to help you write your own.

Requesting Information

Sam says to his boss:

Describe: I have asked you several times to teach me loans. You have replied yes, but you haven't taken any action.

Express: I feel I'm not learning an important part of the job. This is frustrating and undermines my performance.

Specify: I want to arrange with you a specific date when you will teach me loans.

Consequences: *(Positive)* If I learn loans now, I will be able to save time later and do a better job. *(Negative)* If I don't learn soon, I will simply not know my job when I need to, and time will be wasted later.

Results: Sam made an appointment for Wednesday for his

boss to teach him about loans. He learned about loans easily, and felt more competent in his job.

Requesting a Billing Adjustment

Jane writes:

Dear Sirs:

Describe: I deliberately took note of the time your repairman spent fixing my dishwasher. Your repairman arrived at 9:15 and worked until 10:00.

Express: I am surprised by your billing and I am seriously questioning the bill for twenty-four dollars.

Specify: I expect the bill to be adjusted to the correct charge of twenty dollars which, as I understand it, includes travel time (eight dollars) plus three-quarters of an hour labor at sixteen dollars per hour.

Consequences: I am counting on continued satisfaction with your service.

Yours truly,
Jane Doe

Results: Jane received a courteous letter saying that her bill had been reduced to twenty dollars. The billing department had made a mistake.

Requesting Help

Situation: It's a holiday weekend and Sue is overwhelmed with house chores. Her children are lounging and watching TV. They don't offer to help. Her husband and the kids are hoping to squeeze in a few days of fishing and she realizes that when they leave she'll be left with all the work. She takes the initiative and delivers this script to the kids during a TV commercial:

Describe: You are looking at TV even though we have asked for your help with the gardening.

Express: I am annoyed that you relax so much under these circumstances and then complain about not going fishing. If Dad found the garden weeded and spaded he would feel less pressured and would take you fishing.

Specify: The garden must be weeded and spaded before you can go fishing. Will you help do that today?

Consequences: *(Positive)* There will be time for a fishing trip tomorrow only if this job is done today. *(Negative)* If this is not done today, there's no fishing tomorrow.

Results: They agreed they would turn off the TV as soon as the show was over, then go out and spade the garden plot. They all went fishing and Sue enjoyed a quiet weekend.

Requesting a Raise

Situation: Mary feels she is underpaid and has tried to suggest this several times to her boss (a dentist). For instance, she'd casually say, "Well, I've been here two years, time for promotion (ha-ha)." Only it wasn't funny because he never responded. To take action, Mary wrote this script and delivered it.

Describe: I have been working for two years without a raise. My salary is twenty-five dollars less than the average monthly salary for dental hygienists in this area.

Express: I feel unfairly treated. I have worked conscientiously to build your practice. When I started there were barely enough patients to fill one day. Within a year we had more than forty hours filled each week and we have maintained that work load for more than a year now. I think I contributed to that success.

Specify: I want to discuss a 15 percent pay raise and employee benefits. Will you discuss these with me Wednesday after work?

Consequences: *(Positive)* I want to continue working here because I enjoy this office. *(Negative)* But I cannot continue unless my salary and benefits are raised to reasonable figures.

Results: Mary's request was taken seriously because she had documented it with specific information in the *describe* step. They met in two days and negotiated a pay raise.

Saying No to Unreasonable Demands

Situation: Arlene knew she would be asked again to drive for her son's Cub Scout activities. The solicitor who called each year was persuasive, using arguments like, "We need dependable, reliable drivers like you, who can take charge of this important function. Without your help, we would fall apart." Arlene had this script ready by the phone when the solicitor called this fall.

Describe: As I understand it, you are asking me to drive for six Cub Scout functions.

Express: I feel put upon because this is very costly, both in gasoline and my time.

Specify: I'll drive for only three excursions this year, once in November, again in January, and in March. Please mark me down as a parent to call for those months and no others.

Consequences: *(Positive)* That way I'll be happy to help you in future years. *(Negative)* But if you ask me to do more, I'll simply refuse.

Results: The solicitor was taken aback by Arlene's assertive voice, especially when Arlene responded negatively to her guilt-producing plea about how much she needed her for the job. From the tone of her voice, the solicitor was glad Arlene agreed to drive three times.

If your downer disagrees or only partially complies with your DESC script demands, don't be discouraged. Write another script and try again to talk it out with him. And remember the advice of the Bowers: "Good contracts change with the requirements of the situation and the feelings of the people involved. They are tools for improving your life—use them that way!"

19

HOW TO BE AN EFFECTIVE LISTENER

Years before we speak a language, we've already begun the process of learning through listening. But our innate human tendency for self-expression is so overpowering that when we learn words we immediately desire to utter them. Thus listening becomes a secondary process to speaking and we fail to more fully develop a valuable asset.

Listening is an art that is never formally taught to us, yet everyone would benefit if it were. We would understand others better and be a more valuable friend to them if we improved this crucial skill. Here are some strategies to help.

Psychotechniques for Better Listening

1. *Show acceptance.* If someone wants to talk with you, the best first step is to convey an attitude of helpful concern, even before he opens his mouth. It will lower his defensiveness and allow more of his feelings to emerge.

Make eye contact with him and keep it. Your words will sometimes interfere with his expression, so if you can, minimize your responses. Instead, convey with your eyes, face, and body that you are interested in what he says.

2. *Use door-openers.* If your rightful place is to listen to him and he is reticent, encourage him to loosen up with a few "door openers" like, "Why don't we discuss it," or "You might feel better if you get it off your chest." When you do this, however, remember that you have a responsibility of trust about what he discloses.

3. *Focus on what he says, not how he says it.* Although you may feel that what he says is strange or his ability to express it is

poor, always discipline yourself to listen for the value of what's being said. Be guided by the notion: How can I be of help to this person, or what can I learn from him. You're not judging a public speaking contest. Concentrate on ideas not impressions.

4. *Keep your thoughts in order.* When you are listening, use certain guidelines: Try to anticipate what he will discuss on the basis of what he's saying or has said to you in the past. Ask yourself, "What's he getting at? What point is he making?" Mentally summarize what he has stated. If you feel it would help, say something once in a while to help him clarify his thoughts.*

5. *How to handle long pauses.* If he trails off and seems blocked, he may be experiencing strong feelings connected to what he has just divulged or would like to express. If this happens *don't* be abrupt. Keep his train of thought moving by merely feeding back to him a few of his last words. For example, if he says, "Then it hit me. She said she didn't love me anymore. . . ." (long pause), your answer might be, "She said she didn't love you anymore."

6. *Don't interrupt with involved questions early in the conversation.* It's okay to ask short questions to clarify points as he goes along, but allow him time to finish before you ask long questions. A good rule is *Think twice before you speak once.*

If your question may be an upsetting one, save it until very near the end of your meeting. You don't want to so unnerve him that he won't be able to continue.

7. *Help him ventilate.* If he is pent-up with emotion and needs to discharge it, hear him out and try not to interrupt until he is finished. Don't underestimate the good you can do by just listening sympathetically.

Convey understanding and make supportive acknowledgments all along the way like "Yes," "Mmm," "I see," "I understand," and so forth.

Don't stir up other emotions while he is in the process of his catharsis by finding fault with him, asking him to hurry up, pointing out his inconsistencies, or showing disbelief or contempt for what he is saying.

8. *Help him think straight.* When a person has something on his mind, he is often unclear about how he feels. He usually needs

*See point 8 for tips on how to do this.

a sounding board to help him crystallize his thoughts and feelings. You can help by doing these things:

   a. Make reflective summary statements.
   b. Point out relationships with other things he's said.
   c. Discourage "catastrophizing."

Here is an example using these three points: Suppose someone says, "I don't know the reason they fired me. I don't think it was only my work. I recall getting into scrapes with my assistant. If the word gets around, I hope it won't hurt my chances of getting another job in town. That would be a disaster."

You might answer as follows:

   a. (Make a reflective summary statement)—"You think they fired you for the way you dealt with your assistant and you're feeling scared that you may not find another job here."

   b. (Point out relationships)—"You suspect maybe the word will spread around. Isn't that the way you felt when you lost your previous job?"

   c. (Discourage "catastrophizing")—"This surely isn't the end for you. You've been fired and rehired before. You'll do it again. With your skills you could still look for work in Stamford. It's only twenty minutes away from here.

   9. *Don't criticize.* If a speaker hits a raw nerve in you—a pet bias or a sensitive topic—don't jump on him to defend yourself against the indignity. You can also go to the other extreme and support with zeal what you hear. This is equally bad because once a speaker detects which side you are on he will tend to withhold other feelings he has that go against your views.

In either case, whether you're pro or con, it reflects your need to get into the act, a move that often blocks a speaker from expanding on all facets of the subject.

Good listening isn't easy. It takes self-discipline. Over a lifetime we've built up faulty habits of inattention to what others are really trying to say. At this stage, it becomes largely a matter of undoing these habits; and if many thousands in the helping-arts professions have done it, you can too.

Wilson Mizner once wrote: "A good listener is not only popular everywhere, but after a while he knows something too."

20

HOW TO BE MORE ASSERTIVE

With so much assertiveness training (AT) in popular psychology books these days, it seems that one should take a course in it if only to be protected against all those who have already done so.

Yet there is a serious and genuine need for AT among people who are constantly the victims of their own passivity. Their problem extends from dealing with the cocktail party loudmouth all the way to refuting the professional con artist who profits from those who can't defend themselves against his supersalesmanship.

In our competitive society, those who are passive will more often than not lose in the game of interpersonal relationships. They suffer without a whimper the indignities that occasionally arise in human interaction, and they usually blame themselves for their social failings. These are the unsung social "martyrs" of our time.

There are psychotechniques that can help you if you are among those who have trouble dealing with social exploitation. But before we discuss them, a few points should be clarified.

To be assertive means to have an active rather than a passive attitude about life. It's a special form of self-disclosure, which means expressing yourself outwardly rather than inwardly. It does not mean being aggressive, overbearing, or angry. Nor is it the royal route to manipulating someone. Also, it isn't gamesmanship or a self-centered, "to hell with everyone else" attitude. AT teaches skills to help you protect your self-esteem. You train to become a fighter, yes, but one who fights fairly when threatened by a transgressor. AT has other benefits too. Generally speaking, it instills generalized feelings of well-being in people who practice its techniques. It has been shown, for example, that people with phobias who learn to be assertive become less fearful

95

and depressed. Many people with psychosomatic ailments report that they don't have as many aches and pains as they had before they started being assertive.

AT teaches both verbal and nonverbal reactions. For example, a diner may tell a waiter, "This is cold. Please bring me a hot cup of coffee" *(verbal),* or instead he may frown visibly to let the waiter know that his coffee is cold *(nonverbal).*

But assertive behavior doesn't only mean reacting to something that offends or disturbs us. It also includes positive behavior that expresses regard, caring, concern, warmth, and love for another. Thus, if you greet someone with "I hope you have a nice day," or "Can I give you a lift to the station?" these are also assertive acts.

Consider assertive skills as you would any other acquired social skills that help you deal more effectively with others. In the same way that you learned from your parents the social amenities of "thank you," "excuse me," and "pleased to meet you," assertive behaviors, like other social responses, must also be learned. They should automatically come into play to strengthen your ties with others or when you feel that your normal rights have been ignored, refused, or overlooked. Once you have learned them, use them just as you would any of the other psychotechniques in this book.

Assertiveness Psychotechniques*

1. *Use "feeling talk."* Try to bring yourself more into the picture when you speak about the world around you. Be more expressive of what your inner self is experiencing.

Rather than make neutral comments about things, practice expressing your own likes, dislikes, and interests. Instead of blandly saying: "This shrimp is good," or "That's a nice song," say, "I'm really enjoying this delicious shrimp," or "I think that song is spirited and colorful." The *key* to this step is to use more

*Some of these psychotechniques were developed by psychologists Gordon and Sharon Bower, who teach assertiveness training at Stanford University in California. Their book, *Asserting Yourself* (New York: A&W Publishers, 1976) is perhaps the finest book on the subject.

words that describe your personal reactions, such as *I think, I feel, I'm pleased with, I like, I enjoy.*

2. *Boast tactfully.* Don't hesitate to speak about your accomplishments. Mention things you are doing or have done that are interesting and that make you proud. Get used to doing this; it's the equivalent of giving yourself a compliment. Don't feel that others will be bored or annoyed with what you tell them. If you listen closely to most conversations, invariably you will hear people praising themselves for things they've done. If it works for them it can work for you, too. One caution, however: keep in mind that most of us dislike long, boring narratives about the achievements of others, so don't gush!

3. *Use animation when you talk.* We talk with our bodies, too. Remember to smile, gesture, and show lively expression when you speak. The most important thing to keep in mind about body language when you speak with others is to make and maintain good eye contact with them.

4. *Disagree mildly.* Don't feel that life can always be one long agreeable conversation. There are times when we must disagree with each other in our quest for the truth. So, if you find yourself in opposition to what's being said, don't hide it. Disagree mildly, without being irate about it. One good way is to do this nonverbally, by raising an eyebrow in disbelief, looking away, or shaking your head, or even by changing the topic of conversation.

5. *Speak up when you don't understand something.* Whether it's a travel direction, a point in conversation, or a statement at a lecture, don't live with your confusion. Ask that it may be clarified. A good way to begin is to say simply, "I didn't get that last point; could you repeat it for me?" Chances are that if you need to ask a question, others also need clarification but are too shy to ask.

6. *Challenge put-downs.* Use questions also when you don't know how to interpret someone's remarks that made you feel uneasy. Some people who try to put us down with a hint of hostility in their voice often readily back down if challenged to explain just what they mean. Thus, if someone says, "You're trying to be defensive," ask "I don't know what you mean. Would you tell me in what way I'm defensive?" Or if they say, "I

think you're not sure of yourself," ask, "Would you tell me what makes you believe I'm not sure of myself." Or when they say, "Don't exaggerate," ask, "In what way do you think I might be exaggerating?"

If someone tells you to do something that you are not really obligated to do and that you feel is unreasonable, challenge the person with a simple question, like "Why do you feel I should do that?" If it is appropriate, suggest an alternate plan you would rather use.

7. *Don't hesitate to express active disagreement.* If you feel sure of your position and feel the other person is wrong, say so. It could be a golden moment. But don't force him into a corner giving him no alternative but to fight back. Start off with, "I may be wrong but . . . ," then make your point.

Don't mock, criticize, or embarrass him. Try to use phrases like "Perhaps you've overlooked this fact . . ." and "It's easy to be misled by this issue; look at it this way for a moment," or "Well, maybe there's another explanation for what you're saying."

8. *Avoid justifying your every opinion.* This is a cardinal rule in making an assertive stand. When you express an opinion, don't feel that you must justify it with facts and figures. If your opponent keeps haranguing you with "why, why, why," calmly inform him, "These are my values," "These are my feelings," or "These are my own reactions." Answer that you don't have to give statistics to make a point.

9. *Speak up.* Be sure that you speak up with a decisive and vigorous voice. It must have good tone, strong volume, and must convey that you are serious and sure about what you are saying. Speak without hesitation and without tripping over your words. Use plain, direct language. Don't whine.

10. *The "home field advantage."* There is an advantage to being on your own turf if you are to confront someone. Try to set up the situation so that the other person must meet with you in your own home, office, or room to discuss a "touchy" subject. It will give you more of a feeling of safety and familiarity, just as it will tend to give him the opposite feelings.

11. *Practice when you can.* Practice telling a salesclerk you are dissatisfied with an item you've bought. Explain calmly your rea-

sons for returning the purchase, then ask what can be done about it. If the clerk seems unsure of himself, then ask to speak to his superior or the floor manager and keep up the momentum of your complaint.

12. *Learn from others.* No one is completely original in making up social responses. Be alert for assertive behaviors that occur around you and use them when you need them. Don't copy them exactly as you've observed them in others. Use your own style. Try to speak and refashion them to fit in with the way you speak and do things.

Other Psychotechniques to Help You Be More Assertive

Each time we are assertive toward someone, we risk the chance of being put down by him. Passive people usually fear that this put-down will be too devastating to cope with. Dr. Albert Ellis, probably the most prolific writer in the field of psychology, uses a unique strategy. He teaches his clients to go overboard in assertiveness and actually provoke the criticism that they have dreaded all along. When they do this, they realize that the rebuffs they receive are not as catastrophic as they had feared and that they do not respond to the rejection after all. Dr. Ellis believes that once we overcome our faulty self-talk, which tells us we can't deal with put-downs, we become free to develop the skills for coping with them.

We have adapted some of his self-assertive methods here:

1. *Take risks.* Do some things you would like to do but avoid because you feel afraid of social embarrassment. For example:

a. Send a dish back at a restaurant, telling the waiter that it just does not taste right.

b. Wear an unusual article of clothing in public and be sure people see you in it.

c. Eat food while riding a bus or train.

d. At a large public meeting, stand up and in a loud and clear voice ask a provocative question.

e. Without putting him down, tell someone important to you

that you dislike some aspect of his behavior.

2. *Risk rejection by asking for something.* Ask for something you really want, like sex, a special food, some money, or going to a show. It must be something you think will result in a refusal. Risk this by asking for it. When refusal occurs, try to talk the other person into changing his or her mind. If you fail, try again another time with a new request.

3. *Risk saying no to someone.* Deliberately refuse to do something that you usually do against your will and without much satisfaction, like visiting someone, eating a certain dish, or doing a certain chore. You may refuse to do the task or use a stern or even snappy manner just to increase the risk that saying no will result in an annoyed reaction from the other person.

4. *Practice resisting or saying no.* Ask someone to role-play your partner. He or she then makes requests of you, which you refuse. Practice the refusals and exactly how you would phrase them. Give reasons for turning your partner down. Your partner should continue to try to talk you into complying. Continue this rehearsal until one of you feels convinced of the other's viewpoint and gives in.

5. *Set up a mock fight.* If you wanted to go a bit further than just learning resistance to compliance, you might even stage a mock fight and ask a third person to observe it. Set up a specific scene of conflict, say between you and your spouse, or a work associate, or your boss. Decide with your partner exactly what roles both of you will rehearse. After the "fight" is over, ask the observer and your partner to critique your performance. If you don't have an observer, use a tape recorder and replay it later.

6. *Express yourself.* When you show disapproval or when you refuse to do something, do it decisively. Use a decided *no*. Don't hedge or be fuzzy in your answer, and don't leave the decision up to the other person. Don't apologize for your answer.

Never allow yourself to be treated unfairly without pointing this out to your aggressor. On the other hand, don't be demanding or petulant.

When you express annoyance, don't attack or name-call. Instead, use "I-messages" (as we explain in chapter 45) to tell the other person that what he is doing is upsetting you. This means doing three things: (a) tell him about the behavior that annoys you; (b) tell him how it makes you feel; and, (c) tell him the "problem" it causes you.

After each of these actions, observe how you feel and how you cope with the resulting situation. Notice that the world doesn't fall apart as a result of your assertiveness. Pay particular attention to the things you did or said that helped you to succeed with the difficulty. Dr. Ellis, who is founder and director of the Institute for Rational Therapy in New York, concludes:

> If you practice these different levels of assertion and use them discriminately, you can act the way you want to act and still remain on good terms. In taking risks without worrying too much what other people might think of you, you assert yourself while, at the same time, convincing yourself that nothing horrible will happen. Also, you keep learning that you can tolerate the disapproval of others although you may not particularly like that disapproval. This also allows you to feel that no person, including yourself, can legitimately put you down globally or evaluate you as a rotten person when you perform an unpopular act.

Unfortunately, the spate of books on AT that appeared in the mid-1970s stressed being assertive in instances where a personal right is violated. For many people, however, the problem is not expressing opposition to others, but rather expressing (asserting) feelings of warmth or kindness.*

Some methods for doing this follow.

Psychotechniques for Expressing Positive Assertive Responses

1. Deliberately call out "good evening" or "good morning" to someone, even if you think they are not aware that you are nearby.

*The use of the term *assertive* is a sad case of the tail of usage wagging the dog of meaning. It is wholly regrettable that this term has taken hold and stuck. A better term for this type of behavior would be *expressive,* for it covers positive and constructive feelings as well as those which are disturbing or negative.

2. Try to recall a joke or a funny saying and then use it to make someone laugh or smile by repeating it to them.

3. Make a point to say "thank you," "please," "excuse me," "would you kindly . . . ," even in situations where it is not necessarily called for. Try to do this perhaps a dozen times in a day.

4. When you speak to someone you love, interrupt the conversation and say "I love you" to them, and then resume the conversation.

5. *Do small favors.* Hold a door, give your newspaper away on a train, give your seat to a standee on a bus, help someone put on his coat, hold an elevator for someone, let a person go ahead of you in line, offer another shopper your shopping cart when you are finished with it. Don't pass up any opportunity to do small favors. This will help you to be expressive, and give you good feelings about yourself.

6. *Ask directions.* Stop a person on the street and ask for directions. Begin by saying "May I ask you," "Could you kindly tell me," "Would you tell me please." After you receive the information, say "thank you," "I'm much obliged to you," "That's fine. Have a good day," or "Thanks for the help. I appreciate it." Try to let the conversation last more than a few seconds, then smile and thank the person, putting more than your usual feeling into it.

7. *Talk with salespeople.* (Plan this step by making some mental notes beforehand.) Walk into a store and speak to a salesperson about a particular item. Practice asking him or her about the various features of the item. For example, if it's a piece of furniture, ask about the wood, the finish, the material, the manufacturer's reputation, how best to clean it, and any other relevant questions you can think of. Practice conversing with the salesperson and, in a tactful manner, question closely what you are told about the item. Thank him or her for being so helpful and for providing all the information for you. Don't feel guilty about not buying the item! Do this in a number of stores with a variety of goods. This technique is excellent for prompting you to speak out and give praise.

8. The next time you meet someone, look for an opportunity to pay him a compliment. For example:

(To a friend), "I like the rich blue color of your coat."

(To a waitress), "That club sandwich was delicious."

(To a neighbor), "Your lawn is such a healthy deep green this season."

(To a friend), "You're looking well. How is your lovely wife (husband, family)?"

(To a work associate), "How do you manage to keep such a neat desk?"

9. *Learn to receive recognition.* Accept praise or compliments without feeling embarrassed about it. Don't play it down. If, within your heart of hearts, you feel proud of something, then don't be falsely modest about it. Simply agree with the person who is complimenting you and say, "Thank you, it's nice of you to say so." If someone says "I like your hairdo (your home, your car, your dog, etc.)," say, "Yes, I'm happy with it. Thank you. I'm glad you like it too."

Some final words: If you sincerely wish to improve your ability to be assertive, get over the notion that expressing negative feelings such as annoyance, distress, or displeasure is bad or improper. Keep these rules in mind:

1. The best way to get what you want is to ask for it.

2. The best way to avoid something you *don't* want is to say no to it.

3. The best way to stop someone from doing what you don't want him to do is to tell him how his actions affect you.*

Assertiveness training won't solve all your problems. Even if you do all the right things in defending your rights, it doesn't guarantee that you will always get your way. But you will stand a far better chance of winning your point if you are assertive rather than passive.

Ralph Waldo Emerson once said, "A great part of courage is having done the thing before." So it is with assertive behavior. Practice the psychotechniques we've presented here and you'll increase your confidence to deal with those who would put you down.

---

*These rules originated with Dr. Arthur C. Wassmer, psychologist from Kirkland, Washington. They are taken from his book, *Making Contact* (New York: The Dial Press, 1978).

21

HOW TO OVERCOME SHYNESS

Karen is a bright eighteen-year-old who avoids her neighbors. She blushes easily, stammers when spoken to, and hides when company comes. Her feelings of self-consciousness on first dates are almost paralyzing.

Brian is a young bachelor. He has spent most of his life studying music. He is a talented pianist, but has never learned to feel comfortable around people. Although he is popular at parties because he plays so well, he feels ill at ease and goes to them only because he is lonely.

Lisa is an attractive, brown-haired woman of twenty-six. She is efficient in her work as a research librarian, but in social settings it's another story. At meetings she is uncomfortable. At parties she clings to her hostess or goes off in a corner by herself.

These three people suffer from *people* phobia, or shyness. Their reactions are more common than you might realize. The fact is that all of us, no matter how secure we are, can be shy at one time or another when we feel different from those around us.

Children often show a shy, embarrassed reaction as evidence of their basic instinctual wariness of the strange or the novel. In time, however, they gain competence in dealing with the unfamiliar, and they outgrow much of this reticence.

For those who still retain the primitive shyness reaction, social life can be a formidable challenge.

Dr. Philip Zimbardo, a psychologist at Stanford University who is perhaps the nation's leading authority on the subject, has researched over six thousand cases and concluded that some 40 percent of the population suffers from shyness. *Situation* shyness (contrasted with *chronic* shyness) seems to be a universal condition. (It is highest in Japan, where social failure is considered shameful.)

Shy people are almost morbidly concerned about themselves. They fear they will be judged harshly. They are not free to be themselves but, instead, are always on stage, acting to please others and trying for a good evaluation.

The Difference Between Shyness and Unassertiveness

Curing shyness has become a popular area of interest for psychotherapists within the past decade. If you are the shy type, be comforted in knowing that there are tactics available to help you.

A good question to ask here would be whether there is a difference between assertiveness training and overcoming shyness.

Assertiveness training deals with a problem that is far simpler than shyness. It teaches skills of defending oneself and standing up for one's rights. This is a more advanced state of interaction than that which the shy person faces, who, as Dr. Wayne Dyer says, feels "socially immobilized." Shyness training is rudimentary. It provides fundamental social skills and teaches first steps in making the human connection.*

Psychotechniques for Overcoming Shyness‡

You will not reverse your shyness just by reading about it and understanding it intellectually. The key notion running through all the psychotechniques that follow is that you must start a growth process by behaving differently in some way. *You must act.* By doing this you will receive feedback from your actions and know that you are on the right track. This in turn gives you confidence for the next situation.**

---

*In a personal conversation, Dr. Zimbardo asserted that the problems of many shy people are not deep-seated. They have trouble with basics, like small talk, smiling, or even saying hello; and shyness workshops or self-help books can be very helpful. Often, shy people only need permission from an authority in order to try something new that to them may seem bold.

‡Some of the psychotechniques in this chapter have been adapted from Philip Zimbardo, *Shyness: What It Is, What to Do About It* (Menlo Park, Calif.: Addison-Wesley, 1977).
**This principle of action is used in all shyness clinics throughout the United States.

There are five target areas in overcoming shyness:

1. Self-study
2. Controlling uneasiness
3. Improving your self-image
4. Expressing yourself
5. Developing social skills

1. Self-study: The First Step

Keep a shyness diary. Carry a pad with you and list in it the time, place, and setting in which you felt shy. Also record what your behavior was. Look for patterns. Is your shyness related to certain people, circumstances, times, or places? Did others try to put you down? Did you bring on the discomfort through some faux pas of your own?

Keep track of the belittling statements you are repeating to yourself. Were you able to save the day with some response? If you had to relive a particular event, how would you handle it now?

Make a self-contract. After you've studied your diary, sit down and write out a contract with yourself. In it, put the following:

a. What realistic changes you want to see in yourself.

b. The date by which you want to achieve these.

c. How you will monitor your progress. (You might discuss it with a friend.)

d. How you will punish yourself if you fail to make progress (tidy up a closet, clean all your shoes, dust behind the furniture, etc.).

2. Controlling Uneasiness

Relax. Practice relaxation at least three times each day (using chapter 6). This will keep you in a calm frame of mind when social stress arises. Try to make yourself especially relaxed when you are about to meet strangers or enter a difficult situation. Use image desensitization (chapter 8) to rehearse this beforehand.

Try to bear in mind that undue tension will always reduce your efficiency. The more calm and comfortable you are, the better you will cope with others.

3. Improving Your Self-Image

Monitor your self-talk. When you are about to enter a "shyness" situation, try to be aware of what you are saying to yourself. Are your inner messages something like: "I'm a dull person," "I have a poor vocabulary," "I'm funny looking"? These statements are belittling and unfair to you.

Learn to listen to yourself with your "third ear" and you will find that you are often thinking ill of yourself. If necessary, sit down and write out a list of valid praiseworthy statements about yourself (e.g., "I'm intelligent," "I'm well read," "I am very reliable," "I don't push people around"). Let your mind dwell on them before you meet with others. Self-talk can be a powerful influence on your behavior; use it constructively.

Don't be self-biased. If you think of yourself as a disability, this attitude, in itself, will hamper your successful functioning. Many people consider themselves to be shy, yet they act this way only in a limited number of situations. Think of yourself as shy *only at certain times under certain circumstances;* for example, feeling uneasy around your boss, getting flustered when you talk to a policeman, or becoming nervous when you raise a question at a meeting.

If you can trust this perception, you will have to conclude that you do have the ability to act with self-confidence sometimes, so that now it's just a matter of expanding this behavior into other contexts.

Accept compliments. Learn to receive compliments graciously (see page 103). Don't blanch or wince when one comes your way. The important point is never to discount a compliment made to you. If someone admires your coat, don't say "Oh, this old thing." If you do, your complimenter appears foolish and lacking in good judgment.

Develop good feelings about yourself.

a. A good self-perception technique is to look into a mirror. Imagine meeting yourself for the first time. What is your first impression? What is your best feature? What is your worst feature? How would you improve it? How would you describe yourself to a stranger who is to meet you? How would you make a more positive impression? How would you improve your overall appearance?

b. *Your life movie.* Relax—imagine you are watching an hour-long movie of your life. Review everything you can recall about yourself, from the earliest memory to the present. Look for the main plot of the story. Who are the major characters? How are you feeling throughout it? What are the "peak" and "valley" experiences? Which of your present self-attitudes can be traced to your previous experiences with others?

After the movie, list the "ten commandments" that best summarize your family's ideals, values, taboos, and so forth.

c. *Make an "assets-liabilities" list.* List fifteen words that honestly describe your liabilities and your assets. What is unique about you that would be hard to duplicate? List five of the best things that have influenced your life. Do the same for the five worst things.

d. *Write yourself a letter.* Some shy people find that they gain many insights by writing a letter in which they express their feelings on a variety of subjects. Get into the habit of doing this whenever you feel the need to express yourself and there is no one available to listen.

After you do this, put the letter away; then read it a week later.

4. Express Yourself

Like everyone else, situationally shy people have feelings and ideas about everything under the sun. The problem is that they keep them a secret. The more you express yourself the more you will overcome your shyness. Practice the following exercises as often as you can:

a. *Speak to others.* Don't suppress yourself. Speak out even if you are uncomfortable, and when you do, don't forget to make and keep eye contact. This means letting people see your eyes and looking into theirs. Speak louder than usual.

In a bank line, in a doctor's waiting room, or in a supermarket checkout line, speak about medicine, checking accounts, recipes, high prices, new products—anything you can think of. The important thing is to break away from being passively shy. Say hello to a friendly stranger, hold a door or elevator for someone, speak to shop clerks, say more than hello to a friend (chat about the weather or where you're going). Telephone a store to ask about the price and quality of an item, a reference librarian to ask about a book, or a museum or university to ask about a research study. Then get daring and call a newspaper to get more facts on a story, or call a radio talk-program and ask a question. In brief, don't pass up *any* opportunity to express yourself.*

b. *Plan your conversations.* Gather facts about three interesting things each day and then plan to talk about them when you meet someone. Take these from something you've read, heard, or watched on TV. Try to get more information on the subject by looking into a book or two, or call that librarian. If you like, practice your delivery with a tape recorder or a mirror. Become accustomed to being the center of attention without feeling queasy.

c. *Position yourself.* Increase your social visibility at a gathering by sitting in the center of the room. Don't put yourself in a corner and decrease your chances of interaction with others.

d. *Be an authority.* Arm yourself by becoming an expert on some subject. It can be birds, baseball, politics, a news story, taxes, music, seafood, plants—anything. Then speak up on this subject when an appropriate opportunity arises.

e. *Pay compliments* (see page 102). Each day, memorize three pleasant things that you can say to people you expect to meet. Be sincere and natural. If they return the compliment, don't blush; just smile and thank them for it.

f. *Ask questions.* An easy way to fight shyness is to ask questions. This doesn't require you to be on the spot; rather, it places the demand to perform on the other person. Questions do not force you to become involved by revealing the opinions you may have on a subject. At a lecture or in a conversation, think of a question, then, at the right time, ask it. Remember, an intelligent question is often more admired than a brilliant statement of fact, especially if it stumps the other person.**

Also, when you raise a question, don't be satisfied with no

---

*If you're a woman, it may be awkward to speak freely to strange men in public places. Without changing the goal of this step, you will feel more comfortable if you choose, instead, another woman to speak to, then gradually, begin speaking to men. "Safe" places to do this are a library, study group, art gallery, classroom, political rally, or church meeting.
**When you ask a question you are practicing a counterreaction to your shyness. It is similar to the competing response that Azrin and Nunn (page 000) use to break bad habits, and to the relaxation that Wolpe (page 00) recommends as a substitution (a *reciprocal inhibitor*) for fear.

response. Repeat yourself. Shy people often don't bother to pursue a point if what they've said the first time is ignored or not heard. So, repeat yourself if you don't get an answer, and if you're interrupted, get back to what you were saying and be sure to finish it, even if it takes several tries.

5. Developing Social Skills

a. *How to use small talk.* Dr. Gerald Phillips, a professor of communication, has studied social reticence for over ten years. He directs the country's leading shyness clinic, the Friendship Clinic at Penn State University.

He advises, "Don't wait for the other person to make the first overture. Extend your hand and introduce yourself first. 'I'm Phyllis Carter, what's your name?' Be straightforward. Don't be devious with something like 'Didn't we meet before?' Instead say, 'I noticed you from across the room and wanted to meet you.' "

Once you are past the introductions, start the process of small talk in motion. This actually is a misnomer, asserts Dr. Phillips: "It is not trivial by any means. It serves as a cautious prelude to an interaction, like the sniffing out process by which two dogs decide what their relationship will be." A very good tactic is to encourage the other person to talk about himself and then react with interest to what is said.

Phillips teaches clients to keep the ball rolling by using "sayables," like "How did you meet the host?" (if you're at a party), "Where do you live?" "Do you work in town?" "Do you like the city?" "Did you go to school here?" "Were you born here?"; or remarks about the setting, such as "Isn't that a nice picture?" "Aren't these comfortable chairs?" "Aren't these sandwiches tasty?" A good rule: Never be without a "sayable." Prepare and practice them at home or on the way to a social situation. They can be anything of mutual interest to you and the other person.

b. *How to break into a circle.* One challenge for a shy person is to enter an ongoing group. Here are some tips: Stand near the group and listen intently. Show interest and react (nonverbally with facial expressions, gestures, etc.) to what is being discussed. Begin to outline in your mind a question about the topic; then, when you're ready and there's a pause, introduce yourself, smile, and ask the question. Come on gently, and try to support what has already been said. Don't make any dogmatic statements, and, worse still, don't criticize a point, even though you feel like doing it. Simply ask a short, relevant question. It might go as follows: "Excuse me. I'm Marty Wayne. This is an interesting discussion and I was wondering if . . ." (your question). Remember to maintain eye contact with group members.*

c. *How to date.* Shy people feel exceptionally vulnerable in a dating situation because of the intimacy and the emotional intensity that it may demand. "Perhaps for this reason," says Dr. Zimbardo, "more and more dating is becoming a group activity: 'A bunch of us are going bowling. Why don't you come along?' "

We have adapted several dating techniques, which he teaches to clients at the Stanford University Shyness Clinic.

First, make your date by telephone. (You won't have to worry about your body image or your appearance this way.) Use a DESC script to provide you with things to say (see chapter 18, page 86).

Second, plan ahead and have seven specific goals in mind: When you reach your prospect, clearly *identify yourself* by name and, if necessary, explain where you met. For example, "This is Michael Sweeney. We met at the Clark's beach party last week. How are you?" Be sure *you are recognized* in turn. Then, if possible, pay the person a *compliment* related to your last meeting, one that is genuine and shows your regard for her values, ideas, position on an issue, sense of humor, and so forth.

Come to the point in a few minutes and ask for the date: "There's a new Woody Allen movie in town and I wondered if you'd care to join me in seeing it this Saturday?" If the answer is yes, decide on the details of time and place to meet. Be flexible. Then end the conversation smoothly and politely. If no is the answer, offer an alternative to the activity and the day, or suggest a more informal meeting, like a cup of coffee (or a drink) after work or school. If the answer is still no, politely end the conversation and indicate you'll call again some other time.

Use coping imagery. Use image desensitization to take the jit-

---

*Dr. Zimbardo recommends another method: Pick up a straggler (another outsider) and begin speaking with him or her; then slowly work your way into the group using the above techniques.

ters out of a social situation (follow Chapter 8 for this). Do this with a special twist. Imagine a situation that has repeatedly made you feel shy. Go over it in detail, step by step. Now imagine what you could have done if you were self-confident. Think about this positive reaction for a part of each day for the next week. Then, when you enter the actual situation, try to act in the confident way you have imagined.

A final word about shyness: In the beginning, take nothing for granted. Practice the ordinary behavior that is automatic for most of us: smiling, making eye contact, being a good listener, showing normal interest in the other person, paying attention to what's being said, acknowledging someone's needs, nodding, saying "yes," "no," "I see," giving and receiving compliments, starting and maintaining conversation, and so forth.

A useful device for remembering some of the key steps in this chapter is one offered by Dr. Arthur G. Wassmer. He uses the acronym SOFTEN: S—smile, O—open up (be expressive), F— forward (lean forward to meet the other person), T—touch (touch and make contact with the other person when ap- propriate), E—eye contact, and N—nod.

PART THREE
Ways to
Better Health

22

HOW TO OVERCOME INSOMNIA

The Spanish author Cervantes once wrote that "sleep is the best cure for waking troubles." Unfortunately, this aphorism is not true for many Americans whose troubles cause them to *lose* sleep. They suffer from insomnia.

It is estimated that perhaps thirty million of us suffer from some form of sleep disturbance. Sleep clinics around the world have enabled us to study and develop means to cure the harried sleep-loser. If you are one, here are several psychotechniques that will help you to achieve wholesome and natural sleep.

Some Psychotechniques for Overcoming Insomnia

1. Before bedtime, relax as completely as possible using chapter 6 as a guide. Take a warm bath and a glass of warm mllk. (Milk contains the amino acid triptophan, known to induce sleep.)

2. Be sure your environment is right: that your bedroom is quiet, dark, warm or cool enough; that your bedclothes are comfortable, and so forth.

3. Engage in quiet activities for about an hour or so before bedtime.

4. Don't take caffeine for between two to four hours before you retire. This includes cola and chocolate drinks, coffee or tea.

5. Do vigorous exercise about two hours before bedtime. But don't do it just prior to sleeping as this will tend to stimulate you.

Psychotechniques for Overcoming Insomnia by Dr. Charles P. Kelly

One method used for years by many clinicians is that of Dr.

Charles P. Kelly. It is a clinically proven psychotechnique for inducing natural sleep and is based on the research of Dr. Seymour Kety of the University of Pennsylvania.

Dr. Kety's work revealed that carbon dioxide build-up in the blood causes a condition known as respiratory acidosis, which produces sleep. This also occurs when we take most sleeping pills.

Dr. Kelly's method uses breathing exercises to build up carbon dioxide in the blood stream, in addition to muscle relaxation and imagery ("mind pictures," as he calls them). It involves alternating periods of maximum breathing with breath holding. It goes as follows:

1. Lie on your side in bed and inhale until the abdomen is fully expanded and the chest lifted as far as possible. Then exhale completely, being sure to draw in the abdomen strongly at the end of the exhalation in order to expel as much air as possible from the lungs. The abdomen should then be allowed to relax completely but without inhaling. Do this three times.

2. At the end of these three maximum breaths (not more than three are recommended), when the lungs are as empty as possible and the abdomen fully relaxed, hold your breath without either inhaling or exhaling until you begin to feel discomfort. When this point is reached, start three more maximum breaths as you did before. These three maximum breaths are again followed by a period of breath-holding. Repeat this cycle several times. Dr. Kelly summarizes this step as follows: "The maximum breaths and breath-holding should be continued through four to eight periods of maximum breaths and three to seven periods of breath-holding . . . always beginning and ending with a period of three maximum breaths."

3. While you are doing the breathing exercises, Dr. Kelly recommends that you also engage in imagery of nursery rhymes: "Twinkle Twinkle Little Star," "Rock-a-Bye Baby," and so forth. Try to visualize vividly the images they conjure up in your mind. He says: "While repeating the lines [Rock-a-Bye Baby] therefore, clear mental pictures should be formed of the tree, the baby, the cradle, the rocking motion, the sturdy bough, the tree's swing in the wind. . . . In all the breathing exercises the eyes should be turned upward."

Why nursery rhyme images? Dr. Kelly says, "The Mother

Goose lines above have been chosen partly because they are already associated in everyone's mind with sleep."

4. Dr. Kelly also suggests complete relaxation before you go to bed. His sleep method should be repeated each night until sleep comes naturally.

Psychotechnique for Overcoming Insomnia by Dr. Richard R. Bootzin

Other psychotechniques for overcoming insomnia have been developed by Dr. Richard R. Bootzin of Northwestern University in Illinois. Dr. Bootzin, a noted behavior therapy researcher, studied a large number of severe insomniacs whose required time to fall asleep averaged over ninety minutes.

In a one-month period, his six-step method reduced the average time they needed to fall asleep to sixteen minutes. His method, which he calls a *stimulus control technique,* has been successfully used throughout the world. We present it here:

1. Lie down to sleep *only* when you are sleepy.

2. Do not use your bed for anything but sleep. Do not read, write, or watch television in the bedroom.

3. If you find yourself unable to fall asleep in a reasonable period of time (fifteen to twenty minutes), get up and go into another room. Stay up as long as you wish and then return to the bedroom to sleep.

4. If you still cannot fall asleep, repeat step 3. Do this as often as necessary throughout the night.

5. Set the alarm for the same time every morning and get up when it rings, no matter how tired you may be.

6. Do not take naps during the day. Steps 5 and 6 will help you develop a consistent natural sleep rhythm.

23

HOW TO CONTROL YOUR DRINKING

Since we have always been a drink-oriented society, it would be hard to convince Americans that "water is the only drink for a wise man," as Henry David Thoreau once advised.

In this country, there are about 5.5 million alcoholics, who make their lives and those of others miserable because of a crippling habit. So far, science has not discovered a satisfactory cure for chronic drinking. Some experts believe it can't be cured with our present state of knowledge.

In June 1976, the Rand Corporation issued the startling results of a long study funded by the National Institute of Alcohol Abuse and Alcoholism. The study created so much furor that Morris Chafetz, the director of the Institute and himself a supporter of the findings, was forced to resign. The work was based on research with 1,340 alcoholics, and its findings were that some problem drinkers *could* safely resume social drinking if they learned new behavior habits.

Since 1976, many studies have confirmed the conclusion that, indeed, many problem drinkers can learn habits of drinking in moderation.

We believe that there is no self-help psychotechnique that will cure alcoholism. This is a serious condition, which may have a physical basis and could require hospitalization. But we do believe that a program using psychotechniques can be designed to control the amount of alcohol consumption for the person who is not so disabled (the problem drinker), provided he follows the rules.

One of the best methods for controlled drinking is that of Drs. William Miller and Ricardo Munoz. We present an adaptation of it here and have added several points of our own. The approach we present has been tested on hundreds of problem

118

drinkers. It has received the endorsement of many prominent behavior scientists and physicians who now have begun to rethink their strategies about treating drinkers.

A word of caution before you begin: The method is not intended to cure either the compulsion to drink or the extreme tendency toward alcoholism; rather, it is given to teach behavioral skills of self-control over drinking impulses, so that one may continue to enjoy social drinking.

The key to controlled drinking is to break down the process into manageable parts and then to focus on one part at a time. This is what we have done in the following step-by-step program.

Learning About Your Blood-Alcohol Concentration

How you react to alcohol depends on its concentration in your bloodstream. Your blood-alcohol concentration (BAC) is a measure of the number of milligrams of alcohol per 100 milligrams of blood, and it depends on three factors: how much you drink, how fast you drink, and how much you weigh.

Your BAC affects your behavior. Here are some examples:*

A BAC of 20 mg.%—Light and moderate drinkers begin to feel some effects. This is the BAC reached after one drink.

A BAC of 40 mg.%—Most people begin to feel relaxed.

A BAC of 60 mg.%—Judgment is somewhat impaired. People are less able to make rational decisions about their capabilities (e.g., to drive).

A BAC of 80 mg.%—Definite impairment of muscle coordination and of driving skills; legally drunk in some states.

A BAC of 100 mg.%—Clear deterioration of reaction time and control; legally drunk in most states.

A BAC of 120 mg.%—Vomiting occurs, unless this level is reached slowly.

A BAC of 150 mg.%—Balance and movement impaired. The equivalent of a half pint of whiskey is circulating in the bloodstream.

*Adapted from William Miller and Ricardo Munoz, *How to Control Your Drinking* (New York: Prentice-Hall, 1976), p. 11.

Table 1

Approximate Blood-Alcohol Concentration (mg. %) Reached
after One Hour of Drinking, According to Body Weight
and Number of Drinks Consumed

Number of Drinks	Body Weight							
	100	120	140	160	180	200	220	240 lb.
	45	54	63	72	81	90	99	108 kg.
1	30	30	20	20	20	10	10	0
2	60	50	40	40	30	30	30	20
3	100	80	70	60	50	50	40	40
4	130	100	90	80	70	60	60	50
5	160	130	110	100	90	80	70	70
6	190	160	130	120	110	100	90	80
7	230	190	160	140	130	110	100	90
8	260	220	180	160	140	130	120	110
9	300	250	210	180	160	150	130	120
10	330	280	240	210	180	160	140	130
11	370	310	260	230	200	180	160	150
12	400	340	290	250	220	200	180	160

A BAC of 300 mg.%—Many people lose consciousness.

A BAC of 400 mg.%—Most people lose consciousness; some die.

A BAC of 450 mg.%—Breathing stops; death.

Now that you understand how alcohol can affect behavior, you must decide what your limits of drinking will be. There are two limits that you should set: one is for any single occasion where drinking will occur, and the other is for your regular, day-to-day drinking patterns. To do this, look at table 1. If you weigh 160 pounds and you've decided that you don't want your BAC to go beyond, say, 40 milligrams, then run your finger down the column under your body weight of 160 until you reach 40 milligrams. Then slide your finger left to find that the number of drinks you can have is two. If you weigh 120 pounds and set a BAC of 50 milligrams for yourself, then the number of drinks you can have is also two. If you weigh 200 pounds and set a BAC

Table 2
Approximate Blood-Alcohol Concentration (mg. %) Reached
after Two Hours of Drinking, According to Body Weight
and Number of Drinks Consumed

Number of Drinks	Body Weight							
	100	120	140	160	180	200	220	240 lb.
	45	54	63	72	81	90	99	108 kg.
1	10	10	0	0	0	0	0	0
2	40	30	20	10	10	10	0	0
3	80	60	40	30	30	20	20	10
4	110	90	70	60	50	40	30	30
5	150	120	100	80	70	60	50	40
6	180	140	120	100	90	80	70	60
7	220	180	150	120	110	90	80	70
8	250	200	170	150	130	110	100	90
9	280	230	200	170	150	130	110	100
10	320	260	220	190	160	140	130	120
11	360	290	250	210	180	160	150	130
12	390	320	270	230	200	180	160	150

of 60 milligrams, your limit would be four drinks.

The tables for two, three, and four hours work the same way.

Psychotechniques for Controlling Excessive Drinking

Self-monitoring has been found to be amazingly effective in helping problem drinkers to control their drinking; so the next step is to set up a drink diary. To do this, write the following headings across the top of a few three-by-five cards: date and time, type of drink, amount, and situation. Carry a card with you in your purse or pocket and keep the cards for the duration of your program. When you've set your BAC level and your drink limit, note this in one corner of the card.

Now you are ready to begin the program itself. Follow these behavioral suggestions to help you to control your drinking:

1. Your efforts will be more successful if you ask someone to

Table 3

Approximate Blood-Alcohol Concentration (mg. %) Reached
after Three Hours of Drinking, According to Body Weight
and Number of Drinks Consumed

Number of Drinks	Body Weight							
	100	120	140	160	180	200	220	240 lb.
	45	54	63	72	81	90	99	108 kg.
2	20	10	10	0	0	0	0	0
3	60	40	30	20	10	10	0	0
4	100	70	60	40	30	30	20	10
5	130	100	80	60	50	40	30	30
6	170	130	110	90	70	60	50	40
7	200	160	130	110	90	80	70	60
8	240	190	160	130	110	90	80	70
9	270	220	180	150	130	110	100	90
10	300	250	210	170	150	130	110	100
11	340	280	230	200	170	150	130	110
12	370	310	260	220	190	170	150	130
13	400	340	280	240	210	180	160	150
14	430	370	310	260	230	200	180	160

help you by acting as your buddy or partner. Also, tell your family about your plan and ask them to cooperate. Keep the points that follow in mind.

2. Since alcohol is not digested but is readily absorbed in the blood through the stomach and intestinal walls, you won't become drunk if you drink moderately and keep food in your stomach. So it is a good idea to eat, preferably high-protein or fatty foods, before you enter a drinking situation, and keep on munching while you are there.

3. The body can clear alcohol from the blood at an average rate of three-quarters of an ounce per hour, so if you are of medium build and don't drink more than this amount per hour, you are probably safe.

4. Avoid drinking when upset. Alcohol should not be used as a substitute for being with another person. If at all possible, try

Table 4

Approximate Blood-Alcohol Concentration (mg. %) Reached
after Four Hours of Drinking, According to Body Weight
and Number of Drinks Consumed

Number of Drinks	Body Weight							
	100 45	120 54	140 63	160 72	180 81	200 90	220 99	240 lb. 108 kg.
3	50	30	20	10	0	0	0	0
4	80	60	40	30	20	10	0	0
5	120	90	70	50	40	30	20	10
6	150	120	90	70	60	40	30	20
7	190	150	120	90	80	60	50	40
8	220	170	140	120	90	80	70	60
9	250	200	170	140	110	100	80	70
10	290	230	190	160	130	110	100	80
11	330	260	220	180	150	130	110	100
12	360	290	240	200	170	150	130	110
13	390	320	270	230	190	170	150	130
14	420	350	290	250	210	180	160	140
15	450	380	320	270	230	200	180	160
16	480	410	340	290	250	220	190	170

to share your distress with someone rather than drink alone.

5. The notion that you won't become as drunk if you do not mix various kinds of drinks is a myth, but do try switching to types of drinks other than those to which you are accustomed. The idea is to frustrate and alter your well-established habit of drinking certain favorite drinks.

6. The manner of your drinking is also a crucial factor in weakening your drinking tendency. Always sip your drink, never "chug-a-lug" or gulp it. Try to make your drink last longer than usual.

7. Put your glass down after each sip and try to stretch the interval between sips to sixty seconds or more. Try to go as long as you can.

8. Extend the time between drinks. Don't give in to impulses

without a fight. If you feel an urge for another drink, try to let some time go by, say five, ten, or fifteen minutes. The longer you can go between drinks, the more you strengthen your self-control.

9. A word of caution about thirst. Never drink alcohol to relieve thirst if you can drink something else instead. Stay away from salty tidbits (pretzels, peanuts, potato chips, etc.). These foods create a thirst and will cause you to drink more than you need.

10. As a problem drinker, you may be too unassertive in drinking situations. This means that when people pressure you to drink (often without realizing it), you comply. Some drinkers have difficulty resisting this type of social pressure and falter in coming up with the right thing to say to fend off an offer of another drink. You must learn to be assertive here and to practice refusing drinks, perhaps by asking for coffee, water, or soda instead of alcohol. Therapists have found that it greatly helps a drinker to have a supply of retorts ready and waiting. Here are a few:

> No thanks, I've just had my fill.
> I'm not ready for another just now, thanks.
> I can do without another right now.
> I'll pass on this till later.
> I'm leaving soon, thanks anyway.
> Skip me on this round. I'll catch you later.
> No thanks, I'm flying low just now.
> Sorry, I've had enough. I must be on my toes tomorrow.
> No thanks, I've had enough to feel just fine now.
> No thanks. I'm watching my calories.

Keep in mind that there will be much less pressure on you to "have another" if part of your previous unfinished drink is clearly visible to your host.

11. *Being relaxed is important.* It can't be stressed enough that the good feelings of "hanging loose" can go a long way toward curbing your desire to drink. A large percentage of problem drinkers are hypertense people who use alcohol as a tranquilizer. They depend on it to cut their tension level. So practice the deep muscle relaxation exercises in chapter 6 at least three times each

day to keep your tensions down. If you learn to live relaxed you'll never need to lean on alcohol to relax you.

12. Set a definite schedule or timetable of goals for yourself and then reward yourself when you achieve them. You might, for example, resolve not to drink more than three drinks at a two-hour party and have not more than three drinks on any day during the week. Or you could take only milder drinks (wine, vermouth, beer) for several days. If you reach these goals, buy yourself a gift, take in a show, or enjoy a meal out. Be sure to let others know about your progress and give them the chance to praise you. This is the best reward of all.

13. Review your diary cards each week and try to learn from them. Note the times, places, and people that render you most vulnerable. Once you've pinpointed these, try to avoid or eliminate them from your day-to-day activities.

If you tend to drink heavily in a particular place, go there less often; if you drink a lot when you meet or date a certain person, try to avoid him or her; if you tend to sit in a particular place in a bar, change your seat when you go there. The idea is to weaken *anything* in the chain of events that reinforces your drinking habit.

Of course, the opposite holds for those circumstances in which you *can* control your drinking. If you find that when you run into a certain person you tend to drink less, then try to meet him or her more often. Or if a particular tavern tends to slow down your drinking rate, then try to spend your drinking time there. The main thing is to understand what it is about these circumstances that helps you to control your drinking urges.

A final word: Don't be discouraged if you have setbacks now and then. An addiction is not easy to conquer. The only rational thing to do when you slip is to begin again with stronger determination.

24

HOW TO STOP SMOKING*

This [chapter] seeks to round up helpful suggestions from experimental projects that have been carefully evaluated. No sure techniques are offered, no absolute laws of human behavior provided. There are different kinds of smokers and what helps one may not work with another. Individuals must choose for themselves from what is presented here.

Each man and woman makes a personal decision on the important matter of smoking cigarettes. The fact that you are reading this indicates that you are properly concerned.

Many millions have given up cigarette smoking. Although for some people it is surprisingly easy to quit, many find it rather difficult. Psychologists estimate that half of all cigarette smokers can stop without too much difficulty once they make up their minds to do so. They feel only minor or temporary discomfort. Others suffer intensely, almost unbearably for days and weeks. Remember that those who have tried to stop a number of times may succeed this time.

Will you really make the effort? We hope so.

Once You Have Stopped

If you are like most cigarette smokers, you will in two weeks or less say farewell to that hacking, shattering morning cough, good-bye to ugly thick phlegm, adios to smoker's headaches and unpleasant, cigarette-induced mouth and stomach complaints.

You will be saving—how much? Well, how much do you

*This chapter is a reprint of a pamphlet published by the American Cancer Society. Illustrations in the pamphlet have been deleted. Reprint permission has gratefully been received from the American Cancer Society.

smoke up in dollars every week? Could be considerable.

We will no longer burn cigarette holes in clothing, furniture, rugs, or tablecloths. (The National Fire Protection Association says that "smoking and matches" caused a property loss of $80,400,000 in 1965.)

Food will tend to taste better and your sense of smell will return to normal.

Cigarette breath (it can be very offensive) will disappear.

Q Day, cigarette quitting day, might well be renamed K Day —kindness day for both you and your friends.

By quitting cigarettes you are instituting an immediate program of kindness to your lungs, your heart, your stomach, your nose, your throat.

A Garland of Facts

If you are trying to give up cigarettes, you need strong reasons. These warnings were developed by research in recent years and may help you.

Live a Little More

A longer and healthier life is high on our priorities: giving up cigarette smoking is the most important action that the average smoker can take that will improve the physical quality of his daily life, extend his life expectancy, and increase his chances of avoiding lung cancer, heart disease, emphysema and other illnesses.

The More Cigarettes . . . the More Cancer of the Lung

The regular cigarette smoker runs a risk of death from lung cancer ten times greater than the nonsmoker; men who smoke more than a pack a day have about twenty times the lung cancer rate that nonsmokers have. Unfortunately, only about one in twenty cases is cured. With early diagnosis results are better, but early diagnosis of lung cancer is uncommon.

Six-and-a-Half Years, 78 Months, 2,372 Days

Men aged twenty-five who have never smoked cigarettes regularly can expect on the average six-and-a-half years more of life than men who smoke one pack or more a day.

Twice as many men who are heavy smokers (two packs a day) will die between twenty-five and sixty-five years of age, as those who have never smoked regularly.

Give Your Body a Break

Male smokers (ten or more cigarettes a day) between forty-five and fifty-four have more than three times the death rate from heart attacks than nonsmokers. Between the ages of forty and fifty-nine strokes kill nearly twice as many men who smoke as nonsmokers.

How to Escape Work

Cigarette smokers between forty-five and sixty-four miss 40 percent more days at work than do nonsmokers.

According to the Public Health Service, if cigarette smokers had the same rates of illness as those who never smoked, some seventy-seven million working days would not be lost annually and there would be one million fewer peptic ulcers.

A Deep Breath

Emphysema, a relatively rare disease a few years ago, is now a major cause of medical disability in this country. Most emphysema is caused by cigarette smoking. The disease is both a crippler and a killer, causing the lungs to lose their elasticity. Eventually the effort to breathe becomes a constant, agonizing struggle.

Keep Nature's Protection

Cigarette smoke paralyzes the cilia, tiny hairs lining the bronchial tubes, that sweep foreign particles out of the lungs.

Without this protection, healthy lung tissue can be injured, even destroyed by particles in the smoke.

Best Tip Yet

The evidence suggests that the more tar and nicotine you inhale, the greater your risk. As a result of the hot breath of publicity, cigarettes today have less tar and nicotine than those smoked generally in the fifties and early sixties when research was being done to establish the risks. If your tar and nicotine dosage is lower than it was five years ago, you are probably damaging yourself less. However, the best tip yet is don't smoke cigarettes.

Some of the Millions Who Make It

(The following brief sketches are based on fact from letters, conversations, reports, but with names and details altered. They have been selected with the intention of helping others to go and do likewise.)

William . . . is a psychiatrist who decided soon after the Report of the Advisory Committee to the Surgeon General that he ought to stop cigarettes. What triggered his actual decision? He suspects it was a morning cough, but he is not sure. In any case, he stopped and reports that he watched television for several evenings (which he rarely did), ate rather more often than was his custom, did some strenuous skiing, and was happy that his wife cleared the house at once of all cigarettes and ashtrays. He was uncomfortable for a few days, but not climbing the walls. He hasn't smoked for three years.

Joan . . . is a writer who reads seriously. After the Surgeon General's Report she stopped smoking cigarettes. Cold turkey. No gum, no candy, no gaining of weight. Some bad temper for a few days but it was not a big or difficult deal.

Pete . . . is a carpenter who smoked two packs a day for twenty-five years. He was proud, however, that his three sons did not smoke. He wanted to quit but was hooked, he knew it, and he told his boys never to take up the habit. When they believed and obeyed him, he was delighted. He stopped only after an operation in which two-thirds of his stomach was taken out because of an ulcer. He still doesn't discuss the fact that he has given up smoking but he hasn't smoked for a year and he was in the hospital long enough so that when he went back on the job and people began offering him a smoke, he was able to say "no" very calmly.

Bill . . . drives a school bus mornings and evenings and has made it a point not to set a bad example to the boys and girls by using cigarettes in their presence. When he delivered fuel oil—as he did the rest of the day—he used to smoke like a chimney. In the evening he smoked with his food, his coffee, his beer. One night he got into an argument about cigarettes and all at once he tossed his package away and said he was through. His friends didn't believe him, but for a week he took a raisin whenever he wanted a cigarette. Boxes of raisins. Three years later he nibbles on raisins occasionally but he never smokes.

John . . . was a brilliantly successful advertising man who smoked two packs of cigarettes a day: when he began to cough, and this happened half a dozen times in a work day, it took him embarrassed moments to get over it. He had thought of stopping cigarettes, even made half-hearted trials—but at last he decided to go for broke. His first step was to keep a careful record of when he smoked each cigarette, and how much he wanted it. Then he selected a future Q Day and told his family and friends what he was doing. He began to cut down, 50 percent each week for four weeks, and he laid in mints and gum. When Q Day arrived he stopped. It was a rough experience and at one time he was in such a serious depression that he frightened his wife. After a visit to his physician, however, he stood by his decision. During the first three months he gained fifteen pounds, but he lost all this later, his cough is gone, and he feels 100 percent better. He hasn't smoked a cigarette for two years.

Arthur . . . is a biology teacher who switched from cigarettes —a pack a day with deep inhalation—to a pipe with no inhaling, without too much difficulty. He enjoys handling his pipe, filling it, lighting it . . . and he says that he can now talk to his class about the dangers of cigarette smoking and not feel hypocritical.

Bob . . . had smoked two packs a day for twenty years but he gave up the habit suddenly and completely. He credits TV messages and says that they filtered through to him via his seven-year-old son who began asking why he smoked and why didn't he stop?

Bob has always tried to be honest with his children and so after some thought he replied that he smoked because he was stupid and he didn't stop because he was weak. This was a remarkably uncomfortable admission to make to his boy and to himself. Bob decided that a father who was both stupid and weak would not be much of an influence for his son. So he quit smoking.

Joyce . . . is a very competent office manager who smoked more than a pack a day for twelve years. When her husband kicked the habit, she tried but did not make it. Her two youngsters, five and seven years old, worried at their mother's smoking. She in turn worried because her boys did not give up their security blankets. Finally her children volunteered to go to bed without their pacifiers if their mother would give up her pacifier: cigarettes. They made a bargain and have kept it, though Joyce reports she backslides occasionally at parties, but never in front of her boys and never more than two or three cigarettes a week.

Linda . . . reports she really puffed away at cigarettes when she was worried or tense. She was disturbed by stories of the risks of smoking and wished she could stop but continued until (she says) one of the American Cancer Society's announcements gave her just the push she needed. That was three years ago; about the same time her husband lost his job, her four-year-old child broke her arm, her baby had his first nasty cold. Linda wrote the Society that, despite all the tensions, she "came through with a smile and a prayer, but no cigarette."

Harold . . . a reporter of considerable distinction—smoked three packs a day: at the typewriter, before and after breakfast, during lunch, in the afternoon and evening. Any tests would have shown him as a habituated smoker, a bad risk for a withdrawal program. However, he stopped, cold turkey, and has not smoked for ten years. Why? His specialty was science writing and he decided that if the scientists he trusted were right he was a fool to go on smoking. For two weeks he was in considerable discomfort, but with gum and candy he kept going. He says he feels great since he stopped smoking.

You Can Kick the Habit

There are twenty-one million ex–cigarette smokers in the United States: about one in five adult men in this country has dropped the habit.

Those who give up cigarettes report a great sense of satisfaction, of tremendous pride in being able to do it. To learn a new way of living, a way without cigarette smoking, is very rewarding to the ego—and to the ego's mate.

As You Approach Q-Day

Many stress will power as the decisive factor in giving up cigarettes. For them the sense that they can manage their own lives is of great importance. They enjoy challenging themselves and, with an effort of will, they break the cigarette habit.

Thus, some psychologists describe stopping cigarettes as an exercise in self-mastery, one that introduces a new dimension of self-control.

Others, often successful in many aspects of living, find that will power does not help them in giving up cigarettes. They try to stop, they do not, and they feel guilty over their weakness. This is a mistake, since many smokers fail in their first and second, even their fifth attempts, and then finally succeed. Those whose "will" fails in breaking the habit are not weak but different. Their approach must be less through determination and more through relearning new behavior with patience and perseverance.

Self-suggestion, when one is relaxed, aimed at changing one's feelings and thoughts about cigarettes can be useful.

One health educator remarked recently, "Nothing succeeds like will power and a little blood in the sputum."

To think of stopping smoking as self-denial is an error: the ex-smoker should not believe that he is giving up an object of value, however dependent he may be on it. If he begins to feel sorry for himself and broods on his sufferings, they may well become more severe and indeed unendurable. He must recognize that he is teaching himself a more positive, more constructive, more rewarding behavior.

Try Cutting Down

An important first step in the process of giving up cigarettes for many smokers is to set the date for Q-Day, when you are going to stop completely and, as it approaches, to gradually reduce the number of cigarettes you smoke, day by day, or week by week.

A good system is to decide to smoke only once an hour—or to stop smoking between the hours of nine and ten o'clock, eleven and twelve, one and two, three and four, etc. And then extend nonsmoking by half an hour, an hour, two hours.

You may decide to halve the cigarettes you smoke week by week, giving yourself four weeks to Q-Day.

How about smoking half of each cigarette?

In the process of reducing the number of daily cigarettes, try various possibilities; if you have one pocket in which you always carry your pack, put it in another so that you will have to fumble for it. If you always use your right hand to bring your cigarette to your mouth, use the left hand. Is it your custom to rest the cigarette in the right corner of the mouth? Try the left side.

Make it a real effort to get a cigarette:

Wrap your package in several sheets of paper or place it in a tightly covered box. If you leave your change at home you won't be able to use a cigarette machine.

Shift from cigarettes you like to an unpalatable brand.

Before you light up, ask yourself, "Do I really want this cigarette or am I just acting out of empty habit?"

A smoker may find an unlighted cigarette in the mouth is helpful. Others enjoy handling and playing with a cigarette.

Cigarette smoking is a habit that is usually very well learned —learning the habit of not smoking can be difficult. It can help in breaking into your habit chain to make yourself aware of the nature and frequency of your smoking behavior.

Keep a Track Record

Many smokers have found that a useful step in understanding

their smoking is the keeping of a daily record on a scale like that below.

In your gradual withdrawal you may decide to eliminate those daily cigarettes that you find are rated 1, 2, or 3, that is, ones you want least.

Or you may wish to give up first the cigarettes you like most. In any case, keeping a smoking log will give you information about yourself, make you more aware of what your smoking habits are.

You may find that you are largely a social smoker, that smoking makes you feel closer to others, more welcome at a party, that you seem to have more friends. A cigarette may play a surprisingly large part in your picture of yourself as a mature and successful person.

How do you convince yourself that people like and respect you for more important reasons than for your cigarette? Try not smoking and see.

Score Card

Copy this record sheet seven times for seven days. Make a check for each cigarette you smoke, hour by hour, and indicate how much you need it: a mark in the box opposite 1 shows low need, a mark opposite 6 high need, opposite 4, moderate need, etc. Then decide which cigarette you wish to eliminate.

Need	Morning Hours (AM)							Afternoon. Evening Hours (PM)												
1	6	7	8	9	10	11	12	1	2	3	4	5	6	7	8	9	10	11	12	1
2																				
3																				
4																				
5																				
6																				
7																				

Plus and Minus

Write down carefully, after some thought, in one column the reasons why you smoke and in another all the reasons why you should give up cigarettes.

As you turn this exercise over in your mind, new material will occur to you for one or the other columns. Thoughtful concentration on your reasons for giving up cigarettes is important in changing your behavior.

Four Smoking Styles

Dr. Silvan Tomkins distinguishes four general types of smoking behavior. An abbreviated summary of the types follows:

Habitual Smoking

Here the smoker may hardly be aware that he has a cigarette in his mouth. He smokes as if it made him feel good, or feel better, but in fact it does neither. He may once have regarded smoking as an important sign of status. But now smoking is automatic. The habitual smoker who wants to give up must first become aware of when he is smoking. Knowledge of the pattern of his smoking is a first step toward change.

Positive Affect Smoking

Here smoking seems to serve as a stimulant that produces exciting pleasure, or is used as a relaxant, to heighten enjoyment, as at the end of a meal. Here a youngster demonstrates his manhood or his defiance of his parents. This smoker may enjoy most the handling of a cigarette or the sense and sight of smoke curling out of his mouth. If these smokers can be persuaded to make an effort, they may find giving up cigarettes relatively painless.

Negative Affect Smoking

This is sedative smoking, using the habit to reduce feelings of distress, fear, shame, or disgust or any combination of them. This person may not smoke at all when things go well, but under tension, when things go badly, he reaches for a cigarette. These smokers give up often, but when pressure hits them, when there's a challenge, they find it very hard to resist a cigarette. A strong substitute, like nibbling ginger root, may be useful.

Addictive Smoking

The smoker is always aware when he is not smoking. The lack of a cigarette builds need, desire, and discomfort at not smoking. With this increasing need is the expectation that a cigarette will reduce discomfort—and the cigarette does give relief—for a moment. Pleasure at smoking is real, just as the build-up of discomfort at not smoking is real, sometimes rapid and intolerable. The enjoyment of the cigarette, however, is very brief, and may be disappointing—but the suffering for lack of even slight relief is considerable.

For this smoker, tapering off doesn't seem to work: the only solution is to quit cold. Once you have been through the discomfort of breaking your psychological addiction, you are unlikely to start smoking again. The experience of giving up has been too uncomfortable—and too memorable for you to risk having to go through it again.

Some such smokers have found it useful to increase during the week before Q-Day the number of cigarettes smoked, to go from two packs to four, to force themselves to smoke so that their bodies will be in actual revolt against the double dose of tar and nicotine.

The Week Before Q-Day

Think over your list of reasons why you should not smoke: the risk of disease, the blurring of the taste of food, the cost, the cough, the bad breath, the mess and smell of morning-after ashtrays.

Concentrate each evening when you are relaxed, just before you fall asleep, on one result of cigarette smoking. Repeat and repeat and repeat that single fact. Drive home another fact the next night and another the next.

Review the facts that you know about the risks of cigarette smoking. Remind yourself that there, but for the grace of God go you; that a man of twenty-five may indeed, if he continues smoking, lose six-and-one-half years of life, that—if he is a heavy smoker—his chances of dying between twenty-five and sixty-five years of age are twice as great as those of the nonsmoker. Would you fly in an airplane if the chances of crash and death were even close to the risks of cigarette smoking?

Action: Q-Day

Let us suppose that you know, now, when and where and how you smoke. You have suggested again and again to your tired mind that smoking is a dangerous business.

"But what will I do the morning of Q-Day when, mind or no mind, I want a cigarette?"

We hope you will prove that you are stronger than your dependence. Here are some tips that may prove useful when you have an impulse to smoke!

For the Mouth

Drink frequent glasses of water.

Nibble fruit, celery, carrots, cookies, eat somewhat self-pleasing food.

Suck candy mints and/or chew gum (sugarless gum will be easier on your teeth).

Chew bits of fresh ginger when you start to reach for a cigarette. (Take this gently, ginger root is aromatic and pervasive —some experience it as burning, others as clean and satisfying.) Bite a clove.

Nicotine Replacement

Lobeline sulphate tablets, available without perscription, are reported to make it easier for some people to stop cigarettes. Authorities disagree, however, as to whether the tablets provide a substitute that will help satisfy the smoker's craving for nicotine.

(Since some individuals—those with stomach ulcers, for instance—should not use these tablets, check with your physician before trying them.)

Be Vigorous: Exercise

Strenuous physical activity can be very helpful, particularly in working off the irritation—real anger in some ex-smokers—at not having a cigarette.

Vacation is a good time for some people to stop: try camping, mountain climbing, tennis.

Stretching exercises, calisthenics or long walks can be relaxing.

Go "No Smoking"

For some the cigarette after breakfast coffee, at the end of lunch or dinner, is where smoking is forbidden. Ride in "No Smoking" cars.

A spurt of motion picture or theater-going will pass many hours.

Keep away for two weeks from friends who are heavy smokers.

Use Your Lungs

Deep breaths of fresh air can be wonderfully calming.

Inhalers—that clear sinuses—may help tide you over the first few days.

After Meals

For some the cigarette after breakfast coffee, at the end of lunch or dinner, is most important. Instead of a cigarette try a mouth wash after each meal.

If you have a specific pattern that you follow after dinner you may want to change it: read a book instead of a newspaper, skip familiar television programs, sit in another comfortable chair, try crossword puzzles, do some household task you have been putting off, take your dog out for a walk.

On the other hand, you may prefer to do all the things that are familiar and comfortable for you and to which you are used —except to smoke cigarettes. Take your choice.

Reward Yourself

Be sure that you have your favorite food on Q-Day.

Give yourself all the things that you like best—except cigarettes.

When you have saved a bit of money by not smoking, buy yourself a present: perhaps a record, or a blouse, or necktie, book or trinket. When the impulse to smoke is strong, try a substitute: a drink of water, a piece of gum, a walk around the block, stretching and deep breathing.

These substitutes may only satisfy you temporarily—but they will keep you alert and aware and will soften the strength of your desire to smoke. Equally important are constant reminders to yourself of why you are stopping cigarettes. Remember the reasons that you put down for not smoking? Recall the basic data about disease, disability, and death that are caused by cigarettes.

When you stop smoking, you may be exposed to gentle and not so gentle needling from smokers. What are they really saying to you? Perhaps that they wish they could stop, too.

You may be very uncomfortable, but "this too shall pass" relates also to cigarette-less shakes, irritation and temper, the urge to climb walls, depression, anxiety. Time is a great healer.

Unfortunately fear of failure to make it seems to deter men and women from even trying—yet for many, giving up cigarettes while uncomfortable and a strain is by no means agony. After all their terrible expectation, stopping can seem relatively easy.

Questions and Answers

Do You Believe in "Cold Turkey" Quitting?

Yes, for some, no, for others. If you are a really "addicted"

smoker, psychologists favor the sudden, decisive, and complete
break.

For some, gradual withdrawal is less painful and entirely satisfactory.

Some cigarette smokers shift to pipes and cigars—there is of
course some risk of mouth cancer from these but overall mortal-
ity among cigar and pipe smokers is only a little higher than
among nonsmokers, if the smoke is not inhaled.

What about Going to a Quit Clinic?

If there is a clinic or program in your community, you may
find it useful. The American Cancer Society favors such efforts.

Sharing your withdrawal experiences with others and working with them on a common problem can be very helpful. The
clinic may make it considerably easier in various ways to stop
cigarette smoking.

However, remember, no clinic can provide a sure result. In
this matter you must be both patient and physician.

Shall I Make a Big Thing of Q-Day?

Some find it most satisfactory to work on a schedule in which
Q-Day, quitting day, is singled out as the important, decisive day
in their personal lives—that indeed it is. Others who have known
for a long time that cigarettes are bad for them and that sooner
or later they will stop, wake up one day and say to themselves,
"This is it. No more cigarettes."

What motivates them? An obituary, an antismoking commercial on television, a magazine article, a leaflet brought home
from school by a child, a worried look from their son, being fed
up with a repeated cough. There are many possible stimulants to
stopping, but almost always beneath the casual-seeming but bold
decision are months, often years of serious thought and worry.

What if I Fail to Make It?

Don't be discouraged: many thousands who finally stopped
did so only after several attempts.

Some people prefer to stop for just one day at a time. They promise themselves twenty-four hours of freedom from cigarettes and when the day is over they make a commitment to themselves for one more day. And another. And another. At the end of any twenty-four hour period they can go back to cigarettes without betraying themselves—but they usually do not.

Is Smoking a Real Addiction?

This depends on your definition of words. In any case smokers obviously can become very strongly dependent on cigarettes.

However, the discomfort that most feel at giving up cigarettes is not like the painful withdrawal symptoms that drug addicts report.

Giving up cigarettes is much closer to the discomfort and the irritation produced by dieting than to the agony of stopping a drug. As so many know, dieting in an effort to lose fifteen or twenty pounds can be a most uncomfortable experience—but when you have done it, you have a fine feeling.

How about Ashtrays?

One school of thought asks, do you leave a bottle of whiskey near an alcoholic? Their recommendation is to get rid of cigarettes, ashtrays, anything that might remind a smoker of his former habit.

Another school of thought takes a different view and even suggests carrying cigarettes to demonstrate to yourself that you can resist temptation. Choose for yourself.

Shall I Tell Others of My Decision?

Some do, some don't. Some find that the wider they spread the news of their decision the easier it is for them to make it stick. Others regard no smoking as their own personal business and keep it almost entirely to themselves. Will you strengthen your decision if your wife and friends know that you have committed yourself to quitting?

Will I Gain Weight?

Many do. Food is a substitute for cigarettes for many people. And your appetite may be fresher and stronger.

During the first few weeks of giving up cigarettes some psychologists recommend pampering yourself: eating well, drinking well, enjoying those things that are pleasant and fulfilling.

Some people, those to whom self-mastery is vital, get rewards out of controlling their wish for fattening food at the same time that they are licking the urge for cigarettes.

Again, it depends upon the person and his approach.

How about Hypnosis?

There is much interest in this technique by some physicians who report success, particularly with hard-core smokers. Why not discuss the matter with a physician, if you are interested?

Shall I See My Physician?

YES. However, the problem is yours, not his, and he may not feel that he can be helpful. On the other hand, he may be able to give you sympathetic support and may prescribe medication. He can be helpful, also, in suggesting a diet which will prevent you from gaining too much weight.

Physicians as a profession have been leaders in acting on the risks of cigarette smoking: The Public Health Service estimates that 100,000 physicians (half of the physicians who once were cigarette smokers) have kicked the habit. A California study showed that only 21.3 percent of all physicians in the state were cigarette smokers in 1967.

Why Do So Many People Smoke Cigarettes?

Surely one reason is that the cigarette industry spends about $300 million a year in promoting the habit and in challenging the facts that scientists have produced that point to the dangers of the habit.

Another reason is that something in cigarettes, probably nicotine, is habit-forming: smokers become dependent rather rapidly.

Cigarette smoking is essentially a twentieth-century habit, encouraged by wars, by brilliant advertising, and by the development of remarkably efficient automatic machinery that produces those millions of round, firmly packed cigarettes.

It is only within the last fifteen years that we have learned, largely through research pioneered by the American Cancer Society, that this personal and socially accepted habit is extremely dangerous. Cigarette smoking is deeply embedded in our life: agriculture, industry, government, the communications media, all have a stake in it. It is still widely accepted, even though proven to be a most certain hazard to health.

Because promotion is important in maintaining the habit's popularity, the Society believes all cigarette advertising in all media should be terminated. We hope that this goal will be achieved voluntarily and that governmental action won't be necessary.

To Smoke or Not to Smoke?

A story is told of two young boys who were determined to challenge and expose a man who was supposed to be wise. They caught a small bird and decided on a formula that they felt could not fail. They would go to the wise man with their hands cupped and say: "Tell us, wise man, is the bird, that one of us holds in his hands, alive or dead?" If he said "dead" they would release the bird. If he said "alive" a squeeze of the hands would prove him wrong. When they confronted him and asked the question, the wise man smiled, and considered, and finally said, "The answer is in your hands."

Approaches in Giving Up Cigarette Smoking

(If you don't stop immediately and permanently)

1. List the reasons for and against smoking.
2. Select Q-Day—change to a low tar and nicotine cigarette.
3. Chart your smoking habits for at least two weeks: how

many cigarettes, when, the most and least important.

4. Repeat each night, at least ten times, one of your reasons for not smoking cigarettes.

5. Eliminate one category of cigarettes: The most or the least desired.

6. Secure a supply of substitutes: mints, gum, an inhaler, ginger root, etc.

7. Quit on Q-Day—try the different substitutes as the wish to smoke recurs—enlist your spouse or friend in a busy series of events: eating well, going to the movies or theater, exercise and many long walks, moderate drinking.

8. If you are depressed, see your physician and discuss your symptoms.

9. Keep reminding yourself, again and again, of the shocking risks in cigarette smoking.

25

HOW TO LOSE WEIGHT

Americans are suffering from an abundance of plenty, but we are paying the price for our bounty. It is estimated that sixty million of us are overweight. While we are being crushed to death by the cornucopia of edibles, we are starving for diets!

The average fat person goes on and off one-and-a-half diets each year and, between twenty-one and fifty years of age, makes fifteen major attempts to lose weight. Most of them fail. Famed nutritionist Dr. Jean Mayer, now president of Tufts University, once said that those who diet time and time again engage in "the rhythm method of girth control."

A few psychotechniques have proven very helpful for obese men and women who are highly motivated to lose pounds. Dr. Kelly Brownell, an obesity expert from the University of Pennsylvania, has said that we have every reason to be optimistic about such self-help methods. These psychotechniques fall generally into three categories: behaviorial management, nutrition, and exercise. We present their major points here.

Psychotechniques for Losing Weight

Behavioral Management

1. Develop Eating Awareness. Most overeaters tend to underestimate the amount of food they eat. They distract themselves from their habit, but by the end of the day they'd be surprised at how much they have consumed.

The best way to develop eating awareness is to keep a diary. This will help you to study your eating habits. In a small notebook, take one page for each day of the week. Down the left

145

side of the page list the hours of your day, say from 8:00 A.M. to
11:00 P.M. Across the top, mark off these five columns: (1) what
and how much you ate; (2) where you ate it; (3) what you were
doing at the time (watching TV, phoning, studying, etc.); (4)
whom you may have been with; and (5) how you felt at the time
(i.e., lonely, angry, frustrated, etc.). At the bottom of the first
column total the number of calories consumed for the day. Keep
a page like this for a period of at least one week.

Keeping an eating diary takes effort, but almost all research
on breaking bad habits recommends using one. Yours will help
you to learn about the mistakes you are repeatedly making.

2. Make eating a "pure experience." This means don't eat
and simultaneously use the phone, watch TV, read, or study. *Do
not* engage in any other activities except socializing with your
family or friends.

3. Do all your eating only in the kitchen or dining room.

4. Eat only at prescribed times during the day or evening.
Don't waver from this schedule.

5. When it's time to eat, pause from two to five minutes
before you take any food.

6. Eat slowly. It takes about twenty minutes for the stomach
to signal the brain that it is full enough, so *slow down*. Stretch out
the eating period.

7. Place your fork or spoon down after each mouthful. Then
resume eating after you have chewed your food well and swal-
lowed it.

8. Place small portions on your plate; then go back for seconds if necessary.

9. Don't keep food in sight or readily available at work,
school, or home.

10. Shop *after* you eat. If you are hungry it will tend to make
you buy more than you need.

11. Avoid buying "problem foods,"—foods you have trouble
resisting and which are fattening.

12. Aim for only a one-pound loss each week. This will allow
you to gradually relearn new eating habits and self-management
skills.

13. Team up with someone who also wants to lose weight.
Perhaps make a wager on who will lose it faster. You can both

bolster each other through the program.

14. Control your physical and mental moods. Overweight people tend to overeat when they are very hungry. To overcome this tendency, plan to eat three substantial, nutritious meals at definite times each day, or six small meals every two hours (keeping the same total calorie count for each, of course).

Try to avoid boredom as much as possible. It has been found to be a major cause of nibbling. Plan your week so that it will contain interesting and challenging activities.

Many overeaters "snack" as a pickup when they are fatigued. Avoid this by getting a good amount of sleep each night. Tension and frustration can lead to overeating. Reduce your tension level by learning to relax during the day and by planning a reasonable exercise program for yourself.

15. Tell others about your reducing plan and enlist their support in keeping you on target. You'll need all the help you can get.

Nutrition

16. Be conscious of calories. Foods differ markedly in their calorie counts and obese people tend to be ignorant of this. The fact is that many foods may be eaten in large quantities and not be fattening (like vegetables), while some in even small amounts (like apple pie) can add pounds fast. Acquaint yourself with the calorie count of the foods you eat. For about a dollar you can purchase a calorie counter or a nutrition book at a drugstore, which will help you to plan your meals intelligently.

17. After you've studied your week-long diary, consult your book or calorie counter and figure out the adequate number of calories for you. Calculating the correct number for an individual is difficult, but you can come fairly close to what yours should be. An average woman of 128 pounds, for example, requires about 2,000 calories daily, and an average man of 154 pounds needs about 2,700. Dr. Richard Stuart of the University of Michigan advises that a woman should not eat less than 1,200 calories and a man not less than 1,500 calories per day unless they are under the supervision of a physician.

Here are some calorie facts to keep in mind.

High-calorie foods	Calories per serving
Chocolate bar	150
Milk (one glass)	150
Cocoa milk (one glass)	150
Daiquiri	200
Chocolate cake with icing	450
Peach pie	350
Club sandwich (bacon, chicken, tomato)	600
Club sandwich (bacon, lettuce, tomato)	300
Scallops	400
Spaghetti	250
Pork chop	300
Hamburger and roll	350
Roast beef sandwich	300

Low-calorie foods	
Tea with sugar	20
Hard candy (one piece)	20
Cream cheese	100
Egg (boiled)	80
Yogurt	60
Dry wine	80
Sweet wine	150
Peach	50
Bologna	70
Bacon (broiled)	100
Lamb (lean)	150
Steak (broiled)	250
Roast chicken or turkey	150
Noodles, rice, or potato	100

18. When you dine, eat the low-calorie foods on your plate first, then go on to the other foods.

19. When you have the urge to snack, occupy yourself with something else. If you must snack, wait ten full minutes before

eating and pick a small quantity. If possible, try *not* to make it one of your favorite foods. Pick one that is low in calories. Dr. Stuart calls these "free foods," like uncooked celery, carrots, lettuce, radishes, cucumbers, and so forth.

20. Dull your appetite by having a cup of gelatin or sugarless soda one-half hour before mealtime.

21. If you cut out 500 calories a day you'll lose about 1 pound each week, but neither women nor men should allow total calorie intake to go below 1,200 calories in one day.

Exercise

22. It is a myth that exercise increases hunger. It *is* true that exercise burns off calories, so make exercise a daily part of your weight loss plan. Often all a slightly overweight person has to do to be trim and fit is to exercise more.

You don't have to be an exercise fiend. Begin with exercise that suits you best and stick to it. Use the following as a guide to how many calories are lost through exercise: On the average, light exercise (walking, gardening, light housework) burns up four calories per minute. Moderate exercise (bike riding, dancing) burns up seven calories per minute. Heavy exercise (climbing stairs, jogging in place, swimming) burns off ten calories per minute. Don't let weather deter you. I know of a slender, attractive woman who on rainy days runs up and down the stairs several times for her exercise.

23. For the first week of your program try to burn off at least sixty calories each day, then gradually progress to five hundred calories per day.

24. Reward yourself for success. Behavior modification experts agree that new action patterns need reinforcement, so treat yourself after you lose a specified number of pounds—enjoy a show, buy yourself a gift, take a trip.

If you are obese, chances are the temptation to eat will always be a challenge that you must meet and conquer. But think of it as a choice. One slender woman who was a former heavy put it this way: "I finally decided that the taste of chocolate cake just doesn't compare even remotely with the great pleasure I get when I slip into my size 8 dress."

26

HOW TO CONTROL PAIN

It has been said that humans endure pain as an undeserved punishment. Since the dawn of civilization we have toiled to prevent or reduce this drain to both mind and body. In a manner of speaking, pain prevention is the essence of this book. All the steps we describe ultimately are for trying to prevent pain, either psychological or physical.

Modern psychology provides a number of psychotechniques to reduce the pain that wracks our bodies. The underlying theme in many of them is distraction, a simple yet highly effective strategy. We've all seen it used many times by parents. Loving arms caress a fallen child who cries from the sting of a bruised knee. After a few moments of calm and steady reassurance, perhaps with the assistance of an ice cream cone, the crying stops and the child is pacified.

The key to our topic is the ability of the child to endure his discomfort by shifting his focus of attention. It is one of the most powerful methods for conquering pain. When used in conjunction with other techniques, it can achieve pain relief for even more serious physical disorders.

Take the case of John, a sixty-five-year-old retired army officer who experienced chronic abdominal pain. Although he was very active socially, the onslaught of pain embarrassed him so much that he withdrew from people and became a recluse. He managed the pain for several years by self-administering a painkiller.

Eventually, when the drug no longer helped, he sought the treatment of Dr. Phillip Levandusky and Loren Pankratz of McLean Hospital in Belmont, Maryland. John was taught self-control of his pain through relaxation, imagery, distraction, and refocusing of his attention. A year after his treatment he was still pain-free without drugs, and socially active once again.

Dr. Theodore X. Barber, chief psychologist at the Medfield State Hospital in Massachusetts, a leader in the field of pain research, has found that his clients can control up to 100 percent of their pain if they are trained to give themselves self-suggestions. Dr. Barber points out the way to do this as follows:

1. Learn to shift the focus of attention away from the site.

2. Concentrate on the pain sensations and feel them dispassionately and with detachment.

3. Dissociate yourself from the pain as if the afflicted part were not connected to the rest of your body.

At a deeper level, hypnosis has been used very successfully in blocking pain. Stanford University's Dr. Ernest Hilgard, who has probably done more than any other person to advance hypnosis as a science, believes that hypnotic pain control can be taught to patients with a wide range of physical ailments. He maintains that 10 to 20 percent of the population are capable of a hypnotic trance so profound that they can even undergo surgery without anesthesia. We'll have more to say about how you can use hypnosis to reduce your pain.

When Pain Control Should Be Used

A significant instance that justifies pain-control training occurs when the cause of the pain is known and usual methods, (medication, exercises, surgery) do not help. Some years ago, a sixty-six-year-old laborer was struck on the head by an aluminum ladder that fell from a height of four stories. He was left with several crushed vertebrae. After some eight years on a variety of painkiller drugs, he was finally put on codeine, which in time offered him some relief. He grew semi-addicted to this medication and eventually its effects began to wear off. Several specialists told him that he must learn to live with the pain or undergo risky surgery that could paralyze him.

This is the type of case in which pain-control training is called for.

In a more common application, the psychotechniques of pain

control can be especially helpful in day-to-day traumas. Let's say you've slammed a door on your finger, cut your foot, or had a tooth removed. You have throbbing pain, but there may be nothing much you can do about it until your injury heals. These are clear-cut cases in which you know the cause of the pain but still must live with it. The three psychotechniques that follow can be exceptionally helpful in such instances.

The first is that of Dr. Barber, who teaches his clients to control their pain by using distraction, imagination, concentration, and imagery. His many years of study on pain led him to conclude that "some persons can tolerate intense pain by taking a nonchalant, distant attitude, when they can view the pain as something 'out there' and not within themselves."

He says, "We have many bodily sensations and we must train ourselves to think of pain as just another sensation and another part of life's experiences. If we can, then it would lose the hold it has on us. All sensations don't have to be pleasant. We should train children not to dramatize pain, but rather, to accept it matter-of-factly as a part of living." He continues:

> One way to react to your pain is to get really bothered by it. For example, you can say to yourself it's terrible. You can emphasize the negative and the things you don't like. This always exaggerates our pain. The way you'll profit from the exercises which follow has a lot to do with the way you handle problems in living. People react to life problems the way they do to their pain. They look at the negative aspects and emphasize those. They get fussed-up and bothered. But you don't have to think negatively. Try to think positively as you go through these steps.*

Psychotechniques of Pain Control from Dr. Theodore X. Barber

Note: These methods become more complex as you go from

---

*A warning that therapists give on the subject of pain reduction and control is that not all pain is bad. Often it can be a premonitory sign of something potentially serious, which must be cared for before it grows worse.

In general, no one should blunt or mask pain by using hypnosis, biogenic training, or any other psychotechnique, unless the pain has been checked by a physician. So agree at the outset that you will get a medical checkup before you begin any pain-control psychotechnique.

step 1 to step 7. Try step 1 first, then go on to the others if you need them.

Step 1. Lie down in a quiet room and relax. (Use chapter 6 to do this.) Sometimes this is all that is necessary to relieve pain.

Step 2. *Feeling good.* This is an exercise in self-suggestion. Close your eyes and concentrate hard. Repeat positive phrases to yourself as follows:

I feel calm, unhurried and relaxed.
I feel strong and glad to be alive.
I'm growing more at ease each moment.
I have lots of time.
I'm at peace, okay, and I can tolerate this discomfort.

Spend ten to fifteen minutes repeating these or similar suggestions several times each day. Do not repeat these suggestions in a superficial way; instead, try to believe that they will help you. Say them with conviction, sincerity, and emotional commitment.

Step 3. *Distraction through pleasant memories and thoughts.* This method focuses your attention away from the pain. It takes effort but you can do it. Don't focus on the pain at all. Try to be aware of things around you in a way that you never have before. Close your eyes. Pretend that you have just arrived from another planet. Now open your eyes and experience every object as if for the very first time. Be conscious of colors, textures, contours, aromas, shadings, light, even people nearby. Feel the chair, sofa, or bed under you. Divert your attention to anything around you by whatever means you can, even if you do something deliberate like striking a table top, tapping your foot on the floor, or singing a song.

Sometimes you can go back in fantasy to relive a pleasant occasion. Mentally set yourself to recall an enjoyable moment, reexperience the thoughts, feelings, and sensations that went with it. You may also project yourself into the future to an event you look forward to—a visit to a friend or relative, a holiday, a vacation. Try to dwell on this and let it completely take over your thinking and feelings. Do these exercises with conscious deliberation.

Step 4. *Numbness and disappearing pain.* Imagine vividly that you are receiving a large novocaine injection. Visualize how it would be if this actually happened. Try to see the needle entering your body and the anesthesia slowly moving into the pain location. Gradually begin to feel numbness around your pain.

Notice the pain subsiding. Imagine that it is growing more and more numb. Growing dull, growing more and more bearable. Now begin to give yourself direct suggestions or commands that the pain is leaving ... going away ... growing smaller and smaller ... it's reducing ... becoming only a tingle. All through this step, try to remain as relaxed as possible.

Step 5. *Dissociation.* This highly effective method takes a bit of practice but it can be learned. Tell yourself, and try hard to imagine and believe, that the pain is *not* part of you. It is "out there" and you are "here." It is separate from your body and apart from you. The real you is up in your mind, your psyche, your consciousness.

You can take your awareness anywhere and separate yourself from the pain. The pain is something very, very different from yourself. The discomfort is not associated with you, not an integral part of you. The real you is up here in your head. You've cut yourself off—severed yourself from it.*

Step 6. *Analyze the pain.* Focus sharply on the pain itself. Do not let your attention wander. Try to get very close to the sensations—right into them. Then try to study the discomfort. Break the pain down into its component parts. You will find that it usually consists of many kinds of shifting sensations and changing feelings. Don't think of it as pain but, rather, concentrate on all the other changes that are occurring. Notice and look for pressure, soreness, burning, aching, pricking, throbbing, itching, pulling. Observe that it varies from moment to moment. View the pain as an objective occurrence that is happening inside you. See it as a complex thing and not as pain.

Step 7. *Zen Technique.* This is a technique borrowed from the Far East. Here, you *go* with the pain, you allow it to happen, you experience it fully, letting it take you over. You see the pain as an interesting, absorbing experience. It is different, unusual. It

---

*Dr. Barber tells me that he uses this dissociation method on himself and doesn't use novocaine when he sees the dentist. Author Wayne Dyer, another prominent psychologist, has also related to me that he has used dissociation when undergoing root-canal treatment.

arouses your curiosity. You don't have to like or dislike the pain, but study it and allow it to come.

Many of these methods, admits Dr. Barber, are not new. What is new is the notion of consistently and systematically practicing them until they become ready, usable tools for pain reduction. This is Dr. Barber's goal.

Self-Hypnosis

Over four thousand years ago, hypnosis was used by the ancient Greeks to alleviate pain. Today, self-hypnosis is experiencing its strongest revival ever, and its results are somewhat spectacular. Dr. Arthur S. Freese, an internationally known expert on face and head pain, describes in his book, *Pain*, how a doctor, himself a leading authority on hypnosis, successfully withstood injury by using self-hypnosis. The following is from Dr. Freese's account:

> Dr. Robert E. Pearson was a general practitioner in a small northern Michigan town. He had studied self-hypnosis to relieve pain for the hundreds of patients he treated every year for ski injuries. At 11:15 on Monday morning, September 30, 1963, Dr. Pearson heard a call from a contractor he'd hired to tear down a brick chimney. Stepping outside, he was struck by a five-pound brick decending at about thirty miles an hour from some forty feet above. It hit him squarely on the forehead.
>
> He heard an extremely loud noise, had some dizziness and a sick feeling. Without consciously thinking, he automatically used his knowledge of self-hypnosis to control the pain. His first thought was that he had to remain conscious to call his wife to drive him the twenty miles to a hospital. Relaxing later in her car, he suddenly felt the worst pain he'd ever known, but then his self-hypnosis took control again and his pain was quickly gone, not to return again despite the probing of the wound at the local hospital which revealed a severly fractured skull with bone fragments pressed into the brain tissues.
>
> Dr. Pearson arranged for penicillin shots and to be

driven to the nearest neurosurgeon some sixty miles away. Maintaining complete hypnotic control over his pain, he insisted on being discharged on Wednesday (brain surgery on Monday had removed the shattered skull fragments and repaired the wound). He then flew to San Francisco on Sunday for the annual meeting of his medical hypnosis society. He has since specialized in psychiatry and now teaches hypnosis all over the country.

So complete was Dr. Pearson's control of his pain by self-hypnosis that he never suffered from the time of his injury until complete healing, except for those few moments in his wife's car when he relaxed.

This is an uncommon story of total control over excruciating pain. It is inspiring for those of us who suffer afflictions far less serious.

Here is a method of self-hypnosis that you may use to control pain. It has worked well for a large number of patients with a wide range of physical symptoms.

Psychotechnique of Self-Hypnosis for Pain Control

1. First, prepare two signal words: one to bring you into the hypnotic trance (the *in-signal*), and one to bring you out of it (the *out-signal*). These you will use later. The in-signal can be any word like *deeper, trance, sleep, drowsy*. The out-signal can be a word like *up, out, awake, alert*. These are *special* words to use when you either enter or leave the hypnotic state.

2. Before you begin, clearly state to yourself the post-hypnotic suggestion. It is the specific goal or end point of your self-hypnosis. For example, you may say:

"My goal today is to reduce (or eliminate) the pain in my left leg for the rest of the evening."

"When I come out of the trance I will be alert and awake; I will feel relaxed, calm, quiet, and with less pain (or no pain) for the rest of the day."*

*For the first few sessions this step (the post-hypnotic suggestion) should be a conservative one. Say, "I will feel *less* pain than before." Then, as you try more sessions, gradually work up to "I will feel *no* pain for the rest of the day."

"The next time I go through self-hypnosis, it will go more quickly."

"Should an emergency arise while I am in a trance, I will immediately and automatically awaken and take whatever action is necessary."

3. Now you are ready for the self-hypnosis induction. It is an easy step and merely an extension of the tranquil state you achieved when you learned to relax in chapter 6. When you are completely relaxed and tension-free, whisper the in-signal word to yourself and, at the same time, take three deep breaths. Exhale *slowly*.

4. Try to let go and bring on a dreamy state of mind. Be passive. Don't work at it; rather, let it come naturally. Keep trying to move into a floating or drifting feeling. Try to be aware of any changes, subtle or otherwise, in your normal consciousness. Most people who practice self-hypnosis say that they are in the trance state when they have feelings like floating, drifting out of their body, dreaming, softness, calm, inner quiet, and so forth.

5. The hypnotic state is a very private experience. Be aware of any change in your conscious state. When you have reached this point, you are experiencing hypnosis. Describe to yourself just how your body feels and try to remember the sensations so that you can bring them back rapidly in later sessions.

After you have completed step 5, you are ready for the actual pain-control suggestions. From this point go on to use either step 6 or 7, or both.

6. Hand anesthesia transfer. Focus all your attention completely on one hand. Concentrate as hard as you can on it and visualize it becoming numb. Feel it losing all sensation. Think of it as completely insensitive, as if it were injected with a strong anesthetic like novocaine. It is completely dull. More and more, experience your hand as inert and without feeling. Continue to think of it as free of sensations, and when it feels very numb, place it over your pain area.

Think of the numbness being transferred from your hand into the pain area. Visualize the process as a steady draining of numbness from your hand to the site of your pain. See it as an infusion that permeates your entire pain area with its anesthetic qualities.

Feel the aching area calm down and lose its sensitivity, until it becomes as numb as your hand, more and more until you are completely pain-free. Imagine your distress diminishing, growing smaller and smaller until it feels like your hand, completely sensation-free.

7. While you are in this hypnotic state, focus all your attention sharply on the site of your pain and then follow any one of Dr. Barber's seven steps. Although he recommends these methods for use in the waking state, many people find them to be even more helpful while in the hypnotic trance.

The Psychotechnique of Dr. C. Norman Sheely

At the Pain Rehabilitation Center in La Crosse, Wisconsin, the center's founder, Dr. C. Norman Sheely, uses biogenic (autogenic) training for those who suffer pain. Dr. Sheely is one of the world's leading authorities on pain control, and his method has been taught to thousands of patients. He believes that many more patients could benefit from pain-control techniques were it not for the unfortunate resistance of many physicians. He states:

> The idea that the patient can and ought to manage, at least in part, his own pain or illness, flies in the face of traditional medical thinking. The whole thing smacks of too much self-treatment (which is justifiably frowned upon in cases of self-diagnosis, of self-administration of medication) or worse yet it sounds like the bugbear of the medical profession: faith healing! Consequently, even though there is evidence proving its effectiveness, autogenics is often seen at most, as the very last resort for unresponsive cases.

Dr. Sheely believes that "the possibilities for what biogenic training can do for anyone, pain patients in particular, are endless."

We present here a modified version of Dr. Sheely's autogenic method. It has been proven that those who learn it can influence their autonomic nervous system to properly control the functions of internal organs that are not under voluntary control.

1. Lie down in a quiet room and relax (use chapter 6).

2. Say each phrase below to yourself as often as indicated and repeat as often as necessary:

My arms and legs are heavy and warm *(six times).*

My heartbeat is calm and regular *(six times).*

My body breathes itself *(six times).*

My abdomen is warm *(six times).*

My forehead is cool *(six times).*

My mind is quiet and still *(three times).*

My mind is quiet and happy (*three times*).

I am at peace.

I feel my feet expanding lightly and pleasantly by one inch *(two times).*

My feet are now expanding lightly and pleasantly by twelve inches *(two times).*

The pleasant twelve-inch expansion is spreading throughout all the parts of my legs *(two times).*

My abdomen, buttocks, and back are expanding twelve inches lightly and pleasantly *(two times).*

My chest is expanding twelve inches pleasantly and lightly *(two times).*

My arms are expanding twelve inches lightly and pleasantly *(two times).*

My neck and head are joining in the twelve inches of expansion *(two times).*

My entire body is relaxed, expanded, and comfortable *(six times).*

My mind is quiet and still *(two times).*

I withdraw my mind from my physical surroundings *(two times).*

I am free of pain and all other sensations *(two times).*

My body is safe and comfortable *(six times).*

My mind is quiet and happy *(two times).*

I am what I am.

(Pause two minutes.)

Each time I practice this exercise my body becomes more and more comfortable and I carry this comfort with me to my normal awareness. As I prepare to return to my normal awareness, I will bring with me the ideal comfort which I have created in my focused concentration. As I open my eyes, I take a deep comfortable breath and a big comfortable stretch.

27

HOW TO OVERCOME A HEADACHE

Today, a few hospitals and clinics have begun to train patients to utilize their imagination to combat a variety of personal problems, so that we can expect imagery to certainly become one of the more popular research areas in the next ten years.

Here is an imagery psychotechnique for pain control that has been used successfully by dozens of clients. It was developed by the author some fourteen years ago.

To illustrate it, we'll use one of the most common types of pain, headache:

1. Lie down in a quiet room and relax by using the techniques in chapter 6. Keep free of all distracting thoughts and interruptions.

2. Visualize your pain image. Picture your pain in an actual, tangible way. See it as it might appear in a drawing or an animated film. We've all seen TV ads for aspirin. You could, for example, see your pain as a TV commercial might portray it; that is, your head being pounded by a hammer, squeezed by a vise, struck by a bolt of lightning. Make your image as vivid and real as you can. Focus on and experience the pain—feel it throbbing, beating, stinging, burning, tightening.

To help you, here are examples of how some people visualize their headache pain image:

"I see it as a huge hammer pounding away at the top of my head."

"It's a strong rope or cable that twists my head and neck tighter and tighter."

"There's fluid pressure inside my head and it is forcefully pushing out."

"It's like a sharp, jagged bolt of lightning or electricity, which pierces my head."

161

"My neck muscles are tied in a huge knot and it makes my head hurt."

"My blood vessels are throbbing and swollen to the breaking point."

"It's like a burning sensation—a fire inside my temples."

Allow this pain image to persist for about two minutes.

3. The corrective response. Slowly visualize the pain image changing and taking on a new form in such a way that it lessens or relieves the pain. This is the corrective response. It's the change that must occur in order to neutralize or "regulate" the discomfort and have it come out in a manner that will be beneficial to you.

Here are some sample corrective responses to the pain images we gave above:

Pain Image for Headache	Corrective Response
"I see it as a huge hammer that is pounding away at the top of my head."	The hammer begins to hit with less and less intensity until finally it doesn't even touch my head. Slowly the hammer grows smaller and smaller until it disappears altogether.
"It's a strong rope or cable that is twisting my head and neck tighter and tighter."	The rope is slowly loosening and freeing itself. It is shrinking and getting thinner and tattered. It is losing its tight hold on my brain. The rope is dissolving. Now it is completely gone.
"A big rock is pressing down steadily on my brain. It weighs a ton."	The rock is melting away. It is growing smaller and lighter. It is beginning to crumble into pieces. Finally it's only a pebble. Now it's gravel and now grains of sand. Now it has vanished.
"There's fluid pressure inside my	I see the veins that go to my brain

head and it's forcefully pushing outward." now opening up. They are relaxing and allowing blood to flow down into the rest of my body, away from my brain. The blood is gently flowing away from my head the way water flows peacefully in a stream.

Try not to think about the pain during this step. Concentrate only on your personal corrective response and what it should entail. It is an entirely personal image. One client saw her head being lifted into the clouds, where it then lost its sharp stinging pain. It returned to her after a few moments and she felt fine afterwards. So, any corrective response that appeals to you is what you should visualize, even if it is fanciful, unreal, or magical.

4. Some reminders. *Don't rush your corrective response.* Take at least ten minutes for this step and always be sure that in your final imagery scenes you see your head and brain as calm and normal once again. Don't feel that your pain is so special it can't be helped with imagery.

This psychotechnique, of course, is applicable to pain that you may have in any part of your body. Use it on little annoyances like a mosquito bite or for more upsetting discomforts like a throbbing toothache, premenstrual cramps, or a sprained ankle.

28

HOW TO STOP TOOTH GRINDING (BRUXISM)

Have you ever been jolted by someone grinding his teeth? It is a rare parent who hasn't at some time winced at the unnerving abrasion from a sleeping child.

Tooth grinding, or gnashing of teeth, is a habit that is disturbing to others, but, more important, it is highly detrimental to healthy teeth. It is usually a nocturnal activity, but sometimes this *occlusal neurosis,* as it has been called, can occur during the day.

Dentists and psychologists have long believed that *bruxism,* or tooth doodling, is the result of psychological conflict or inhibited emotion. Dr. Alexander Lowen of New York City, developer of the bioenergetic theory of neurosis, states that all body tensions reflect psychological dispositions and that we localize emotions in our musculature when we can't adequately solve our personal conflicts. He believes that when jaw muscles are tense, it often is a sign that the bruxist is making a determined effort to do something, such as pass an exam, become popular, face an adversary, and so forth.

Frequently, tooth grinders possess blocked emotions, like rage, fear, and worry. In his therapy, both Dr. Lowen and the patient use a variety of techniques to release muscle tension and break up the blockage. When this is done, emotional conflicts often surface into awareness and the patient has a better chance to work out his problems.

For many years, bruxists were treated either with oral devices such as bite guards or through psychotherapy. More recently, however, the condition has been handled as nothing more than a habit disturbance, and the treatment is based largely on bioenergetic theory. It is a relatively novel psychological approach to a vexing dental problem, which involves a massed-practice technique.

Psychotechnique for Overcoming Tooth Grinding.

There are two goals in curing tooth grinding: one is to improve the tone of the jaw, mouth, and neck muscles; and the other is to become aware when these muscles are tense and to learn to relax them.

Do the following:

1. Open the mouth wide and move the head as far back as possible. Then close and open the mouth a dozen or so times. Feel the muscles of the jaw, mouth, and neck straining when you do this. Try to be aware of the difference between tension and relaxation. Then bring the head forward a few inches and allow all muscles to let go and completely relax. The more you keep these muscles relaxed and calm during the day, the better.*

2. In conjunction with these exercises, there is a conscious habit that you should cultivate. Dr. Nathan Shore, a distinguished dental researcher, describes it as, "lips together and teeth apart":

> One of the most important steps in breaking the habit of clenching and grinding teeth is to become self-conscious when it occurs. . . . One excellent way to avoid clenching is to [remember] to keep the lips together and the teeth apart. . . . [This] will relax the very muscles that become tense and taut. Keeping the lips together and the teeth apart also permits normal positioning of the various components of the temporomandibular joints.
>
> The more [you become aware of this] very basic procedure of relaxing jaw muscles, the faster you will master a new and beneficial way of overcoming a harmful habit. Gradually, you will find yourself waking up in the morning without your teeth clenched. But you must persevere. . . . Remember that it will not vanish overnight.

*This is a technique developed by Dr. Jerome B. Ackerman of New York City.

You must make a conscious effort to separate your teeth
[and] at the same time, keep your lips closed. Repeat to
yourself several times a day: "Lips together, teeth apart."
An extra dividend: you'll find this facial posture will improve your expression and appearance."

Incidentally, should you wish to do something immediately
when you notice a sleeping child grinding his teeth, it is helpful to
take a few minutes to massage the jaw muscles at the sides of the
face, gently in small circles to break up the tension there.

29

HOW TO STOP WORRYING

Worry is a distinctly human experience. There is hardly a man or woman alive who doesn't spend some part of each day worrying about a money problem, a job, an upcoming exam, the health of a loved one, and so on.

Of course, if we didn't do some worrying about our responsibilities, they might never be fulfilled. But there is a point beyond which worry turns into preoccupation and then begins to take its toll on our happiness. It could even escalate to an obsession and become a serious mental condition. If we give any disturbing thought a chance to gain momentum, it may become stronger and then spiral out of control; and even though we realize that worry does not help us, it is a pointless activity that automatically persists.

An example is the case of Ann, age twenty-seven. Her mother died of cancer about a year ago. Since then, Ann has managed a fairly good adjustment. But one day, after seeing a movie in which the heroine was stricken with cancer, Ann formed the idea that she herself might develop the dread disease. As the weeks went by, her fears became stronger and more frequent until one day they finally began to interfere with her concentration at work.

A similar case is that of John, who is married and the father of two young children. His company has begun to lay off people and he is worried that after seven years with the firm, he too will lose his position. His family expenses have been skyrocketing and he can just about make ends meet.

For the past few months he has grown irritable and sullen about his job, and it has reached the point where it is now affecting his health. He eats less, loses sleep, and is temperamental with the children.

167

There is a very simple psychotechnique that both Ann and John might use to help themselves overcome their preoccupations. It involves interrupting a disturbing thought with a voluntary action. It was developed by Dr. Joseph Wolpe of Temple University. He was the first to suggest that by simply yelling *stop* to ourselves (or even thinking *stop)* as soon as worrisome thoughts gather, we can momentarily disrupt them. If the word *stop* is repeatedly paired with the disturbing thought, the latter decreases in frequency.

Here are steps to follow in using this thought-stopping method to overcome a disturbing preoccupation. They are a blend of several approaches, which represent a refinement of Dr. Wolpe's original approach.

Psychotechniques for Overcoming Worrisome Thoughts

1. Write out a list of at least six assertive statements or arguments that contradict or oppose the self-defeating nature of the worry you have. They should be antagonistic to your distressing thought. For example, if, like John, you worry that you will lose your job, you might write if it is appropriate: (a) I have a good work record; (b) I have had other job worries before, which never materialized; (c) When out of work in the past, I succeeded in landing a job; (d) I have marketable skills; and so on. Or if you have a worry similar to the one Ann has about becoming ill, you might write: (a) I am in good health; (b) I feel fine; (c) My doctor says I've passed all my medical tests; (d) The father of my friend Mary died years ago of cancer and she has been perfectly healthy for years; and so on.

It's a good idea to discuss your worry with someone close to you. Ask him or her to help you construct convincing statements.

2. Next, select a "distraction prop" such as a picture of someone, television with the sound off, or a mirror, which is capable of holding your attention.

3. Choose a quiet time and place, sit in a comfortable chair, and relax by using the steps in chapter 6.

4. Deliberately bring on the disturbing thoughts. As soon as they form in your mind, shout the word *stop* in a commanding

voice and simultaneously slap your leg, a table, or a chair audibly for emphasis. Say the word loud enough to hear it. When you shout *stop*, it must be strong enough to momentarily interrupt your thought stream. (After you have used the word *stop* aloud for fifteen or twenty times, you can begin to say it to yourself so that it is a private, internal message you and no one else can hear.)

5. It will help even more if, as you say the word *stop*, you form a vivid mental stop-image, such as a stern-looking policeman with hand upraised, or a bright red light, or a large stop sign. The livelier the image, the better.

6. After you say *stop*, immediately direct your attention to the distraction prop, concentrate steadily on it, and at the same time repeat to yourself an opposing statement to your ruminant thought.

7. If you find that at this point you have become somewhat tense, repeat to yourself a word like *calm, relax, quiet,* then let go and relax all your muscles.

8. Each time you become aware of the disturbing thoughts, repeat this entire sequence: saying *stop*, slapping, concentrating on your prop, repeating an assertive statement, then relaxing.

Keep these points in mind:

1. Thought-stopping should be done as soon as you are aware of the disturbing thought, even if you are away from home.

2. Thought-stopping should be done as often as necessary.

3. Don't become upset if at first the worrisome thoughts just seem to rush over you more frequently than they do normally. This may happen because you are highlighting the thoughts by drawing attention to them.

4. At first when you shout *stop*, you will notice that you do indeed succeed in breaking the train of your worrisome thoughts, even if only for a few seconds. This might not seem like much at first, but in time this break will grow longer and the thoughts will decrease in frequency.

5. The reason thought-stopping works is that by repeatedly interrupting your worrisome thoughts, you weaken the likelihood that they will recur.

6. These methods can be taught to your child.

Another thought-stopping technique is that of Spencer

Rathus and Jeffrey Nevid. It requires a tape recorder. You may wish to try it as a variation on the above.

1. Outline clearly the content of your ruminative thoughts, then make up three assertive statements to oppose them.

2. Record in a forceful voice the command *stop,* then follow it with the two or three assertive statements, spoken clearly and affirmatively.

3. Lie down or sit down comfortably with your fingers ready to press the play button of the recorder.

4. Start deliberately to ruminate on the distressing thoughts or ideas.

5. When they begin to form in your mind, immediately press the play button and listen for the *stop* command and the assertive counter-ruminative statements that go with it.

6. Rewind the recorder to the beginning.

7. Repeat this procedure ten times in a row, three or four times a day, for two weeks. After that, do it ten times in a row once a day for another two weeks.

These authors state that clients typically report their disturbing thoughts cease by the end of the first two weeks after using this recorder method.

PART FOUR
Overcoming
Bad Habits

30

HOW TO BREAK BAD HABITS

Perhaps the best proof of the existence of the unconscious is the fact that we carry on many activities without being aware of them. Jane has a habit of raising one eyebrow when she is afraid, Jim has a mannerism of saying "you know" after almost every sentence, and Carol smiles a lot, even when there is nothing to smile about. Unfortunately, other automatisms are more extreme and are commonly known as "nervous habits."

Even the most erudite speaker can lose credibility when the audience becomes aware of a motor habit like stammering, nose touching, or fussing with lecture notes.

In day-to-day living, such habits detract from our image. They distract others and connote that we are unsure of ourselves.

There are psychotechniques available to us to reduce or eliminate such annoying traits, and in the next seven chapters we will describe them. But first, there are several preparations to be made before we begin.

Develop Habit Awareness

1. To eliminate a habit you must first study it. Most habits occur automatically, while we pay attention to something else. Drs. Nathan Azrin and R. Gregory Nunn, experts in curing habit disturbances, recommend keeping a diary. This will be your progress record. Each day for two weeks, note in it the number of times the habit occurs, its duration, intensity, and location. Continue using the diary through the entire program. By doing this you will obtain a habit count which serves as a baseline; then, later, you can easily determine if the habit is diminishing.

The diary also serves as a daily reminder to keep working at

173

your psychotechnique. Keep it handy in your purse or pocket.

2. Another good way to develop habit awareness is to ask a friend or relative to help you. Let him read this chapter, then ask him to point out immediately when he notices you performing the habit. This can be done with an innocuous signal like raising a hand, clapping once, or saying something like, "yes, yes," "now now," or "one, two, three."

Pay particular attention to the occasions when your habit appears. Does it crop up in the presence of certain individuals? In special places? At definite times? Try to figure out how these circumstances make you feel. Ask yourself the question, "Is my habit a response to this feeling?"

3. You should also develop awareness by deliberately practicing your habit before a mirror. Do this slowly. Try to notice any preliminary movements you may make. For example, if you bite your nails, you will probably find that your hand generally begins to linger in the area of your face before the biting starts. When it does begin, study it closely. Notice exactly how it happens, what movements you make, and what other parts of the body may be involved (i.e., lips, eyelids, cheeks, etc.).

It is helpful to write out just what you see happening in the mirror. By studying the habit closely you will be able to define exactly what it consists of and which muscles of the body are used in its execution.

4. *Learn to relax.* Tension often brings on an annoying habit. So, when you *begin* to realize that you are entering a "habit situation" learn to relax quickly. (Follow chapter 6 for the relaxation psychotechnique.) Increase your ability to relax so that you can do so in a few minutes, even while standing or sitting.

A word about symptom substitution. Don't worry that when you conquer your "nervous" habit, another one will crop up to take its place. This was a belief in psychiatry for many years, but studies show that it rarely occurs.

31

HOW TO OVERCOME
THE HABIT OF NAIL BITING

Many people, when they are under pressure, resort to oral activities like overeating, drinking, and smoking. One of the more innocuous oral "tranquilizers" is nail biting. The psychotechnique for this habit is as follows:

1. First, establish a competing reaction for nail biting. A competing reaction is a voluntary response that, in a sense, undoes or blocks the undesirable habit. Many authorities recommend hand clenching. Do it as soon as you are aware of any preliminary actions that usually precede the habit. The most common precedent to nail biting, as we have said, is moving the hands up to the face area, often because an itch is felt there.

2. Do not tighten your fists too hard, but just enough to feel tension in them. You may grasp a nearby object, like the arm of a chair, a book, a table edge, or telephone. Practice the clenching until you are sure no one will notice it.

3. If you must interrupt the competing reaction, get back to it as soon as possible.

4. The competing reaction should make you aware that the habit does *not* occur while you are using it.

5. Practice the competing reaction before a mirror.

6. Always repair broken nails as soon as possible after you've chewed them. This acts as a post-habit competing reaction. Carry a nail file with you at all times for this purpose.

7. Don't spend too much time repairing your nails. After you've finished, perform the hand-clenching competing reaction again for three minutes.

8. Practice the competing reaction in imagery several times each day, *even though you are not engaged in nail biting*. This step

is similar to image desensitization, which we described in chapter 8.

Let's review it for a moment. Relax and imagine a situation in which your nail biting is *likely* to occur. Now, in imagination, see yourself going through the competing reaction successfully. While doing so, actually perform the competing reaction.

9. Remember to keep a record of your day-to-day progress.

32

HOW TO OVERCOME
THE HABIT OF HAIR PULLING

This habit often begins by playing with the hair, and then, in time, it progresses to more aggressive pulling and tugging. As this harmless stroking or fingering of the hair at the beginning becomes more firmly entrenched as a means of discharging tension, the habit progresses to the pulling and tugging stage.

1. The same competing reaction may be used here as for nail biting; that is, hand clenching. Follow the same instructions.

2. The post-habit competing reaction that will be useful for hair pulling is to comb, brush, or straighten your hair after you've pulled at it. Always carry a comb or small brush with you for this purpose, or an eyebrow pencil if you pull at your eyebrows. Make repairs as soon as possible, then repeat the hand clenching for three minutes afterward.

33

HOW TO OVERCOME NERVOUS TICS*

Tics are involuntary muscle contractions. They can occur in small muscle groups, such as around the eyes or lips, or they can involve larger areas like a leg, an arm, or the neck. They often appear when we are under stress. There are many types of tics, the more common of which are head jerking (either backward or to the side), shoulder shrugging, foot tapping, and twitching of various parts of the face.

The muscles involved in tics (as well as all the muscles of the body) have opposite partners called *antagonists*. It is the job of these antagonist muscles to check the movements of their partners. For example, when we reach for a door, we don't overreach because at some point in the process, our antagonist muscles hold back our arm.

The muscles that give rise to a tic are usually overdeveloped. Their antagonists are much weaker. The aim in overcoming a tic is to restore the tone and strength of these antagonist muscles so that they can inhibit the tic response. As in the two previous chapters, again we use a competing reaction, but in a different form.

The competing reaction for a specific tic consists of a hard tensing of its antagonist muscles. This is done through isometric contraction, which means tensing a muscle, yet not producing any movement in the part of the body controlled by that muscle. For example, if you press both hands together, you will notice that your body does not move. This is an isometric exercise.

---

*Many of the psychotechniques in this chapter have been adapted from Nathan Azrin and R. Gregory Nunn, *Habit Control in a Day* (New York: Simon & Schuster, 1977).

Head Tics

If your tic is one of jerking the head backward, the competing reaction for this involves locating the muscles that are opposite (antagonistic) to the backward movement.

When you are alone, practice identifying these muscles by letting your head go back, then slowly but firmly bringing your head forward with steady pressure. This will make you aware of the neck muscles responsible for *forward* head movement.

In public, should you find youself in the middle of a tic response, you would contract the muscles you've identified, in order to counteract it. Then, if possible, continue the competing response for a full three minutes after the tic stops. *Do not* contract the muscles too hard, as the strain will cause the tic to reappear. When you do this exercise you strengthen the antagonist muscles and reduce the chance that the backward jerking will occur.

Another isometric competing reaction for backward head-jerking is to keep your head centered, then contract your neck muscles slowly until the jerking stops. Hold this position for a full three minutes. While doing this, you may use your palm to exert pressure on your chin, which will cause your neck muscles to contract even more.

Both these competing reactions for backward head-jerking will make you aware of the muscles in the front of your neck that need strengthening. Repeat these exercises several times daily, especially before you are about to go into a tic response.

If your tic is one of jerking the head to the side, the same principles apply:

1. First locate the antagonist muscles.

2. For the competing reaction, keep your head centered, then place your hand on the side opposite to which you jerk your head. For example, if you jerk to the left, push your head with the palm of your right hand.

3. Exert gentle pressure on your head in the opposite direction to that of your tic. Feel your neck muscles tense up.

4. Once you've identified the correct competing muscles, you must do this exercise each time your head starts to jerk. This is to be done privately, of course. Continue until the tic stops, then

keep your palm pressed to your head again for a full three minutes afterward. You are strengthening the opposing muscles.

Remember, practice this competing exercise several times each day, whether or not you are in the process of a head-tic episode.

In brief, the psychotechnique steps involved in inhibiting any tic are:

1. Find the competing reaction by locating the antagonist muscles to the tic.

2. Exercise these muscles daily.

3. After using a competing reaction successfully, continue it for a full three minutes afterward.

34

HOW TO OVERCOME
EYE BLINKING AND TWITCHING

The competing reactions for both eye blinking and eye twitching are the same, for which we quote Drs. Azrin and Nunn:

> The competing reaction for eye blinking and eye twitching is to voluntarily blink your eyes about every five seconds, while keeping them open fairly wide between these blinks. Avoid "hard staring" by shifting your gaze at frequent intervals, no less than about every ten seconds. For some people, the eye-blinking habit consists of blinking at a very high rate, once every second or even more, and doing so fairly continuously. For other people, a rapid flurry of involuntary blinking and twitching of the lids occurs after long periods without blinking. The voluntary blink every five seconds in the competing reaction will cause the blinking in both instances to be normalized in frequency.

To summarize the psychotechnique for eye twitching and eye blinking:

1. Open your eyes a bit wider than normal, then blink every five seconds.

2. Shift your eye gaze every five to ten seconds, thus reducing strain. Move your head freely as you do these exercises.

35

HOW TO OVERCOME
THE HABIT OF THROAT CLEARING
OR A NERVOUS COUGH

How many times have you heard someone remark, "Oh, he has a nervous cough." The implication is that the sufferer does not have a true infectious throat condition, but one based on psychological causes.

If your doctor has ruled out any physical basis for your habit, it is probable that it is a reaction to a stress situation. If stress is the cause, then smooth breathing and relaxation of the neck and throat muscles are the primary psychotechniques to use.

The psychotechniques for overcoming a "nervous cough" are:

1. Review chapter 6 on total body relaxation.

2. Concentrate especially on the chest, throat, and neck areas. Vividly imagine these muscles letting go as much as possible.

3. Visualize your neck, throat, and chest as tensely bound up; then form a picture of these structures loosening up and calming down in a competing reaction (just as an animated TV commercial might show a cough medicine working).

4. Use an additional competing reaction, which is related to breathing: We cough because our stream of breath is broken, so try to maintain a smooth cycle of breathing. Practice a regular rhythm of breath control with your mouth slightly open, and try not to stop the pattern even for a moment.

5. Another competing reaction has to do with throat stimulation. We ordinarily cough or clear our throat because its mucous-membrane linings are dry or have trapped a foreign

body. Remember to *keep the throat moist* by sucking on a lozenge or frequently sipping liquids (preferably warm) during the day.

Continue these procedures until the habit stops.

36

HOW TO OVERCOME STUTTERING

If you stutter, you are not alone in your problem. There are over one million stutterers in this country, who must wage a constant battle against the tendency to stumble over the spoken word.

We will describe two methods to help you overcome your stutter problem. The first is by Dr. Nathan Azrin, of Southern Illinois University, and Dr. R. Gregory Nunn, of the Chicago Clinic for Habits and Tics. The second is by Dr. Wendell Johnson, noted speech authority and former professor at Iowa State University.

Both psychotechniques focus on different aspects of the stuttering process, and they nicely supplement each other.

The Psychotechnique for Stuttering by
Drs. Azrin and Nunn—A Behavior Therapy Approach

1. First review chapters 30 and 31.

2. There are two competing reactions for stuttering: one is *relaxation* and the other is *breathing control*. They are to be used when you are in a situation in which you feel you may stutter.

3. *Relaxation.* Nothing contributes more to stuttering than tension, so it's important to be as relaxed as possible throughout the day (use chapter 6). Pay particular attention to relaxing the muscles of the throat, neck, shoulders, and abdomen.

4. *Breathing control.* Deliberately practice breathing in and out slowly and deeply through your mouth. When you are about to speak, always start on the exhalation part of the cycle—after you've expelled about one-third of your air.

5. Practice at home by reading a paragraph aloud, using the following method: While exhaling, say one word for each com-

plete breath cycle. Gradually build up to two words per breath cycle, then three words, and so on, until you are saying phrases of five or six words in each cycle.

6. Should you stutter, stop immediately and start again on a new line. Your goal is to read aloud a complete line without a stutter. If the deep breathing makes you drowsy, stop for a while, then resume.

7. When you are outside your home and are ready to speak, don't rush. Try first to think out what you wish to express.

8. Then inhale and smoothly exhale about one-third of your air.

9. Begin to speak and do so while exhaling, not inhaling.

10. Try to speak only in short phrases. If you are speeding up, tell yourself, "slow down," "relax."

11. Avoid a monotone voice. It helps stutterers to accent words slightly as they speak. So instead of saying in a flat tone, "When will the bus for Glendale be arriving here?" use animation and say, *"When* will the bus for *Glendale* be arriving *here?"*

12. If you can, use minute, natural pauses in your speech. For example, you might say: "When I arrived home *(pause)* I found the phone ringing *(pause)*. When I answered it *(pause),* it was Mary Lewis *(pause)*. She wanted a favor *(pause),* my sponge cake recipe."

13. Should you stutter, stop immediately, inhale, then exhale about one-third of your air and start to speak again.

In brief: Use the competing reaction of deep breathing and speaking on the exhalation when you feel you may stutter. This means inhale slowly, then smoothly exhale about one-third of the air before you speak.

The Psychotechnique for Stuttering by Dr. Wendell Johnson*

1. Try to adopt the right mental attitude. Don't think of yourself as a disability. Pay attention to those times when your

---

*Adapted from his book, *Stuttering and What You Can Do about It* (Danville, Ill.: Interstate Publications, 1961).

speech is acceptable and normal and try to duplicate the essential elements you find helpful.

2. Read aloud a great deal as expressively as you can when you are alone, or with anyone who will listen.

3. Listen attentively to seasoned speakers at lectures and in movies and television. Try to feel along with them as they speak. Try to imitate them, getting the feel of what their normal speech is like.

4. Read aloud in chorus with someone. If you make a mistake, stop and start again.

5. Occasionally, when alone, read aloud as fast as you can and then direct yourself to slow down.

6. Study your mistakes. When you stutter try to figure out what caused it. Were you momentarily distracted? Did you feel your listener was angry, bored, unbelieving, impatient? Were you upset?

7. Do more talking. This does not mean to make a pest of yourself with others, but it does mean that you should, as Professor Johnson advises, "make a special point of not avoiding the talking that is yours to do in the ordinary course of daily living, the talking you would have been doing more fully all along had you not been holding back."

37

HELPING CHILDREN WHO HAVE BAD HABITS

Dr. Odgen Lindsley of the University of Kansas has successfully trained parents to be the behavior therapists of their children. You can help your children to overcome bad habits with the psychotechniques we have outlined here if you are mindful of two points that Dr. Lindsley stresses:

1. Pinpoint the behavior you want to alter. For example, if your child bites his nails, wets the bed, and stutters, pick a single target. Focus on only one habit, preferably the simplest one, which in this case is nail biting.

2. Reward any gains the child makes with praise, a gift, a coin, a movie. Try to give rewards as close as possible to the time when the child shows the desired behavior.

A caution about relapses: It is best to anticipate that you or your child will occasionally lapse back into your old habit. Don't blame or torture yourself with self-recrimination. The thing to do is to redouble your determination and get right back to breaking the habit as soon as possible.

PART FIVE
*Improving Your
Love, Family,
and
Child Relations*

38

HOW TO STRENGTHEN YOUR
FAMILY TIES

Some people have the wrong idea about marriage. They expect or even demand that their partner be perfect. But this illusion is never attained, and it is a wise woman who does not expect her spouse to be the perfect husband any more than she can be expected to be the perfect wife.

In a marriage, there are bound to be moments of strong disagreement and anger. But a happy family is one in which members know *how* to quarrel and express feelings constructively. It is far more damaging to sulk, secretly retain anger, and express it in indirect ways.

Blackboards and Bitterness

Dr. Thomas McGinnes, former president of the American Association of Marriage and Family Counselors, presents it this way:

> If I am annoyed by something you do or say but I never tell you so, you will soon sense my annoyance in my bearing, facial expression, tone of voice and actions (or by the way I break dishes or slam doors), but you may have no idea of what is going on within me and between us. We are like blackboards THAT ARE NEVER erased. The new material is written over the old, and presently neither of us can read anything written there.
>
> A constructive fight that leads to a resolution is a cleansing process like the erasing of a blackboard. What-

ever is at issue can be spotlighted, pinpointed and dealt
with. Then it is far less likely to distort future communications. Both parties know where they stand with each other.

Dr. McGinnis, needless to say, advocates more openness in
marriage. He describes a "healthy fight" as having five ingre-
dients:

1. Feelings are honestly expressed and not used as weapons
against the members. (Better to say: "I am angry," but not "You
louse.")
2. Each person respects the other.
3. Neither is trying to destroy the other's self-respect or in-
jure the other.
4. The fight is between equals and not a power struggle to
gain supremacy, and it's not the kind of fight where one wins and
the other loses.
5. The quarrel is not left hanging but is resolved fairly by
mutual negotiation.

Here is a psychotechnique that will help you express feelings
of love or anger toward a family member. We have adapted it
from Dr. McGinnes's book.

Psychotechnique for Expressing Feelings Toward a
Family Member

1. Sit facing each other. Ask your partner to remain silent
while you look directly at him, and then tell him some of the
moments when you feel love for him. Use brief sentences that
begin with "I," such as: "I feel love for you when you share your
worries with me," or "I feel love when you show warmth or kindness to me or others." Then let your partner reply similarly with
some of the moments he feels love for you, while you remain
silent.
2. Next, use the "I" sentences to express those moments
when you feel anger toward the other, then let the other do the
same. For example, you may say, "I resent you when you criticize
me in front of our friends." Or your partner may say, "I get
angry when you make lame excuses not to be with me."

3. *Evaluation:* Compare the two sequences of "I feel love" and "I feel anger." Which group of feelings was harder to express? Do either of you ever take love for granted? Are feelings of resentment and anger kept hidden? Can you have negative angry feelings toward a person and still love him at the same time? What is the outcome of this experience? Do you feel closer to him or more distant?

4. *Follow-up:* Try this procedure with another family member.

There is a lot more to family life than resolving angry conflicts. Many families, even though they *can* resolve conflicts or keep them to a minimum, are still basically unhappy. The growth of love within them has been strangled. They just drift along without aim or purpose. In a word, they need to be revitalized.

But the sad fact is that most people don't know how to go about this process of family change. So they give up and settle for an existence of family mediocrity. Their members are like tracks in a railroad bed, always running parallel, always nearby, but never touching one another.

Dr. McGinnes has developed a number of psychotechniques to strengthen the bonds within the family, and we give three of them here:

Psychotechnique for Dealing with Conflicts of Expectation in Your Marriage

In private, each partner lists those expectations of his marriage which he feels are not being completely fulfilled. Then he lists those expectations about which he feels happy. When this is done, the partners exchange lists. Each reads aloud the lists prepared by the other. Partners should not interrupt the reading or attempt to defend their positions. This is an opportunity for each to learn how the other feels, not to take issue with those feelings.

Evaluation: Are there any surprises? Any conflicting expectations? Single out the one expectation on each list that has been the most irritating and difficult to manage, and discuss it fully. Listen attentively and meaningfully to your partner, and ask him to do the same for you. Also, discuss those expectations that have been fulfilled, and express appreciation to the partner for his contribution.

Psychotechnique for Communication through Words

Pick a partner and sit facing each other. Talk to each other in the manner suggested below. Observe how you feel as you do so. Also, be aware of how your partner is giving and receiving these messages.

1. Talk two or three minutes to each other using only statements that begin with the word *you*. (Examples: "You seem tense." "You look very attractive.") Ask no questions during this interchange. Discuss the experience with your partner.

2. Now talk to each other using only statements that begin with *I*. (Examples: "I am nervous." "I am wondering what you're thinking.") Again, no questions during the interchange. Discuss and compare it with your previous experience with *you*.

3. Now talk to each other using only statements that begin with *we*. (Examples: "We need more recreation." "We are getting tired.") Again, no questions should be asked during the interchange. Discuss and compare it with your previous experiences with *you* and *I*.

4. Now make any statements you wish, as long as the word *but* is included in each sentence. (Example: "I'm enjoying this, but I'm also bothered.") Discuss what effects the *buts* have on the statements.

5. Now make any statements you wish, using the word *and* in each sentence. (Try repeating some of the sentences you made with *but,* substituting *and* for *but,* and notice the effect on the message. Example: "I'm enjoying this and I'm also bothered.") Discuss and compare what *but* and *and* do to statements.

Psychotechnique for Increasing the Feeling of Connection with Another Family Member

Set aside at least half an hour to be alone with a family member. Pretend you are strangers who are going to interview one another. Decide who will be the first interviewer.

The interviewer asks the interviewee questions about the following: his present life-style; early childhood and family relationships; current feelings about himself; his marriage and family; satisfactions and dissatisfactions; critical health problem; greatest secret; most intimate experience; a period of loneliness; a time of joy.

Conduct the interview as if you know nothing about each other. Make no assumptions and give no opinions or evaluations. Inform the interviewee that, as in any good interview, he doesn't have to answer a particular question.

When you have finished, reverse roles.

Evaluation: Discuss this experience together. Do you feel you know more about each other? Was the experience exciting or boring? Did you experience each other as real people? Did it result in any special feeling of connection or greater involvement with each other?

Follow-up: Try this with other family members.

39

HOW TO USE THE FAMILY COUNCIL

It is a truism in group psychology that people tend to support and defend what they create. This is no less valid in a family setting. When a decision is made in the home with equal input from all members, the plan adopted will have a much better chance to succeed than if the parents alone participate in its creation. This democratic function is the notion behind the family council, an idea devised by the late Dr. Rudolph Dreikurs, who was professor of psychiatry at the University of Chicago Medical School.

Every family should have a time when it meets to discuss topics of individual or mutual interest. It is a chance for each member to raise a problem that bothers him or her, and it is done in a democratic atmosphere, with all members—parents and children alike—given an equal voice.

1. To begin, designate a regular time and place for the council each week.

2. Appoint a chairperson for each meeting, beginning with a parent for the first few times.

3. The first meeting should last no more than fifteen minutes.

4. Plan an agenda. Some topics that might be discussed are:

a. Special projects (planning vacations, making a trip to a distant relative, throwing a party, etc.)

b. Unusual situations that have arisen with neighbors, friends, teachers, and so forth

c. Financial expenses for the past week and the coming week

d. The family calendar for the coming week (doctor and dentist visits, school events, community activities, etc.)

5. Some rules to announce:

a. Everyone must be on time.

b. Everyone must be present.

c. Talking out of turn or making insulting remarks is not permitted.

d. No fighting or arguing.

e. Anyone five years or older must attend.

6. The council should be action-oriented and have as its central idea, "We have a problem; what do *we* do about it?"

7. The family council is a learning experience for children who can witness the benefits of democratic decision making. In addition to showing interest in the issues they bring up, you should also be aware of opportunities to help them develop their ideas and present them convincingly. Teach them to look for flaws in another person's argument, and then to negotiate with that person. Dr. Dreikurs believed that "children will learn more from these experiences than they will learn from words or from parental impositions."

8. Have patience. The family council is an excellent way to bring a family together and to foster (or rebuild) mutual trust. But he forewarned that although the council has proven eminently worth the effort, it may be a slow and taxing process for everyone involved, especially for the parents. Patience is needed in the beginning. Group process always moves slowly.

9. An important caution: Children occasionally become heady with power, and, in the first few sessions, you may become uneasy about giving them an equal voice in family matters. But after several sessions you will learn to tolerate their misjudgments. The family council is the very place to evaluate such mistakes.

10. If possible, plan some relaxation or entertainment immediately after the meeting (even an ice cream cone for all will do). The point of the family council is that it be a pleasant experience, which will carry over to other activities.*

---

*Excellent, detailed information about setting up a family council can be found in Dr. Loren Grey, *Discipline without Fear* (New York: Hawthorne Books, 1974).

PART SIX
Helping Your Child

Men and women may march bravely into the competition of the business world or try to fulfill the varied demands of household problems, but the challenge of raising children is the ultimate test of a human being's versatility. As any parent can testify, it calls on every possible skill and insight in the human repertoire.

One of the most difficult hurdles parents face is the one that calls for motivating and disciplining their children. Perhaps in no other area do they make so many poor judgments, which later bring forth distorted attitudes, resentment, and out-and-out rebellion in their children.

A growing trend in child guidance is to teach parents to be the therapists of their own children. For those who remain skeptical that personality change can be achieved through lay coaching, we can mention one of Freud's most celebrated cases, that of little Hans. The boy was an intelligent, well-cared-for child of a wealthy family. During his fifth year, he developed a phobia for horses, which grew so intense he was unable to leave the house. It was then that the boy's father consulted Dr. Freud. In time, Hans was treated and cured entirely by his father, a layman to psychiatry, with Dr. Freud acting as a guide and resource person.

The success of the child's therapy shows that an intelligent, determined parent can bring about a behavior change, *if he or she is given the proper guidance by a professional.** The next seven chapters, and chapters 52, 55, and 57, will teach you to help your child overcome a number of life difficulties.

---

*The case of Hans substantiates our viewpoint even more when we consider that the father communicated with Dr. Freud exclusively through letters and that the boy *maintained his cure* despite the subsequent divorce of his parents.

40

HOW TO USE REWARDS WITH YOUR CHILD

One of the fastest and most effective means of inducing a child to change his behavior is to give him a reward of some kind. There are some important considerations about these mini-incentives that you should bear in mind.

1. First, remember that a reward is anything a youngster might value or desire, like a candy bar, a walk, money, a game, clothes, a bike ride, ice cream, going to a party, watching TV, or hearing a story.

2. There are two kinds of rewards: intrinsic (a child feels inwardly good about himself for doing something that either he or society feels is desirable), and extrinsic (a child feels good because he receives a concrete reward like a toy or candy).

3. The idea in all reward systems is eventually to get the child to behave mainly on the basis of intrinsic rewards. It is important to remember that at some point you must discontinue frequent tangible rewards and bring your child around to performing the correct behavior on his own simply with praise (social reward) or an occasional gift.

4. The psychology of motivation tells us that there is no age limit for using a reward system. It works with any age group, provided the recipient appreciates the prize as an incentive worthy of changing his behavior.

5. You're in trouble when you've made up *your* mind about a reward that you believe would be "just fine," but your target only half-heartedly goes along with it. This is why it's important to give your child a role in deciding on a reward for a specific behavior. Don't assume it will motivate him until you negotiate it together.

6. Using rewards with young children: One of the easiest ways to reward a young child is to give gold stars. On a sheet of

paper make seven columns, one for each day of the week, and post this in a conspicuous place at the child's eye level. The refrigerator door is a good spot. Each time he earns a reward, praise him and present him with the star, so that he can put it up himself. At the end of the month say, "Tommy, you did many things right this month and you've made Daddy and me happy by winning all these stars." Then translate the stars into something tangibly enjoyable for the child. Say, "Now it's time for your prize." (This can mean that ten stars equal a movie, a small toy, candy, etc.)

7. Time is important. When you give rewards, don't present them too late. They should be given *as soon as possible* after your child performs what you want. If the two of you are away from home when he does the proper thing, show him that you are making a note of it so that when you get back home he will receive a reward.

8. Be firm and consistent. Once your child catches on to your reward system he may try to inveigle you into giving rewards for almost anything he does correctly. Do not fall into this kind of barter trap. Choose only a few specific tasks for which you will reward him, and hold fast to these. It is a good idea, however, to occasionally reward actions for which you haven't contracted or asked. For example, if a child does something like take his dirty dishes to the sink after dinner, or help you set the table, you might surprise him with a small reward.

9. Are rewards bribes? A bribe is compensation for something dishonest or illegal; a reward is a tangible appreciation for something worthwhile. It is not a bribe to give a Nobel prize or to pay a weekly salary or to award an athletic letter. These are tools that help us to convey recognition for worthy human performance. Don't feel guilty about giving rewards to your child. Studies on incentive motivation show that human beings work harder, better, and achieve more if they receive either social praise or material goods.

10. Take small steps and be patient. Remember, reward in *small* steps at first and don't expect too much; or, as one writer put it, make a large-scale fuss about a small-scale accomplishment. Don't overuse a reward; consider it something special. Lay out a program that the child will understand, and then stick to it.

There will be ups and downs, but don't become discouraged. Rewards really do work.

41

HOW TO DISCIPLINE YOUR CHILD

The Psychotechnique of Logical Consequences

Lorrie calls her daughter Lisa to dinner. Ten minutes pass and the girl, age thirteen, still does not come. Lorrie calls again and again. Finally, Lisa comes to the table twenty minutes late. How many times has this happened to you? Dr. Rudolph Dreikurs is credited with a psychotechnique that he called *logical consequences,* which is an effective way to deal with such stubborn behavior. It is a method for teaching children and adolescents correct behavior by having them directly experience the painful or distressing results of their own misdeeds.

Lisa's case, for example, presents an excellent chance to use the method. Here is what Lorrie might do:

Some time before dinner is to be served, she should ask Lisa how much longer she will be and then agree on a time with her to come to the table. If the child does not come by the agreed time, then the family should proceed to have dinner without her, leaving her meal on her plate. No further comments should be made, nor should there be scolding.

Another example: Sharon, age six, dawdles and plays with her food. Each time she does this, her mother pressures her to eat faster, but Sharon ignores the warnings. Finally, when her mother becomes exasperated, she scolds and then spanks Sharon. The child then begins to eat.

A better way to approach Sharon is to tell the child calmly that there will be a time limit to eating. For example, she might say, "Sharon, at exactly 6:30 everyone will be finished eating and the table will be cleared." Since the child is so young, the mother should give one or two reminders that 6:30 is approaching; then, at exactly that time, she should calmly remove all food from the

205

table, saying, "It's exactly 6:30, time to clean up."

After this, nothing else should be said about eating and no food given to Sharon for the rest of the evening. If the child protests, her mother's attitude should be, "I'm really sorry about this, but I've decided on this rule and I just can't be unfair to myself about it."

It takes perhaps one or two of these sessions to break a child of such feeding delays without any health consequences to consider.

Another example of logical consequences is Bruce, age ten, who has formed the annoying habit of leaving his sneakers in remote parts of the house. He does this with some of his other toys as well. Scolding him doesn't help.

Bruce's mother should use logical consequences in the following way: The night before Bruce must take his sneakers to school for sports, she should find them and hide them in a closet. The next day the boy should be told in a calm, even-tempered tone, "You have misplaced your sneakers and there is no time to look for them. You must get along without them and use your shoes instead for school play today." He should be told that this will be the solution each time he misplaces his sneakers until he finally learns to put them in their proper place.

The idea behind logical consequences is that the child learns from his own experiences, even though, as we recognize, the end results must be arranged by the parent in order for it to be a learning experience.

Setting limits in this way is a matter of daring to take a firm stand, a difficult task for parents who easily feel guilty about using discipline. But remember one thing: When you lay down the law, you must feel kindness in your heart and not vengeance toward your child. You love him and want to help him avoid trouble with authority figures later on. When he grows up he'll appreciate the self-discipline you've taught him.

The "Time-Out" Psychotechnique for Disciplining Your Child

There comes a time when a parent must do what figuratively will hurt himself more than it does the child. Every parent shuns the task of punishment, but a responsible parent must uphold his authority and carry through in these moments of interpersonal stress. The *manner* of doling out punishment, however, can make or break the shaping of a child's behavior. If it is either too lenient or too harsh it won't help him to learn his lesson.

One strategy of fair discipline involves depriving a child of his freedom for a short period of time. It's called "time-out" (T-O) and it works best with young children between the ages of about three to ten years. It involves the following:

1. T-O means time-out from pleasure or enjoyment. It requires that a child be sent to a place where there are no toys, games, or people; in short, nothing to play with. It should not be a dark or frightening room. The best place is the bathroom.

2. When you use T-O select only one behavior you wish to change, such as teasing, yelling, or spilling milk. Say, "I want to teach you to change your bad habit. From now on, each time you tease, I'll say 'go to time-out' and you will go to the bathroom and stay there till I tell you to come out."

3. Don't lecture or scold during the T-O period, which by itself should be sufficient to get your message across. But remind your child that in the future when he misbehaves, you will use T-O again to punish him.

4. Try to keep the distance and the travel short to the T-O area.

5. To start, T-O's should be brief. Three to five minutes usually works well. Then, if necessary, gradually build up to fifteen or twenty minutes.

6. Try to keep an eye on the child during his stay in the T-O area. You must be sure he doesn't enjoy his time there or make a game of it.

7. Use a warning signal or cue to tell the child that he is misbehaving and that a T-O may have to be used if he continues. Say, "Michael, you will have to stop teasing the baby or go to T-O."

8. It is better to give several brief T-O periods of five or seven minutes each, rather than one or two very long ones of fifteen or twenty minutes.

9. The T-O time starts *after* the child quiets down in the T-O area.

10. After a T-O punishment, praise the child for being quiet there and get him back into the ongoing family activity.

If T-O doesn't work at first, don't give up. It probably means that you haven't tried it enough times or you did not use the right room. Generally, it takes a few trials before T-O begins to have an effect. Once underway, it should produce good results.

42

HOW TO PERSUADE YOUR CHILD
TO DO SOMETHING

It was once said that thought convinces men, but feelings persuade them. This aphorism is even truer for children. Persuasion for them is seldom an intellectual process. More than likely it's a selling effort—an appeal to emotion, desire, and value.

Most parents are not born persuaders, especially of children. But they play this role when they believe a child must be guided into a proper course of action or belief, and when a rational appeal will be too complex to understand or accept.

Here are several psychotechniques that will help you to be more persuasive with your children:

1. *Use bandwagoning.* Your child's natural instinct of group-mindedness is a strong force in getting him to comply with your request. If he is told that many other children are doing something, chances are he will want to do it too. Some parents tell their children, with good success, that famous children in movies or on TV are doing "it," and the child should do "it" also. Group suggestion is a powerful tool; take advantage of this fact.

2. *Point out personal positive benefits.* Nothing helps more to convince someone to do something than to point out "what's in it for him." Try to relate your request to something that is meaningful to your child. For example, "Lisa, if you brush your teeth every day, they will be white and shiny. You'll have a very pretty smile, too, and you won't have to go so often to the dentist for fillings." Or, "If you share your toys with Kathy, next time when you go to her house she'll let you play with her puppy." Or, "If you'll take a nap now, when you wake up we'll visit the seals at the zoo."

3. *Pick the right time.* The cliché tells us that there is a time

209

and place for everything. This also applies to the art of persuading children. It's common knowledge that gaining compliance is easier when your target is in a happy frame of mind.
Children themselves often use this tactic; they are on their best
behavior just prior to asking for a favor. If you can, try to choose
a moment when your child is in a calm, relaxed mood. Better still,
approach him when he is enjoying himself—while he is delighting
in a new toy, playing a fun game, or happily munching his favorite food.

4. *Dramatize the benefits.* Don't appeal just to a child's reason in convincing him of a course of action. Rather, remember to
stimulate his feelings and desires as much as possible. Use imagery as dramatically as you can by painting an attractive end
result if he complies. You might say, for example, "Patty, if you
eat all your food and take your vitamins each day it will give you
beautiful long curls, which all your girl friends at school will very
much admire." Or: "Jimmy, if you help me to clean up the back
yard and paint the porch, it will look perfectly neat and sharp for
when your friends come over next week."

One mother, to dramatize her request, taped a big picture of
a new bicycle on the kitchen wall as a constant reminder to her
daughter of what she'd receive after she'd passed her history
course.

5. *Accentuate the positive.* Don't use negative suggestions
with your child. The mistake that Grandmother Moore made
(see chapter 3) was that she began every request to the children
with an admonishing negative. If you say, "Chrissy, don't scatter
your toys," she knows what she must *not* do, but it is not clear
exactly what you *would* like her to do. It is better to say, "Chrissy,
please keep your toys in the play box in your room after you've
used them, then they'll be ready and waiting for you the next time
you want them."

6. *Make it fun by creating a challenge.* For most children, chores
are boring. To offset this, dare to use a little color or imagination
to encourage your child's cooperation. The best way to do this is
to speak a child's language, which is play. Play is also the means
through which you can reach him most effectively. Be alert for
the possibility of turning a mundane request into a novel, playful
game or contest. Keep it simple. For example, you might say:

"Nancy, I'll give you three guesses about what you should do in this room to make it neater." Or: "Scott, I'll bet you a penny you can't run upstairs and get my slippers before I count to twenty-five." Or: "Pam, I'll race you. Let's see who finishes first. I'll wash the dishes and you sweep the floor."

A bit of imagination will help you to be more persuasive, and, with practice, you will become quite proficient at it.

How to Help Your Child Follow Through on the Chores You Give Him (The Rule of Successive Approximations)

Children usually become confused and discouraged when they are given a task that is huge or complex. They lose confidence in themselves, or they may think that you are unfair and expect too much from them.

There is a technique for assigning chores which a wise parent can use to insure that children will be treated fairly and that they will readily accept as guidance offered to them by loving parents. Like all of us, children learn in steps, and their steps are small. You will reach your goal easier by "shaping" the child's behavior through rewards for each successive approximation to the overall goal that you have in mind. So, break down a larger job into manageable parts, what psychologist Dr. Ernest Dichter calls "taskettes." Then ask the child to tackle each part, one at a time.

For example, Judy, age eleven, has an untidy room. There's a better way to get her to clean up than to command, "Judy, straighten up your room immediately." You should begin first by asking her to arrange her books on the shelves and tidy her desk. When she completes this assignment, praise her accordingly. The next day, give her another job to do, like dusting her bedroom furniture or sweeping the floor, and reward her again. Keep giving her assignments over a reasonable period of time until the job is complete.

Remember to reward a child with praise or a small gift (a candy bar will do) each time he or she succeeds. By doing this you give a youngster the chance to easily fulfill your demands. At the same time you build confidence that they can achieve a large job if it is tackled one part at a time.

The idea in the beginning is to expect little and reward much. In time, you must drop the rewards and use praise alone.

Shaping desired behavior requires patience and consistency, but it is one of the best ways to train children.

43

HOW TO HELP YOUR CHILD OVERCOME FEARS

Children are not born with self-confidence. They learn it through successful coping. One of the corrosive aspects of low self-confidence is fear. When a child fears that he cannot cope with a challenge, he is saying that he lacks confidence.

There are psychotechniques that you can use to help your child build self-confidence to cope with his fears. They were developed by Dr. Arnold Lazarus of Rutgers University.

Dr. Lazarus describes how he helped a nine-year-old boy with a school phobia by using comic book characters and imagery. He asked the boy, Peter, to imagine that Batman and Robin gave him a wrist radio and asked him to help catch a criminal who was operating at school.

The boy was told that in his school locker there was a secret message, which he was to read and then destroy. Peter was then asked to imagine that he went straight to school the next day. The boy visualized himself riding the bus, getting off, and walking toward the school—all the while wondering what that secret message was.

He saw himself walking across the schoolyard into the building and down the steps to the locker room. Dr. Lazarus then had Peter describe at length and with feeling, all that was going on, and the boy reported that he was at school doing all the things Dr. Lazarus suggested. The plan was to enable the child to see himself back at school without feeling anxious. "Of course," Dr. Lazarus told Peter, "you don't want to tell Batman and Robin about your fears, so you go to school the next morning and head straight for your locker."

Dr. Lazarus continued the imagery with Peter by having him

213

visualize a green slip of paper in the locker. It had Batman's emblem on it. He continued, "You slip it into your pocket and it says, 'we will signal you on your wrist radio during your first recess. Over and out.' You go to class and the teacher gives you some work to do. You are sitting at your desk working. You wonder what Robin will want you to do next. You carry on with your work."

To conclude the story, in place of fear Peter was feeling excitement, and curiosity about the secret note. He was slowly being desensitized to the idea of returning to school, and in just one session with Dr. Lazarus, Peter overcame his school phobia.

The point to this is that parents can do the same for their children, and Dr. Lazarus gives a psychotechnique for them to follow. His four-step method to help a child overcome a fear is presented here. But before you proceed with it you should read chapter 8 on imagery desensitization. This will make it easier to understand Dr. Lazarus's method as it applies to children.

Psychotechnique for Helping Your Child to Overcome Fear by Dr. Arnold Lazarus

Step 1. Try to establish, by means of sympathetic discussion, the range, intensity, and circumstances of the child's fear. What produces the fear? When is it a little better, and when is it the worst? How does the child cope with it? Attempt to draw up a graduated list from the least feared to the most feared situations.

Step 2. Try to establish the nature of the child's hero-images, usually derived from TV, movies, radio fiction, or the child's own imagination. You are searching for some powerful and reassuring companion to weave into stories involving the child's fear.

Step 3. As described in our example above, you then ask the child to close his or her eyes and you describe an imaginary sequence of events that is close enough to the child's everyday life to be credible. Within the story, you introduce the child's favorite hero, or alter ego.

Step 4. Each time the fear-arousing scenes are presented (starting with the least fearful events) introduce the hero-image as a natural part of the narrative. Immediately afterward, ask the child if he or she felt afraid, unhappy, or uncomfortable. If so, introduce more and more pleasant scenes involving the child and the hero-images, and do not move to a more difficult item until the child no longer feels any tension or fear when picturing the less fearful scenes.

44

HOW TO BE A GOOD LISTENER
WITH YOUR CHILD

The cliche, "a communication gap," often describes why parents and their children have misunderstandings about each other.

The next two psychotechniques were developed by psychologist Dr. Thomas Gordon. They will help you to get along better with your child.

The Psychotechnique of Active Listening

Dr. Gordon has successfully taught this method to thousands of parents. It is based on the work of Dr. Carl Rogers, who discovered client-centered counseling, and it should be used when you suspect your child is upset or troubled.

Active listening calls for paying attention to the underlying feelings that are being expressed, and not so much to the content of the statements themselves. For example, if a child says, "Won't Johnny be coming over to play with my new game today?" it would be only partly correct to respond to the content of what he's saying by replying, "No, he had to go to the dentist," or "No, but we'll ask him to try to come over tomorrow."

It may be true that you are offering an alternate solution to the child, but you miss the child's underlying feelings. Using active listening, you would answer something like this: "You are feeling disappointed that Johnny isn't coming today."

Active listening enables you to immediately get to the heart of what's bothering your child. It demonstrates to him that you really understand him. You are feeding back to him the meaning behind his words.

216

Most parents are not used to this type of responding, so here are some more examples to help you learn this psychotechnique:

CHILD: I'm upset with the way I missed the correct answer on the quiz.
PARENT: You're annoyed with yourself because you didn't get the right answer.

CHILD: I don't want to have to have to beg Mickey to play with me.
PARENT: You feel small when you have to ask Mickey to play with you.

CHILD: I hate to go into that dark room alone.
PARENT: You're scared to go in there by yourself.

CHILD: I'm slow at math. I don't think I can do well at it.
PARENT: You feel you're not smart enough for it and so you doubt that you will ever catch on to it.

CHILD: Where do people go when they die?
PARENT: I guess you've been thinking about death, haven't you, and maybe wondering about what happens afterward.

These are examples of active-listening answers to remarks of troubled children. If you train yourself to respond in this way, you will do much to improve communication with your child.

A legitimate question: You might ask, "How do I know that I will reflect the correct feeling of my child?" The answer is that you won't know until you try a response. If you miss the feeling, your child will tell you so. Here's an example:

CHILD: I don't like to be late for school because then I have to walk in front of my friends in class who come in early.
PARENT: You feel silly being late, don't you.
CHILD: No, that's not it. I'd feel embarrassed by it.

Active listening provides a sure way of knowing if your feedback hits the mark. It is a simple, nonthreatening way to keep your child talking to you for more than one or two statements.

Dr. Gordon's book, *Parent Effectiveness Training,* has created what *The New York Times* called a "national movement." Using his method of active listening will bring both you and your child a number of benefits. It will

1. Teach you not to moralize or be judgmental, and thus it will help you to create a trusting atmosphere in which your child will more readily open up to you.

2. Help your child to discharge his feelings more easily, feelings that otherwise might be bottled up and damage his self-esteem.

3. Help your child to accept his own feelings, too.

4. Convey to your child a sense of deeper caring on your part.

5. Make it easier for your child to listen to someone else's point of view.

6. Help your child to think for himself and discover his own solutions.

Active listening is a small addition to the already ongoing relationship with your child. It should not form the entirety of your talks with him. You still, for example, will take a stand on an issue, give advice, correct his misinformation, give kindly counsel, and assuage his sentiments when he is hurt.

It is a useful technique when he is troubled about something and has difficulty understanding or accepting his feelings. It is another tool that you can use to build his trust in your understanding of him.

45

HOW TO GET THROUGH TO YOUR CHILD USING "I-MESSAGES"

Most parents unwittingly create what Dr. Thomas Gordon calls "roadblocks" when they talk with their children. This means that their talking often blocks rather than opens communication.

Some of the more common roadblocks for parents are: ordering, warning, moralizing, advising, judging, name-calling, psychoanalyzing, and probing. Statements along these lines usually contain a high number of "you-messages," for instance, "you stop that," or "you mustn't do that," or "you should know better," or "you're nasty." They are always judgemental evaluations of the child's character rather than his actions, and they are child-oriented.

Although "you-messages" may be useful at times, Gordon feels a more effective type of message could be used that far better enables a child to understand how its parents feel about its annoying behavior. Gordon calls these "I-messages." They are, by contrast, parent-oriented. They communicate to the child just what he is doing that bothers you, and what he should do to please you.

Here is an example: A child leaves a mess in the kitchen. A parent could respond as follows: "Johnny, you left a mess in the kitchen. You're so sloppy, can't you be neater?" Faced with this remark, a child will probably feel put down and justifiably guilty, but he doesn't feel he has the chance to take some constructive corrective action.

A typical I-message, on the other hand, could be: "Johnny, you left a mess in the kitchen. This irritates me; now I'll have to take time to clean it up and get you to help me."

Here you've told him three things:

1. *What he did that bothers you* ("you left a mess in the kitch-en")

2. *How it makes you feel* ("This irritates me")

3. *The problem it causes you* ("I'll have to clean it up and get you to help me")

Let's use another example: A child runs around the house making noise while you try to get some rest. The difference between a typical you-message and an I-message might be:

"Marie, you're being a noisy brat, please stop the racket" (you-message).

"Marie, the noise you're making really bothers me and I can't rest" (I-message).

The you-message focuses on the child and tells him essentially, "You are bad or wrong." It denies him the opportunity to do something out of consideration for what his parent needs.

The I-message is not vindictive or judgmental; it gives the child a chance to think of what his responsibility is. It is a statement of fact, and it should always contain the three parts enumerated above.

Remember, the whole purpose of the I-message is to get children to change their behavior by building up their self-reliance. It's not enough to tell them what they did or how it bothers you, you must also tell him *why*. Tell them the problem it now causes you.

Gordon's work with over a quarter of a million parents shows that when children are given the reasons why their parents feel distressed about them, they usually change for the better.

He cautions that I-messages do not insure that a child will cooperate, but they will provide a much better chance that he will than if you use a you-message.

Sending I-messages should be used in conjunction with active listening (see chapter 44) for the very best results.

46

HOW TO TOILET TRAIN YOUR CHILD

Toilet training has always been a problem for parents, yet, until 1957, there were few studies on exactly what parents do to train their children in bowel and bladder control. In 1957, psychologists Robert Sears, Eleanor Maccoby, and Harold Levin conducted a nationwide study that shed important light on the subject. Their findings showed that, on the average, mothers began to train their children somewhere between the ages of five and twenty-three months. The average age for starting was eleven months, and the average age of completing the task was eighteen months. The training took an average of seven months. Some mothers managed it in a few weeks; others took as long as eighteen months. As might be expected, the older the child was, the faster he learned. About 20 percent of the mothers were rated by the psychologists as "severe" in their methods. Also, the degree of warmth that a mother expressed to her child was a crucial factor in his learning speed. Mothers who had high anxiety about sex generally started training sooner than those who did not. The early starters also had the lowest rate of success.

The Practicalities of Training as Soon as a Child is Ready

A moment's thought about the frustrations of childhood incontinence can only lead one to conclude that a shorter method of bowel training is needed. An average child soils himself about seven or eight times daily. If it takes about ten minutes to clean and diaper him, a mother spends about nine hours each week just tending to this unpleasant chore. This may be the least of a family's worries when we consider that laundry or disposable-diaper bills may well run into the hundreds of dollars each year

PSYCHOTECHNIQUES

and that there are restrictions on a family traveling with a child who might have an accident at any time.

The Psychotechnique of Toilet Training

After hearing these facts, the frustrated parent might well ask in exasperation, "Can anything be done?" Fortunately, the answer is yes. Perhaps the best method of toilet training to date is that given by Nathan Azrin and Gregory Nunn. It is an intensive one-day program, which can be carried out at home. Anyone who has a good relationship with the child can administer it.*

General Considerations Before You Begin

If your child is twenty months or older he is probably ready for this psychotechnique of toilet training, though younger children often will benefit from it as well. Here are three tests you should perform to determine your child's readiness for training.

1. *Bladder-control test.* Ask yourself three questions: (a) Does my child urinate a considerable amount at any one time rather than dribbling throughout the day? (b) Does he remain dry for several hours? (c) Does he give "signals" (squirming, leg crossing, etc.) which indicate that he is about to urinate? If the answer to two out of three of these questions is yes, then your child probably has attained sufficient bladder awareness and enough control to benefit from this toilet-training psychotechnique.

2. *Physical Maturity Test.* Does he have enough finger and hand coordination to handle objects easily? Would he be able to lower, then raise, his pants by himself?

3. *Instructions Test.* Can he follow simple instructions, such as bringing you an object from the next room, showing you the parts of his face, imitating a simple task like clasping hands?

If your child does not pass these tests, wait until he is more

*The procedure has been successfully tested on two hundred children who ranged from twenty months to four years of age. The average child learned in four hours, some in as little as thirty minutes, and some required two days (fourteen training hours). Girls were slightly faster than boys.

developed before using this psychotechnique.

Preparations You Must Make Beforehand

1. Gather the following materials: a doll that wets (preferably the same sex as the child), a potty chair, a variety of tasty snacks, drinks, potato chips, and cookies, several pairs of loose-fitting training pants, and a "friends-who-care list."*
2. Select a place in the kitchen on a day when you and the child will be quietly together all day long. Try to have no one interfere with your training session.
3. Tell the child about the potty chair (i.e., where to sit, the pot inside, etc.).
4. For a day or two before you start, allow him to watch you or others in the family going to the toilet. Have an open-door policy.
5. Point out how pants are lowered, and how to sit on the potty.
6. Teach him to lower and raise his pants several times.
7. Teach him to flush the toilet, tell him about the bowl, the water, where the waste goes, and so forth.
8. Teach him the meaning of key words you will use, like *pants, wet, dry, flush,* and *toilet paper.*
9. Teach your child to tell you: (a) when he has wet or soiled himself, (b) if possible, when he is wetting or soiling himself, (c) when he feels he is about to "do." These sensations prepare him to be aware of body cues. If you notice these signals, point them out to him, saying, "Tommy is doing now (has done, will do, etc.)."
10. Use the doll to play "toilet." Pretend that the doll wants to go to the bathroom and let the child practice lowering its pants and placing the doll on the potty.
11. Teach him to wipe the doll, then to wipe himself (while he is clean).
12. Give him all he wants to drink to increase the frequency

---

*This list contains names of people the child loves and respects. It may include fiction characters like Bugs Bunny, Yogi Bear, and Santa Claus.

of his urination. The more he drinks the better. Remember, salty snacks increase thirst.

13. Use gentle manual guidance to lead your child to the potty when it is time to do so.

14. Try to maintain a cheerful, warm attitude throughout.

15. Follow each step in the program carefully, explaining them to the child as simply as possible.

16. Try not to show disapproval of the child if an accident occurs during the training.

The Training Steps

Now you are ready to begin.**

1. Engage the child in play with the doll for at least an hour. Play games by saying: "Now Tommy (the doll) is dry. Feel his pants. Soon he will want to go. Then how will his pants feel? Wet, that's right." Proceed to have the doll wet itself, and then instruct the child to remove the doll's pants and help him to put clean ones on.

2. Next, tell the child to place the doll on the potty and say: "Now Tommy will go in the potty. See how he does it?" After the doll "wets," let the child see it; then you empty the potty into the toilet and let *him* flush it. Some children are distressed when they produce a bladder or bowel movement which you promptly flush away. But this needn't be a trauma if the child does the flushing himself.

3. When the doll is dry be sure to praise the doll enthusiastically, and try to speak for the doll when appropriate. (For example: "Now I wish Michael would change my pants because I just wet myself," or "I will try to tell Michael when I feel like going.")

4. After some minutes begin to train the child to pull the doll's pants down and place it on the potty *before* it wets. After

---

**Many modern mothers have been brought up on Freud, so we would like to put your mind at ease from the start. For many years, the theories of Sigmund Freud held that bowel training functions were intimately related to personality development. You needn't worry about this idea. There is no evidence that it is correct, and rapid training should not adversely affect a child's personality.

some trials with wetting on the potty, begin to pretend that the doll has defecated, and then teach the child, by guiding his hand, to wipe the doll clean and dry. When the child doesn't notice, make the doll wet or soil its pants, then mildly scold the doll and let the child do the same.

5. Inspect the child's pants about every five minutes.

6. When you feel the child's pants to be dry, praise him and reward him with a candy, and teach him to speak to the doll and ask "Are your pants dry Tommy?" Do you have to go to the potty?" and so forth.

7. After the doll-play ends, begin to teach the child to lower and raise his own pants. (He has already done this in step 6 on page 223.) Then sit him on the potty until he urinates. After this, praise him and coach him to raise his pants, praise him and give him more to drink.

8. Repeat these trial sittings and allow him to sit for about ten minutes each time, then gradually reduce them as necessary.

9. As time goes by, indirectly suggest that the child go to the potty to urinate. For example, say "Maybe it's time for Michael to go to the potty." Remember, all through the trials, encourage him to drink as much as possible. Also, it is important for you to reinforce him with immediate praise when he urinates, so the very moment you are aware that he is wetting in the potty, praise him in a spirited manner. When you are praising, use all the means at your disposal: snacks, drinks and treats, the friends-who-care list, even a phone call to grandmother.

10. After a few trials, your child will begin to walk to the potty by himself. Begin praising him immediately after he takes the first few steps. For example, say "Michael is a good boy, he's walking to the potty all by himself." (Toward the end of the training period, you will begin to decrease the frequency of praise.)

If an accident occurs during the training period, let the child feel the wet pants and show your disapproval (e.g., "Michael, you wet your pants and I don't like that.") Always try to criticize the *behavior,* not the child. Do not show anger. Don't forget to maintain his desire to urinate by giving him fluids.

11. After he has completed three successful potty trials himself, begin to phase out the snacks and the approval. Continue to inspect his pants every half hour or so until the end of the day.

Don't be discouraged if you must go into a second day of traning. Be prepared for this. Naps should be given as usual, but training should be resumed when the child awakes.

12. As his potty trials proceed, he will eventually defecate, and when this occurs, teach him to wipe himself with sufficient toilet tissue by guiding his hand over his anal area and dropping the paper into the potty. When your child is finally trained, you must make it a grand event in his life. It should be told to his aunts, uncles, and so forth; or perhaps you can reward him with a toy or a visit to the zoo. He should know that the extra satisfactions he gets are related to his achievement.

A final note: This toilet-training psychotechnique is a taxing routine. It will demand your patience and resourcefulness. Plan to meet many frustrating moments, but don't give up. When it's over, you too deserve a reward. So, treat yourself to dinner or a show after the job is done.

PART SEVEN
Succeeding at
Work
and at School

47

HOW TO OVERCOME TEST JITTERS
(AND BOOST YOUR SCORES)

Each of us knows the terror of examinations. We've borne the pallor of midnight cramming and struggled through the anxiety before and the forced euphoria after our baptism by fire.

When college students are asked about their number one worry, they invariably say it's passing exams. There are probably more mental breakdowns on campus because of examination phobia than from any other single cause. Perhaps in a youthful fantasy, we believed that it would all be over after we left school; but unfortunately, exams continue as a way of life wherever we go.

Jobs in government and private industry, most state licenses, many company promotions, and, of course, school diplomas all require passing tests of some kind. Even championship contests in football, baseball, tennis, gymnastics, and so on, when it comes down to it, are tests of ability, and the job we hold ultimately is a test that we must pass in order to remain on the payroll.

Behavior therapy literature is replete with studies that report success in desensitizing people to the fear of exams. In addition to using our desensitization techniques (in chapters 8, 9, and 10) to help you calm down before test time, there are a number of well-validated tactics you can use to boost your scores as well. So, if you have test anxiety, use those chapters and this one for maximum benefit.

First, try to alter your attitude toward tests. They are not designed to be torture events. Know right from the start that there is no magic formula for passing them. Pretest anxiety can hurt your scores, and the best antidote to it will always be study and more study.

If you are a college student, you should take your work seriously. Regard your schoolwork as you would any job for which you have agreed to work certain hours for certain pay. Dramatize this point to yourself by imagining how long your father would last on his job or how much your professors at college would be capable of teaching you if they were to assume the lax habits of many careless students.

Important Things You Should Know about Tests

We can speak of either a timed test or a power test. The former has a definite time limit; in the latter, time is not a factor. If you are over fifty-five years of age and you have a choice, it is to your advantage to choose a power test.

Tests that require many short answers are more reliable than tests that call for fewer but longer answers. *Reliability* means that they give a more consistent measure of a testee's ability.

There are two types of exams—objective and essay—and they each require a different plan of attack. Objective tests usually require short answers and are of the true-false, multiple choice, completion (fill-in), matched-columns variety.

When you are scheduled to take an exam, question your examiner about it. Find out as much as you can about the material to be covered, how long it will be, and, if you're a student, how much it will be worth in the final grade. Ask him if it will be essay or objective, or a combination of both. If you can't find out what kind of exam it will be, study as if you were going to take an essay test. (We'll discuss this later.)

If it's an objective type, find out if wrong answers are penalized. This means that for each incorrect answer you lose slightly more than one point. The penalty for a wrong answer is usually the amount of credit of the answer multiplied by the probability of guessing it correctly. Thus for a true-false item worth one point, the penalty for a wrong guess would be $1 \times \frac{1}{2} = \frac{1}{2}$. If you took a 100-item true-false test, where each item was worth 1 point and you got 20 wrong, your score would be 80 (items you got right) minus 10 = 70.

People who are unaware of penalties become dejected when they receive a score lower than they expected. So always find out what the scoring system is before you take an objective test.

Psychotechniques for Taking Tests

Objective Tests

1. *When you study* for an objective exam, review main ideas, but also keep track of supporting details and take note of unusual phrases, striking words, sayings, mottos, and key sentences.

2. *When you take objective exams,* read the directions twice, then underline key words like *always, never, sometimes,* or *usually* before you tackle the questions.

3. *To save time* answer each question as you read it. Pass over those which are difficult or of which you are unsure, and return to them later if you have time.

4. *If you can't understand a question,* carefully change or alter the wording of it to help you understand it better. For example, a true-false question like "Not all Haitians were exclusively descendents of the Carib natives of the Caribbean," might be changed to "Some Haitians were not exclusively descendents of Carib natives."

5. *If there is no penalty* for wrong answers, fill in every blank. Don't start guessing, however, until you finish the entire test.

6. *On completion questions,* usually more than one answer is correct, so even if you are penalized, you should write in an answer if you have a hunch about it. But no wild guesses.

7. *Don't go back* and change your guessed answers. Studies show that your first hunch is usually right.

Essay Tests

1. Essay exams are more complicated and need different preparation. When you study for an essay test, pay attention to principles, concepts, and main ideas along with supporting

points. Look for relationships between the various topics, sections, and chapters.

2. Make as complete an outline as you can of what you study. Jot down key words, phrases, and quotes.

3. When you are ready to take the exam, carefully read the directions twice. Then, unless there are many questions that require only a few words for an answer, read through all the questions. As you do this you are priming your blocked preconscious memory to begin working.

4. When you answer a question, write an outline first. List all facts you can think of; then, when writing your final answer, just flesh out the outline with these as you go along.

5. Think before you write. Don't let your pen lead your thoughts. Stay calm and composed, and when an idea jells, write it down.

6. If it's a timed test, keep a sharp eye on your watch. Budget your time according to the credit given for the question:

7. When your answer ties in with another one you've given, be sure to mention this. It gives your answer extra clout.

8. First tackle questions you are sure of and leave some space between answers for facts that may come to mind later.

9. A good rule is "think more and write less." When you begin an answer, start by making a summary statement, then elaborate on it. For example, "The first moon landing occurred in 1969." Then go on to tell who, what, why, and so forth to flesh out your answer.

10. *Underline* key words that require you to do something, like *name, describe, compare, discuss.* Keep these suggestions in mind.

When asked to *name, list,* or *outline,* your task is to simply jot down a number of items that are connected with the subject discussed, not to explain anything.

When asked to *compare,* always take the two items named and show their similarities and/or differences. When asked to *define, describe* or *explain* something, present it from several points of view. Try to think of the unusual points about the subject, which most people would miss. Use short sentences.

When asked to *discuss* (the most difficult direction), follow your outline carefully. Take a separate sheet of paper for this and use numbers or letters to help you divide your answer into sections. One of the important elements in a discussion question is credibility. Always give examples, illustrations, or quotes, when you can, to bolster your answer.

11. We remember by associations. When we hear *knife* we think *fork;* when we hear *chair* we think *table.* Make full use of this natural associative process. If you're frustrated in remembering a particular fact, try to bring it back by recalling its relationship with other things around it. For example, try to visualize the book in which you read it, where you were sitting at the time, what the page looked like, and any pictures, tables, or graphs nearby.

12. No matter what type of exam you face, remember to write legibly. This is especially true for essay questions. To some degree, your score depends on your examiner's subjective evaluation of your answers, so why irritate him with a scrawl?

13. Always proofread your paper before you hand it in.

What to Do before the Test

1. Your score will depend very much on how you prepare for the test. Cramming will help before an exam, but it will give you only a short-term memory. After several days, you won't recall very much of what you've studied. Also, cramming is not good if you do it as a last-minute effort to learn something for the very first time.

2. Try to stretch out your study over several days or even weeks and always review each unit as soon after class as possible.

3. For several days before an exam, try to get extra rest and relaxation. The night before an exam, be sure to get a sufficient amount of sleep.

4. Before exams, never use alcohol or drugs of any kind; they may affect your brain's efficiency. Know that some medicines you may be using (cold preparations, for example) can bring on drowsiness. And don't overeat before a test; if anything, it's better to go in hungry rather than full.

5. If you feel particularly insecure about the subject, predict questions you think might be asked and practice answering these

at home. Put some pressure into your practice session by timing yourself. This is especially helpful for math problems you might encounter.

6. An important point: The night before an exam, *do not allow any activities to intervene between the time you finish studying and the time you go to sleep.* This includes reading, watching TV, listening to the radio, having prolonged conversations, and using the telephone. This rule also applies on the day of the exam itself. Try to go directly to the test without any interruptions.

7. Don't discard old exams. Review them as study aids and analyze them to find and correct your weaknesses. Consider any good test a learning experience and part of your overall education.

8. If you are not satisfied with your test performance, ask your professor or supervisor his impressions about what you might do to improve your scores. Remember, it's not what you know in your mind, but what you let him know you know that counts in an exam.

48

HOW TO STUDY UNDER PRESSURE

How often does it happen that you find yourself in a pressured learning situation? If you're a student or a business or professional person, meeting deadlines of this kind is a way of life. But it needn't be a frustrating chore, for there are a number of study techniques, thoroughly researched by psychologists, which are available to you. One that is particularly useful is the PQRST method (Preview, Question, Read, Static, Turn back).

Psychotechnique for Studying Something

Before you begin to study, try to clear your mind of any random or persistent thoughts. Relax, lie down if you wish, and allow thoughts to come and go freely for a few minutes. Jot down any tasks that will need your attention, and take care of them later. Concentrate your entire effort on the assignment at hand.

Step 1: *Preview.* Reading or studying something without a preview is like starting a car trip without first scanning a road map to know where you're headed. So, take a few minutes to make a quick survey of the material. If it's a chapter in a book, take special note of the chapter heading. Read the first paragraph or two; they generally give a quick overview of what's to come. Read all titles and captions, pictures or figures. Note the main divisions of the chapter and how each of these is divided. Read concluding paragraphs and summaries carefully. You may find at times that you don't completely understand what you're reading, but you'll gain a familiarity with what the writer considers important. This will help you to read selectively when you actually get to the material.

Step 2: *Question.* Look away from the book and ask questions on what you'd expect to find in the assignment. You don't have to know much about the subject to ask questions. For example, for a chapter on combat neurosis during World War II, you might ask, "How many servicemen got it? What brought it on? How was it treated?" Questioning gets us actively involved in our reading. It creates an anticipatory set that helps the learning process.

Step 3: *Read.* Read the material. Focus on ideas, not words. Vary your rate of speed depending upon your purpose, the chapter's difficulty, and your previous familiarity with the subject.

Read with a red pencil. Feel free to underline, make brief comments to yourself in the margins, and write questions that challenge the author. Notice connections with other things you've learned. Jot down key words. Don't take notes yet.

Step 4: *State.* After you've finished reading, state in your own words what you have read. If the chapter is very long, make statements about a few pages of a section at a time. Think through what you state. This is a very important step and probably the one most likely to be overlooked by readers. Most experts recommend spending two-thirds of the study time in stating, reflecting, or recitation; few advise spending less than one-half the total time here. This short review right after a learning period can increase your chance of recall by almost 50 percent.

Step 5: *Turn Back.* Turn back and reread the chapter selectively. Don't necessarily read everything, but spend more time, if needed, on difficult and key passages. If, after you read the first few words in a paragraph, you seem to recall what will follow, skip it and go on. Don't spend time rehashing what you already understand. Now is the time for making notes, in outline form and in your own words (not the author's), with the book closed, if possible. If you've followed all these steps faithfully, the notes will almost write themselves.

Remember, it is not enough only to understand the PQRST method; it must be practiced frequently. Study aids are like muscles—the more they are used, the more effective they become.

49

HOW TO BE A BETTER STUDENT

1. Understand just what your assignment covers before you begin to study, so that you do not waste time doing unneeded work. Studies have shown that when a student has a clear idea of a task, he will learn it better and faster.

2. Do some easy studying first, thus getting yourself into the swing of studying before you tackle the more difficult task. Your mind is similar in this way to your muscles, it needs a warm-up period.

3. Study your most difficult subjects while you are fresh and, if possible, break the lesson down into small, manageable units.

4. Allow yourself a solid block of time for study, so that you will not waste time starting and stopping again and again. Be sure, though, to take rest pauses every hour or so.

5. When the time for study comes, begin promptly. Don't allow yourself to be distracted even before you begin.

6. Set up a definite study schedule and do not allow anything to interfere with it. Do this by dividing an entire week into hour-long segments and then marking off each of these for a specific activity.

7. Reserve a few moments shortly before each class period to review mentally what you have studied. Try to do this by only glancing at your notes and not reading them.

8. Use a definite system of notes (and note-taking) and try to take notes in outline form only.

9. Take sufficient time to make thoughtful and careful notes on your readings. Leave plenty of space in your notebook for additions and corrections.

10. Put only the most important points in your notes. Do not record long, detailed passages.

11. Record in your own words the main ideas in your reading

or listening. These will make more sense to you later on, when you reread your notes.

12. Aim to work things out for yourself, but if you are still confused, seek advice *before* you get discouraged.

13. Keep a neat notebook. A disorderly set of notes will discourage you from studying.

14. Strive to keep your work up to date. If you have work to make up, it will be on your mind and prevent you from feeling free to learn new material.

15. Read in sufficient light. Bad light has been shown to make students irritable and unreceptive to new learning.

16. Have a systematic plan for a brief rest after school hours. The best time for this is right after you arrive home or just before dinner time. Remember, you can't keep a fresh mind in a stale body.

17. Keep mentally alert throughout the study period. Take a brisk walk, deep-breathe before an open window, do calisthenics, or throw cold water on your face. An excellent refresher, which also provides a ten- or fifteen-minute break, is to take your "morning shower" during your evening study period.

18. Try to ignore noise and distractions while studying. If the noise bothers you and you can't do anything about it, start looking for another place to study.

19. Practice taking timed tests at home with "one ear on the bell."

20. Reserve a special place in which to study. Don't hop around the house reading here and there. Try to establish what educational psychologists call *place habit*. It will help your learning process.

21. Try to forget all personal worries during study periods. If you can, settle any unanswered questions that are on your mind before you sit down to study. If you are tense, use the relaxation exercises in chapter 6 to put you in the right mood. Remember— learn to relax and relax to learn.

21. Keep a pad next to you to jot down any outside problems that come to mind while studying, thus allowing yourself to concentrate on the lesson at hand.

22. Always keep an eye on your own study habits to discover where you can improve. Don't hesitate to experiment with a new

technique. It may prove worthwhile.

23. Take note of yourself to find out during what hours your mental efficiency is at its peak; plan your activities accordingly. People have different biorhythm patterns, and if you can determine yours it will help you to learn better.

24. Compare your study habits with those of others in order to get suggestions for improving your own. Also, don't hesitate to ask teachers for suggestions.

25. Use a straight-backed yet comfortable chair for studying. Don't be too comfortable, however. Studies show that a slight state of muscle tension improves our ability to learn.

26. Do not stay at any task so long that you become nervous or overfatigued. Take a few short breaks rather than one long break during an evening.

27. Consciously watch in your everyday living for opportunities to apply your new learning. Knowledge that is applied is retained better than knowledge that is merely stored.

28. Test yourself to see if you are learning; ask yourself questions that you think might be included in an exam and see if you can answer them.

29. Participate in group and class discussions whenever possible as a means of furthering your understanding. The more you can articulate an idea the better you will comprehend it.

30. Take a complete rest or change if you feel stale, restless, or irritable. Sometimes the solution to a problem comes easier if you "let it lay" and then return to it later.

50

HOW TO MANAGE OTHERS SUCCESSFULLY

"Wherever your life touches ours, you make us stronger or weaker . . . there is no escape—man drags man down, or man lifts man up." This quotation from Booker T. Washington well describes the meaning of interaction in human affairs. We often find ourselves with the responsibility of managing someone else, and in that role we can greatly influence their behavior for better or for worse.

Take the examples of John, Judy, and Diane. John was a like-able family man who enjoyed helping people. He had many friends and, all in all, he was popular and generally happy. Happy everywhere, that is, except at work. He supervised one hundred employees in a department store where he became manager after twelve years as a successful buyer.

He hoped the promotion would lead to a vice-presidency with the company, but things were not working out well for him. Although he could easily make people like him, in actuality he was a weak manager. He could not lay down the law, and consequently his workers walked all over him. John was making the mistake that many new executives make: he was trying to gain the approval of those he directed.

It was also tough going for Judy. Her students were constantly out of order. They missed assignments, cut classes, failed their tests, and were tardy. She was a good teacher, a top-flight student in college, and was well respected by her colleagues. But she was doing something wrong.

Diane, a busy mother of four teenagers, had always been an efficient person before the children were born. But gradually, as they grew up, she was loosing control over them. Getting them to do chores like cleaning their rooms, helping with the laundry, and shopping for groceries was a big problem for Diane. It had escalated to the point where it now caused serious friction between Diane and her husband.

These are examples of once-adequate people who were now finding themselves facing difficult obstacles beyond their capacity. If we look closely, we would see that each person has partially contributed to his or her own problem. Unwittingly, each has *strengthened* the habit of opposition in those they direct. This opposition habit, in turn, is a wall that John, Judy, and Diane now find insurmountable. Conflicts like these are common in human affairs and they often lead to nervous breakdowns.

In a book on psychotechniques, we must be quick to say that human relations constitute an enormously complex area, and no amount of techniques will ever solve all the problems.

But with the idea in mind that it is better to light a small candle than to curse the darkness, there *are* some strategies that our three perplexed combatants can use to help them deal more effectively with those under them.

The following psychotechniques were originated by psychologists D. Tosti, J. Loehr, and L. Homme. Their rules for dealing with others through what they call *behavioral contracts* are paraphrased here:

Rule 1: *At first, ask for and reward small achievements of new behavior.* Initially, don't request too much of the other person (we'll call him *the target*). Divide the overall task into manageable components. For example, if Johnny's room is a mess, start first by asking him to clean up only his desk, or his closet.

Rule 2: *Use immediate rewards.* As soon as possible after your target accomplishes the task, reward him for it (with praise, money, a favor in return). Don't delay praise; but remember, adhere to the "first work then play" principle and don't reverse the order.

Rule 3: *Reward often at first, then gradually less often.* Try to reinforce nearly every action that is in the desired direction, no matter how meager it is. This will keep the new behavior going as you reward progressively less often.

Rule 4: *Be consistent and systematic in your dealings with the target.* Once you and he agree on a plan (contract), stick to it. Don't suspend it unless there is a very special reason to do so. Be firm. For example, if you and your employee agree he'll type nine letters each afternoon before leaving, don't stop him after eight because you're a bit guilty about his working so hard that day (or because *you* might want to leave early too).

Rule 5: *Reward specifically.* Don't reward *general* obedience or a target's good intentions. Pinpoint your goals and ask for and reward specific jobs completed. For example, if a student is fairly well behaved all day, don't reward her by saying, "Janet, you were a fine girl today. You didn't give me any trouble." Do say, "Janet, you didn't talk out of turn once today. You got through all your arithmetic problems (or house chores) and that's good."

Rule 6: *Request high-quality performance.* Keep your standards high for the task you want your target to accomplish. Let him know exactly how well you want him to do his job. Don't reward shoddy performance. For example, if your subordinate does manage to meet a deadline you've both agreed on, but has made a number of errors, call them to his attention and let him redo the work. But (following rule 1) *do* reward him partially for that portion of his performance which is acceptable.

Rule 7: *Ask for active, not passive, behavior.* Ask for *positive* rather than negative actions. For example, remember Grandmother Moore in chapter 3. She tried to get the cooperation of her grandchildren and her husband but made the mistake of using negative suggestions instead of positive ones. Say, "Do this" rather than "Don't do that," when you describe what you want done.

Rule 8: *Keep your agreement (contract) with your target simple and clear.* For example, Judy should say to her students, "Please hand in neat, legible term papers," not "Don't hand in sloppy, illegible term papers." Describe specifically what behavior you expect. Be concrete, don't be fussy. For example, say to your spouse, "If you clean the aquarium, I'll wash the car," rather than "If you help me around the house, I'll help you with your office reports."

Rule 9: *Always be fair and honest.* Don't use gimmicks or manipulation. Your target should agree that the reward you offer is worth his efforts. Never withhold a reward if it is justly deserved.

Rule 10: *Transfer the initiative as soon as you can.* As soon as it is practical, shift the responsibility for the new behavior over to your new target. Ultimately, what you're after is his own self-management. When this is done, it will be easier for you and it will help him to grow in self-confidence.

All in all, managing others is an art—but even an art has some rules that can be learned. Furthermore, as your skill increases you will undoubtedly create your own psychotechniques, which will improve even more your ability to manage others.

51

HOW TO HANDLE DISCIPLINE AT WORK

Most of us who work for a living reach a point when we are not just responsible for ourselves, but must also direct the actions of others. This pertains as well to one laborer given authority over another, as it does to a corporate executive who manages an entire department.

At the very moment when you cross the line from being a worker who takes orders to one who must give them, you become part of the supervisory team of your company. And at one time or another in this capacity, you will have to grapple with the task of disciplining someone.

Although you may be skilled in many aspects of your work, chances are you have never been taught the art of disciplining another person. Sometimes, when you must deal with a tough problem, you may even secretly hope it will resolve itself so that you will be spared the confrontation with a worker. Or you may be suffering from what Harry Maynard calls "hardening of the categories," by not keeping an open mind to all the facts in a discipline case. In any event, if disciplining is an important part of your job, you must master it and use it constructively.

If you feel uneasy about giving reprimands, it will help if you believe that your comments can assist a worker to be more effective.

Here is an example that illustrates poor discipline methods: Supervisor Mary Smith found Nancy, one of her assistants, away from her work post for over an hour. This caused a backlog in orders for an important customer. Mary, an excitable woman, angrily blasted Nancy in front of several other workers and demanded an explanation for her absence.

This is an example of a serious type of supervisory error.

Emotional impulse is what prompted Mary to disregard some basic rules, which are:

1. Deal with the worker privately and unemotionally.
2. Hear his or her side of the story before you comment.
3. Try to find the cause of the violation and offer some constructive help.

Mary's mistakes in dealing with Nancy very likely will lead to a number of destructive reactions in others nearby, such as the following:

1. Bystanders will try to avoid the same violation, not out of their own free motivation to cooperate, but out of fear of public denunciation and scorn by their peers.
2. Nancy's social prestige will be injured, especially among competitive peers, because her faults were exposed for others to see.
3. Animosity may be generated in her, particularly if she feels Mary set her up in front of the others as a "sacrificial lamb."
4. Others might well identify with Nancy and also feel angry at Mary for exposing her to public ridicule.
5. A low trust–high fear atmosphere may be created, so that if someone makes a future mistake, she's much more apt to cover it up than bring it out in the open to Mary.

Here are a number of strategies you can use to avoid some of these pitfalls and make your job easier when you face that inevitable discipline session with someone.

A Dozen Psychotechniques for Disciplining Someone

1. Try to have your talk as soon after the infraction as possible, but don't have it if either you or the worker is upset.
2. Allow a cooling-off period, then begin in an informal, relaxed manner.
3. Start with some praise, if possible. For example, "John, you've been with us for a long time and your work is generally quite good . . ."
4. Describe the infraction as accurately as possible without

making judgments. For example, "Some records caught fire in your work area, Joe. Can you tell me what happened?" Not, "You left your cigarette on a crate and you set fire to some records. Why did you do that?"

5. Be patient; let the worker talk. Many times he will beat you to the punch, see his mistake, and offer corrections himself.

6. Don't undermine his self-respect. This means don't blame, accuse, berate, or belittle. Any action you take should have a constructive aim. It should help the worker to perform better and be happier in his job. It should not be revenge or punishment.

7. Don't be content with simply identifying the mistake; try to get to the cause of it. Going back to our example, Mary might have probed why Nancy was away from her work. Perhaps there was a strong personal or health reason for her absence. Another case might involve a person who is sloppy in part of his work. It may be that he hasn't received adequate training on a new procedure, and he is simply too proud to tell you he doesn't understand how to perform the task properly.

8. A good manager tries to see things from a worker's point of view. No one likes to be told to do something without knowing the reason why, and workers generally obey a rule readily if they know the reason behind it. For example, if you mention a no-smoking rule, you might explain that oil drums nearby make smoking a hazard, or that the company suffered a sizable loss from a fire some years ago. Any other true incident that would back up your explanation would be appropriate.

9. If it is absolutely necessary for you to correct or admonish someone publicly, a good rule to follow is to do it quickly and briefly, then discuss it privately with him as soon as possible.

10. Be sure to get his reactions to the talk before you dismiss him. The air should be cleared and there must be no hard feelings. He must be absolutely certain about how you feel and what he should do in the future.

11. If you are trying to resolve a quarrel between two workers, don't see them together until you've had a chance to see them individually. Always try to be nonjudgmental and willing to learn. Many times a hothead needs only a chance to blow off steam in order to come back to his senses.

12. Finally, it's a good idea to follow up a discipline talk some days later; but keep it brief and show genuine interest in the worker's corrected behavior.

52

HOW TO HELP YOUR CHILD WITH SCHOOLWORK

School is a major hurdle for most families. When children succeed there, everyone is happy; but when they bring their failures home with them, parents relive their own childhood frustration with education.

The trouble is that parents are not given the proper training to help their children. Yet they must do this to the best of their ability, usually with only the aid of an occasional article or possibly a book on the subject.

There are a number of psychotechniques you can teach your child that will improve his school performance. Not only will these help him, but they will bring a measure of peace of mind to you as well.

1. *Diagnose his difficulty.* The first step is to learn the worries your child may have about his schoolwork and what he may be doing wrong. To get this information, start by having a relaxed, nonthreatening conversation with him. Let him know that you'd like to help him become a better student. Begin by just talking to him about his schoolwork in general. Remember, do not be judgmental; you are on a fact-finding mission during this talk. Start off with open-ended questions (questions that can't be tersely answered yes or no, but that ask the child to give an extended answer on a subject). For example, you might ask, "Judy, tell me about your history class," or "Allen, how would you describe your teachers this term?" or, "Mary, tell me about your favorite subject."

Don't make the mistake of becoming bored when he does start to talk, because he may close up and you will have defeated your own purpose.

2. *Speak with his teacher.* Ask any questions that form in your mind based on your talk with the child. Try to get the teacher's opinion about what your child needs to be a better student, and follow any instructions she may suggest. Tell her about your plan to help your child and arrange another meeting with her later in the term to review his progress.

3. Check his study area. Be sure that the lighting is right, the heat is adequate, the chair is firm and strong, and the desk is uncluttered and gives him ample writing space. He must have a comfortable place to study.

4. *Help him to set up a definite study schedule.* Block off seven columns on a sheet of paper for the days of the week and a column for each hour in the day. List his class time, play time, study time, and so forth for the week. Try to encourage him to stick to this schedule as closely as he can. Let him help you to organize and make up the schedule.

5. *Start using rewards.* If he has great difficulty settling down to study, begin on the first day by asking him to study for only fifteen minutes. Then when this time is up, stop him, reward him promptly for it (by giving praise, a candy, etc.) and make no other demands for the rest of the day.

On the second day, ask him to study for twenty-five minutes, then reward him, and again dismiss him for the rest of the day. Keep doing this until he is up to the desired number of study hours necessary for his work load. Remember, proceed slowly at first, then gradually increase your demands on him.

6. *Review subjects before class.* Teach him to set aside a few moments before each class to review the subject. Ask him to check over his homework on the topic and to be prepared for the upcoming class.

7. *Study with a plan.* Teach him to study his easiest, most interesting lessons first. This serves as a warm-up and prepares the way for more difficult subjects. Later, he should tackle his more troublesome assignments, but not so much later that he will be too tired.

8. *Study in one spot.* Discourage him from moving from place to place in the house. He should study in the same location every day.

9. *Chat with other pupils.* Teach him to compare his study

habits with those of other children, especially those who are doing well.

10. *Help him to be a better reader*. Study your child for several minutes as he reads silently. Keep in mind the following "don'ts," which are bad habits that will slow his reading:

Don't let your child point to words with his finger or a pencil. This will slow him down. Teach him to read with his eyes only.

Don't allow him to move his lips or whisper while he reads. Again, this slows him down and will not permit him to read faster than he can speak. If he has trouble giving up this habit, let him hold a pencil between his teeth.

Don't let him rock his body or move his head while he reads. This is tiring and also will slow him down. Teach him to move just his eyes.

Don't let him dive right into reading a chapter without first previewing it.

Don't let him read in poor light. Not only will this cause eye strain and irritability, but it will decrease his ability to concentrate.

11. *Teach him to preview*. When he is to read a book or a chapter, teach him to skim through it first. An author gives definite signals about what he will say, and if your child can spend a few moments reading these, it will greatly help him to understand the message of the book.

Teach your child to read the book jacket carefully (if there is one), the title of the book, the preface or introduction, the table of contents, the chapter headings, section headings, underlined words and phrases, and the summaries (if any) at the end of the chapters. He should also look carefully at any pictures, graphs, or figures. All these guideposts will help him prepare mentally for what lies ahead.

12. *Review together*. At the end of the day, just before the child goes to bed, try to spend at least ten minutes with him reviewing the day's work. Ask or answer any questions that might have arisen, and encourage him to discuss with you some of the main points he has covered.

Finally, take any of the study skills from chapter 49 (How to Be a Better Student) that might apply to your child, and teach him how to use these to improve his school performance.

PART EIGHT
Dealing with
Crisis Situations

53

HOW TO BANISH NIGHTMARES

It is estimated that some twenty million people in this country suffer from nightmares, and many of them are children. The fear of having a nightmare is a frequent cause of insomnia. This fear is similar to a phobia, in which the phobic person is preoccupied with losing control of the situation. In the same manner, the dreamer fears losing control over his nocturnal destiny. At various sleep clinics throughout the world, this notion of control has been the cornerstone of successful therapy for sleep disturbances. The goal is to help the patient restore his feeling of control in the dream.

Experiments going back a hundred years have shown that dreamers can influence their dreams by stimulating one or more of their senses or by giving themselves waking suggestions during the day or right before bedtime.

Work done at the Psychological Center of Georgetown University in Washington, D.C., has shown that nightmares can be controlled or banished completely. Dr. Arnold Mysior instructs his patients there, many of whom are children, to suggest to themselves that they will be able to face their dreaded nightmare and bring it under control. The method involves self-suggestion before bedtime. One young girl had a recurring bad dream of falling off a cliff. Dr. Mysior's prescription was simple: "Fly," he advised her. After several nights of such self-suggestions, she dreamed that she flew, and from then on her nightmare disappeared.

Dr. Leonard Handler of the University of Oregon cured an eleven-year-old boy who was haunted by a "monster" in his dreams. The child had as many as seventy-two such bad dreams in a six-month period. He was taught to command the monster to leave and never return. During the following six months, the boy

253

had only two nightmares, neither of which was about the monster. And shortly thereafter, he was completely symptom-free.

Psychotechniques for Overcoming Nightmares

This is a five-step method. It can easily be taught to children.

Step 1: *Formulate an exact dream solution.* Write out as clearly and briefly as you can, exactly what you would like to have happen in the dream. For example, "I would like to stop dreaming about having an accident in my car. I would like to see myself driving on a long trip safely and with complete confidence. I would like to see myself overcoming any dangerous driving situation."

Step 2: *Do something during the day which is related to the nightmare.* Continuing with our example, take a short, relaxing ride in your car. Test the brakes, horn, steering, and so forth. Reassure yourself that the car is in good working condition and that you are handling it well. Sit in your parked car. Close your eyes, relax, and visualize yourself in the dream, driving without worry.

Step 3: *Read the description you've written (in step 1) several times a day and visualize yourself conquering the dream.* Write notes about it, tell it to others, if possible sketch it on a sheet of paper. The general idea is to keep the suggestion of the solution very much alive and in the focus of your attention.

Step 4: *Review chapter 6 on relaxation.*

Step 5: *Review chapter 8 on image desensitization.* For the imagery sequences, see yourself dreaming. Gradually give yourself images that lead up to the end point (conquering the problem or obstacle in the dream). Following our example again, see yourself preparing to go for a drive, leaving the house, walking to the car and starting it, putting it into gear, and so on. Keep presenting vivid images to yourself slowly, until you finally see yourself completing the drive successfully.

It requires persistence to influence the course of your dreams. After a few weeks, many people do succeed in altering the outcome of their dreams, and in overcoming their nightmares.

54

HOW TO OVERCOME DEPRESSION

Winston Churchill called it the "black dog." It gripped him like a vise and plunged him into moods of despair. He was victimized by the common malady of our day—depression.

Famous creative minds like Beethoven, Van Gogh, Tchaikovsky, and Edgar Allen Poe lost the spark of inspiration when melancholy hit. Statesmen Warren Harding and Abraham Lincoln had attacks so severe that occasionally they could not function in office for days at a time.

We can easily empathize with anyone who is depressed because, young or old, rich or poor, we have all felt it ourselves. It spares no one.

Depression is by far the most common type of psychological problem. The vast majority of patients in mental hospitals suffer from it. But contrary to popular belief, most people recover from it.

Some authorities, among them Dr. Nathan Kline, an outstanding psychopharmacologist who has treated more than five thousand cases, hold that sadness has a physical basis. Others, like Dr. Martin Seligman of the University of Pennsylvania's Mood Clinic, believe that it is mostly "learned helplessness," and that to some degree we can relearn the skills needed to be happy, or at least not to be depressed. This is also the position of Dr. Arnold Lazarus, professor of psychology at Rutgers University, a leader in the field of behavior therapy. He teaches that people's moods are governed by their anticipations of future events. He has developed a strategy of using imagery for coping with gloom. He maintains that "most of our optimistic and pessimistic anticipations take the form of mental imagery," and that "words, ideas, values, attitudes, beliefs, are all replete with imagery. Find the image and you will understand the behavior. Furthermore, find the image and *if* you desire, you will probably be able to change the feelings and the behavior."

We cannot deny that images affect our moods and feelings. When we imagine a succulent steak, a tasty wine, or a creamy custard pie, we often desire it. And how often do our sexual images lead to sexual feelings? Indeed, the image is father to the feeling and, as we shall see, Lazarus uses this principle in a number of imagery psychotechniques to combat depression. They will provide you with good beginning steps to overcome gloom. After you've practiced these imagery psychotechniques, proceed to those of Dr. Aaron Beck and to ten more in this chapter, which require your active participation.

Psychotechniques Adapted from Dr. Arnold Lazarus for Overcoming Depression

1. *Pleasure imagery.* List about fifty things you do reasonably well and that you find interesting, stimulating, and enjoyable. These can be ordinary acts like gardening, fishing, bowling, cooking, hiking, singing in a choir, or attending a party. Then lie down in a quiet place and relax (using chapter 6). Next, imagine as vividly as you can actually doing some of these things. Try to see your images in detail. Look for colors, textures, sounds, aromas, and so forth. The closer your image is to the real situation the better. Spend fifteen minutes on each item you choose. Do this at least two times per day. Let your mind roam and drift. If it begins to dwell on something sad, say *stop,* then relax, wait, and proceed with the imagery.

Allow yourself to feel as much pleasure as you can. One of the reasons for gloom is that people momentarily forget they still have the capacity to create happiness for themselves. The imagery in this step will restimulate these recollections.

2. *Time projection.* The ancients had a saying: *sub specie aeternitatis.* It was a form of mental set that advised that a person would be better able to accept his present circumstances (woeful or otherwise) if he viewed them in terms of eternity. This wisdom applies as a psychotechnique for depression.

Again, relax completely. Imagine that you are in a huge time-machine, which can project you into the future. First, try to go two weeks forward in time. Next, try for four weeks, then eight weeks, until gradually you have gone six months or even a year ahead. Imagine that you are involved in constructive living, and see the things you would probably be doing then—where you would be living, the people around you, and so forth.

When you are fully into this scene, begin to look back on today. Slowly recall the upsetting incident that made you depressed. Don't try to see it as bland or unimportant, but rather as an event that was sad but tolerable.

The more you practice projecting yourself into the future, the more your present trouble will lose its emotional impact and allow you to gain a more balanced perspective.

3. *Coping imagery.* Dr. Martin Seligman, as we mentioned, believes that sad people have erroneously learned to think of themselves as unable to overcome obstacles. Drawing on this concept, Lazarus has refined a well-known "coping imagery" psychotechnique, in which you mentally rehearse successfully doing various jobs that you have done well in the past.

First, list several small tasks in which you feel competence, like making a home repair, sewing a dress, or writing an interesting letter. Imagine yourself doing them with good success and receiving the acclaim of those around you. Again, try to see all scenes as vividly as you can. Do not minimize the power of imagery rehearsal. It is a respected and genuine behavior therapy technique.

Coping imagery serves a dual purpose: first, by concentrating on your positive skills and not on your negative ones, as gloomy people usually do, you will remind yourself of your potential to snap back and reduce your depression; second, your imagery scenes serve as goal rehearsals for actual achievements you anticipate later on.

The psychotechniques of Dr. Aaron T. Beck, Professor of Psychiatry at the University of Pennsylvania, emphasize the cognitive aspects of depression. They pick up where those of Dr. Lazarus leave off. Beck agrees with others that the important characteristic of depression is inactivity, so he requires his clients actually to do something in real life to dissolve their sadness.

It is also Beck's belief that gloomy people tend to interpret their situation incorrectly. They make errors in thinking by engaging in belitting self-statements, and he teaches them to recognize and change these thoughts.

Psychotechniques of Dr. Aaron T. Beck for Overcoming Depression

1. The double-column technique. Whenever you first notice the blues coming over you, think back and recall exactly what thoughts either triggered or increased your feeling of sadness. Write these in a column on a sheet of paper. Chances are your thoughts contained negative opinions of yourself ("I've failed as a friend," "I'm a sloppy worker," "I'm not good looking"), or they contained pessimistic attitudes about your future ("I'll never be able to pay off my debts," "I won't ever get well"), or feelings of being overwhelmed with responsibility ("My job is too tough for me," "I'll never be able to adjust to my divorce").

These negative beliefs, which are automatic, probably seemed perfectly plausible to you at the time you had them, but if you calmly look back on them days later, you will be surprised to learn that often they were unjustified.

2. After you have listed your negative thoughts, correct them objectively. Answer each item as if someone else had related it to you and sought your advice. Look for the positive side of the statement, and then, in the second column, write this more balanced reply to your negative thought. Dr. Beck gives an example: "A housewife was feeling gloomy and neglected because none of her friends had telephoned for a few days. When she thought about it, she realized that Mary was in the hospital, Jane was out of town and Helen really *had* called. She substituted this alternative explanation for the negative thought, 'I am neglected,' and began to feel better."

3. Dealing with the "impossible." We often become unhappy when faced with a challenge we feel is insurmountable. This can happen to a student who is failing a difficult course, to the parent of an unmanageable or handicapped child, or to a person who despairs because he can't find a job.

If this is your type of depression, begin first by writing down in order every step you will have to take to meet and conquer your challenge. Don't allow your mind to race—when it does, it will usually think "failure." Now rank these steps from easiest to hardest, and begin to do them one at a time. This "parts method" is a proven technique in learning a hard procedure, and it works eminently well. Most problems *can* be mastered by breaking them into smaller, manageable parts.

4. Another reason for feeling overwhelmed has to do with your "repetition compulsion," the tendency to use the same action or solution for your problem. What you need is a fresh approach to an old set of facts. If you are frozen in this way, speak with others about how they would handle the situation. Then write down and study these alternate solutions. Don't assume that people cannot be helpful, even if you see them as less intelligent or less sophisticated than you. They may have had a similar problem and worked it out well.

Other Psychotechniques That Have Been Helpful in Fighting the Blues

1. Increase your satisfactions. Get as much enjoyment as you can. Make a list of at least thirty activities that have brought pleasure in the past, preferably things you do well. These needn't be complex tasks. They may be as simple as riding a bike, playing chess, listening to music, choosing a good restaurant, visiting a museum, shopping for bargains with a friend, going to an auction, or playing tennis or golf.

Next, grade these in difficulty from the easiest to the hardest to do and complete one or two of these activities each day.

Be unconcerned with any immediate change in your mood; don't even look for it. Simply follow through on each and every item on your list, robot-fashion, without worrying, "What will this *really* do for me?" The idea is to break through your inactivity block to some small degree and allow your depression to lift naturally, in the course of things.

2. If you don't have a pet already, buy one and take good care of it. Many people are distracted from themselves in a healthful fashion by a dog or cat they own and love. If you are like thou-

sands of others who have no one else with whom to share warmth, owning a pet would probably help you.

3. Socialize. Do something sociable every day. Take part in a discussion group, have a cup of tea with a neighbor, chat with a grocery store clerk. This simple ritual will help you to penetrate the isolation that usually shrouds a person when he gets the blues.

4. Pleasuring. Get as many body pleasures as you can. Eat tasty foods, drink good wine, make love, take warm baths, listen to good music, seek pleasant surroundings, smell sweet fragrances, wear comfortable, pleasing, and flattering clothes; in short, enjoy as much sense pleasure as you can. Look forward to these moments of minute pleasure in which you momentarily forget your discontent.

5. Be assertive. One of the best antidotes for dejection is assertiveness. Lazarus speaks highly of this psychotechnique: "Training the depressed person to emit assertive responses is probably the single most effective strategy in these instances."

Being assertive not only means standing up to others when your rights are trampled, but also actively getting out of your shell. Don't turn down any chance, no matter how insignificant, to bring satisfaction either to you or to someone else. This even means doing little things like buying someone a cup of coffee, sending someone an article you read, giving a coin to a beggar, saying thank-you to an elevator operator, complimenting someone about his clothes, or doing a small favor for a friend.

Also, try new things. Don't miss an opportunity to do something different. Experiment. Take small risks with new situations and new people. Don't expect miracles. Keep reminding yourself that these psychotechniques have worked for others, and chances are some of them will work for you.

6. For the time being, don't associate with people who are gloomy, sad-sack types. They will influence your moods more than you realize. If you do happen to meet them, listen especially for inconsistencies in what they say, and vigorously speak out about their pessimistic attitudes. Let them know that they may be wrong in their thinking; if you assert yourself with them it will have an uplifting effect on you. Of course, the corollary to this point is to spend as *much* time as you can with people who are

cheerful, outgoing, and happy about life.

7. Keep your daily life as organized and as uncomplicated as you can. Be especially neat and orderly about your appearance, belongings, appointments, and your work. The more organized you are, the less you will waste time and energy, valuable resources you'll need to overcome your depression.

8. Depressed people suffer from lack of a future. This means they have no goals, which are the best antidote for gloom and depression.

Make a list of ten reasonable goals to achieve. They needn't be stupendous, like writing the great American novel. Keep them modest. Some might be, having friends over for a special dinner, selling old items in your closet, doing volunteer work with youngsters, taking a do-it-yourself course, enrolling in a lecture series, joining a book discussion group, taking training to improve your job skills, joining your chamber of commerce, or getting a job.* If possible, discuss your list with someone.

Set and pursue goals for yourself *even if your heart isn't in it at first.* Tell yourself: "This psychotechnique *has* worked for others, why shouldn't it work for me?"

9. Stay healthy. Keep in good physical shape by eating and sleeping adequately. Give yourself every possible chance to overcome your gloom. Remember, concern about your health will only add to your worries.

Depression worsens when we are weak, ill, or malnourished. Also, a person's blue moods deepen toward the end of the day, which indicates that fatigue is an important factor.

10. Exercise. If you're in good health, do something physically strenuous each day. Dr. Thaddeus Kostrubala, chief of psychiatry at San Diego's Mercy Medical Center, uses jogging as therapy for many of his moderately depressed patients. He says, "The most immediate effect on the patient is elation and an amelioration of depression." He believes it would be beneficial for most patients. His contention has been verified. Neurologists have found that muscle action does release certain substances in the brain, which in turn have a moderating effect on our moods.

All through your struggle to battle the blues, remember that

---

*A National Institute of Mental Health survey in Kansas and Maryland showed that wives who work are *less* susceptible to depression than those who do not.

there is no *one* cure for them. Try every method we have suggested here, plus those from elsewhere. Have realistic expectations that some may work, others may not. But keep trying.

55

HOW TO EXPLAIN DEATH TO A CHILD

To a child, death is an abstraction that cannot be grasped. The magical thought that it is a reversible state of being is reinforced daily in the course of play, when soldiers, dolls, and toy animals fall mortally wounded on the field of imaginary battle, only to rise and play again. Even in the movies and TV cartoons that are so much a part of a child's existence, characters seldom, if ever, die permanently.

Unfortunately, these naive conceptions collapse when a child's parent or sibling suddenly passes away. For many children, this is a trauma that profoundly affects the rest of their lives.

But children can be helped to accept the inevitability of death, and we present here some techniques that can minimize a child's despondency when death strikes the family circle. They should be used with the understanding that all children differ as individuals in their ability to tolerate stress.

Psychotechniques for Helping a Child to Accept the Death of a Loved One

1. When death strikes, it is a time when your child will need extra love and affection. Love will go a long way toward comforting him and making up for his loss. Even if you're not a demonstrative person, make an effort to have more body contact with him; give more touches, kisses, and hugs than usual. In a child's mind, these translate into emotional reassurance. Step up sense pleasures by giving more ice cream, candy, toys, and other things to help keep him happy. Avoid the pitfall of well-meaning pity. It can do more damage than you realize. Pity demoralizes rather

than comforts. It can undermine a growing child's strength and replace it with a feeling of insecurity.

2. Stay close. It's not a good idea to separate yourself from a child soon after the death of a significant person. A child often feels abandoned when a loved one dies. He needs your physical closeness, your tangible presence, to reassure him that he won't be deserted by you.

3. About funerals: If a child is old enough to understand, he should be allowed to attend the funeral. It is a ritual that conveys finality, and it will help him to accept that which is irreversible.

Children under the age of six who can't show the constraint and calm necessary at a funeral should not be allowed to attend. If you feel that it would be hard for a youngster to witness a funeral, you may dissuade him by asking a leading question, like "You don't wish to go to the funeral, do you?" and then proceed to talk him out of it.

If he does attend, he should be told in advance what to expect (this also applies to attending the burial site), that is, that the deceased will be in a coffin, and that people will be sad and even crying. He should be told he can change his mind about attending if he wants to. At the services, he should sit in a place where it will be easy for him to leave if he wishes to do so.

If the child's immediate family cannot sit with him, then someone else should. It is not a good idea for a child to be alone.

Never force a child to attend a funeral.

4. Don't associate death with sleep. When you are at the funeral, avoid saying that the deceased is asleep. Some children develop fears of falling asleep after this explanation, thinking the obvious—that if they sleep they too may die.

Another common mistake is to tell a child that God loved the deceased so much he called him to heaven. A child might then conclude that if he is loved by God, he too will be summoned to heaven. Children often become confused over this explanation in other ways: They are told, on the one hand, that heaven is the ultimate goal of us all, yet everyone at the funeral is crying and sad. This paradox can be very puzzling and upsetting to a child.

It might be more useful to simply say that the deceased has gone away and won't be returning, but that he or she wants us to carry on until we all meet again someday in heaven.

5. Encourage him to express his grief. If he is an older child, show him by your own example that he needn't be embarrassed to show his feelings. Tell him to cry if he wants to; that this is his way of showing that he loved the deceased. Explain that it is better to shed tears than to keep the hurt inside.

6. If the child begins to speak about the deceased, don't hesitate to talk warmly about him or her, yet don't dwell unnecessarily on this. In time, you should be able to recall and discuss loving anecdotes about the person, which had special meaning to the child. You might say, for example, "Remember when Daddy used to make a penny disappear and then take it out of your ear?" or "Sharon liked to put sugar on her apple. Remember the face she made one day when she put salt on it by mistake?" These recollections help to desensitize the child to the pain of separation.

7. Death should not go undiscussed. Feelings that are strongly suppressed can create anxiety and depression. If you are sure that the child has the subject on his mind but isn't bringing it up, you should carefully raise the issue. You might start off with a question like: "That little boy we met at school reminded me of Timmy. Did you think that, too?" or "I had a dream last night about Timmy. He was very happy. Do you ever dream of him?" Then gradually draw out the child's feelings.

When he begins to ventilate his thoughts, remember that a child's emotions are volatile, but they are also short-lived. So don't be rattled if a crying outburst occurs; it will pass. Allow the child to express his feelings as fully as possible. But don't be oblivious to the fact that a child may have deeply repressed feelings, which could result in symptoms like twitches, tics, irritability, insomnia, loss of appetite, enuresis, and so forth. For reactions like these, professional help should be sought.

8. In time, a question that will most likely arise is, "Mommy, will you die too and leave me the way Daddy did?" Your answer should be immediate and loving, and it should convey the notion that (a) Daddy didn't die because he did not love the child, (b) he did not leave voluntarily or abandon his family, and (c) Daddy's death is not a punishment to Daddy or the child for being bad.

Reassure him that you won't leave him, then distract him by saying that there are many enjoyable things to plan for in the future. Your answer to this question, then, might go as follows: "No, Daddy loved you very much, but he didn't leave us because he wanted to. He became very ill and died. I love you very much too, and I won't die for a long, long time to come. It is so far into the future that we can't even know when it will be. So let's try to plan happy things to do for later on. Shall we go to the beach next Sunday?"

9. Some children want their surviving parent to promise never to remarry and thus replace the deceased parent with a new one. If you honestly do not know what you will do about this, don't fully hide your ambivalence from the child, but answer truthfully. For example, "I don't know what the future will bring; that is a long way off. We'll see. We'll talk about it then," and so forth.

If you have decided to remarry even if there is no immediate prospect, don't promise your child that you won't. As time goes by and another partner comes into the picture, the nature of the child's relationship with the new person will most probably cause him to re-form his conclusions. He'll then make the necessary adjustments in his thinking about your remarriage.

10. Be alert for signs of guilt. Like adults, children too will often reminisce about the times when they said such things as "I hate you" or in other ways offended the deceased. Explain that we all grow irritable with others once in a while, but that this does not mean we wish someone harm or death. Here's an example:

JOHNNY: I feel bad 'cause I broke Anita's doll last summer. That was wrong. I shouldn't have done it.

MOTHER: You loved her very much and she loved you, too, Johnny. Sometimes we become so annoyed with someone that we do a foolish thing to them without thinking. But time passes and then we realize how silly it was, when all along we loved them so very much.

Another good tactic is to counter an "offense" with a compliment. For example, Johnny's mother might have added: "If you add up all the good things you did for Anita it would make up for it [breaking the doll] a thousand times. Like the time you bought her a dress out of your savings, or when you climbed the roof to get her ball, or when you helped her fix her carriage."

11. Often children can learn to accept death more readily if they have already experienced the death of a pet. If a pet dies, you should use it as an opportunity for the child to express grief. Discuss it openly and help him deal realistically with the situation.*

12. It is not a good idea to remove belongings (pictures, furniture, books, etc.) of the deceased unless they are causing adverse reactions within the family. Rather, they should be regarded matter-of-factly as belonging to "sister who died," or whomever.

13. Under certain circumstances, dealing with your child's reaction to a death should begin even before it occurs. If someone like a grandparent is gravely ill and death is imminent, prepare the child for the inevitable by hinting at it or briefly mentioning it. Allow questions to surface, and answer them with the amount of realism you believe your child can accept.

In brief: When you must explain death, the important thing is to know your child and his individual tolerance for powerful traumas. Expose him to only that amount of anxiety that you believe he can withstand. Don't overwhelm him.

Keep alert for any unusual reactions he may have, and be ready to correct these as they arise. It is not incidental that in the process of helping your child to accept death you also help desensitize yourself to its impact.

Remember that you yourself are the best influence on your child; you are the model for him to copy. If you can accept a loved one's death and still function after it, then this is the most important lesson you can teach your child.

---

*Sometimes parents replace a pet quickly and do not allow a full-blown grief reaction to set in. Some experts think this is a mistake that deprives a youngster of an opportunity to learn coping skills in a bereavement situation.

56

HOW TO DEAL WITH THE DEATH OF A LOVED ONE

Death is the ultimate trauma we face. It has always been a taboo subject in our country. Like incest and suicide, it provokes so much anxiety that it is not brought up, or it is only briefly mentioned and then dropped. For most of us, death is simply not real. As with other unsolvable problems, we often deal with it irrationally. We may withdraw from thinking about it, or we may even deny that it exists.

Our silence on a taboo topic is related to our tendency to be superstitious. Have you ever heard someone cry out, "Don't say that," when something unspeakably evil was mentioned? Within us we have the irrational capacity to believe, if only for a brief moment, that what is spoken could possibly come true. (The Romans called it *nomen est omen.*)

As children we saw the world in a simplistic way. Reality was mixed with fantasy, and thinking about something often made it appear true. As adults, many of us still retain this vestigial quirk in our logic. Somehow, just talking about a subject seems to bring it a bit closer to reality.

Yet talking is largely what must be done to deal adequately with the crisis of death.

In a chapter on how to deal with death, there is an unanswered question lying beneath every thought: Can death ever be explained satisfactorily to anyone? We think not. But we do believe that its acceptance could be easier if we avoided some mistakes that only add to our difficulty in a time of grief. Here are some suggestions.

268

Psychotechniques for Dealing with Death

1. Breaking the news. If you can, avoid using a letter or a phone call to tell someone about what has happened. The best procedure is to go personally to inform him or her. It is preferable to have someone along to help you. And if you have the option, make your disclosure early in the day rather than late in the evening, to minimize the bereaved's loss of sleep.

If the news must be given by phone, it is preferable to first speak with a third person (a husband, wife, brother, sister) who can then relay the message in person.

2. Mourning helps. Freud called mourning "grief work." He believed that it sets in motion an entire process within the psyche which helps us to accept the death of a loved one. You should take part in formal mourning rituals if it is your family's custom to do so. Mourning will help to stabilize your feelings and at the same time give you the chance to be close to those you love. This, especially, is a time to attend religious services, pray, meditate, and seek the counsel of your clergyman.

3. If you're having difficulty functioning in your job, at school, socially, or at home, don't hesitate to see a psychiatrist or psychologist. There are useful methods for treating grief reactions that have helped others, and they may help you as well.

4. Don't isolate yourself. Even though you may not feel like it, keep up your contacts with people. Socialize with others, and stay close to family members. Allow yourself to be consoled. Let emotion out, don't hold back, and don't reject offers from someone you like who wants to help distract you from your sadness. Permit yourself to lean on them a bit more at this time.

5. If you can't sleep, concentrate, or eat, it's also a good idea to go for a medical checkup. If your doctor prescribes sedatives or muscle relaxants, take them even if you have prided yourself on not needing them in the past. Convince yourself that this is a special time of stress and that you will take them for a while until you feel better.

6. Fatigue and poor physical health will definitely deepen your melancholy. So avoid exhaustion, loss of sleep, and overwork. This is a time when you must conserve your energy and keep as healthy as possible. Many people find it helpful to take

hot baths, long walks, massages, and do gentle exercises. Try to eat nourishing meals and get plenty of rest and relaxation.

7. Stay away from morbid situations. Don't go in for "heavy" movies or TV shows, or lectures on sullen topics. This rule applies socially as well. Avoid people who have a pessimistic nature and are themselves morose or angry. Rather, associate with those you know who in the past have given you a "lift," those who are optimistic and have a cheerful disposition.

8. Resume a satisfactory living rhythm. Get back to your usual routines quickly, or if you don't have any established routines, try to "regularize" your daily habits as much as possible. If you're a housewife, for example, look for a job that will interest you or do volunteer work. Don't remain idle; but also, don't overcrowd your schedule. Keep yourself as well organized as possible.

9. Sometimes your anguish may be so great that you will want to break away from it all immediately by taking a vacation. This often proves to be a wrong move. A break might be advisable after a few months; however, a vacation too soon after the death of a loved one places you in unfamiliar surroundings, with people who may not understand or care how you really feel. This "vacation" often turns out to be a period of isolation, albeit in a restful setting, and isolation is not a good way to overcome depression.

10. Don't plan any radical changes in your life pattern for at least several months. Some bereaved spouses, trying to escape their gloom, may sell their homes, quit their jobs, move to other locations, remarry, give up school, and so forth. Consider that your depressed state of mind may affect your judgment. What appears wise to you now may be regretted when your feelings stabilize in a few months.

11. Dealing with guilt. There is scarcely a bereaved person who does not suffer from some guilt connected with the death of a loved one. It is a natural tendency for some of us to search the past recalling times when we offended or rejected him or her. It is the memory of these instances which elicits guilt in us.

Decide that there is only one reality about the past—that *nothing can be done to change it*. The only thing we *can* do is to atone for our past misdeeds.

It will help you if you pledge something or dedicate yourself to a plan that will absolve whatever "mistakes" you have made concerning the deceased. For example, after his wife died of lung cancer, one man vowed that he would give up smoking. A young housewife promised to care for her deceased husband's aging parents. A teenager who lost his sister in a car accident took an oath never to speed again. And a young woman whose little brother drowned vowed to give time each summer to teach children to swim.

There are other, more total kinds of dedication that can provide us with good feelings about ourselves. These are efforts that we might dedicate to the memory of a loved one, like doing volunteer work for organizations that try to eradicate the disease which claimed his or her life (e.g., the American Cancer Society, the American Diabetic Association, the American Heart Association, etc.).

When we are faced with a death in the family, the riddle of our existence comes into bold prominence and insists on a hearing. At these times, religion often makes the trauma easier to bear and understand. Dr. Elizabeth Kübler-Ross, prominent writer on the subject, says, "Truly religious people with an abiding relationship with God have found it much easier to face death with equanimity than those who do not."

57

HOW TO PREPARE YOUR CHILD FOR GOING TO THE DOCTOR OR THE HOSPITAL

Going to the hospital is always a frightening experience for a child. It is even more painful for parents, who feel there is nothing they can do but passively stand by and let medicine take its course.

If you are calm and open with your child, you can put his mind at ease about his hospital stay. Here are some constructive psychotechniques you can apply to help your child and yourself as well. These tactics can also be used when your child is frightened about a visit to the doctor.

1. The very first thing to keep in mind is your attitude. There is no stronger force to influence a child's feelings about a medical procedure than how *you* think and feel about it. So, try to discuss with your doctor at length what is bothering you about your child! Be sure to ask him to explain in detail what the operation entails and what will happen at the hospital. Try to accept the situation as realistically as possible. Chances are, if you are composed your feeling will filter through to your child and make your job of reassuring him a lot easier.

2. You are bound to feel depressed if your child is seriously ill. If you think this stress might be too much for you to bear, then discuss it with your doctor. Ask him for a referral to a professional counselor who can help you through this critical period.

3. Do not hesitate to ask your doctor for his help in emotionally preparing your child for an operation. Some parents are reluctant to bother the "busy doctor" about such matters, or they feel that he won't fully cooperate. If you are confused about a certain point, ask him to clarify it. In reality you are making the

doctor's task less complicated if his little patient has the right spirit and is not overly fearful about the procedure.

4. Put a definite time aside and allow your child to talk to you about the hospital and the operation. Let him raise questions about it and try to answer them as honestly as possible without raising undue alarm. Permit him to express his fears and concerns. You might say, for example, that many children go through times like this and that (perhaps) even you went through it when you were a child or an adult. Here, a story about how mother went to the hospital to give birth to the child might be appropriate.

Another idea is to arrange a visit with another child who has already been through an operation. While you are present, encourage both children to talk.

Your child should *always* be given the reassurance that everything will be all right after the operation is over.

5. If the child is below the age of nine, it will be helpful to have a play session in which both of you play out the hospital situation. Do this on the day before he is to leave. Use dolls, puppets, and other toys. Your dialogue might go: "Here is a little child (don't make it your child) who is going to the Parkhurst Hospital (name your hospital here) with his Mommy and Daddy. He is not afraid. He knows that he will be stronger, healthier, and will be able to play much better when he comes back home." Follow along step by step through the entire hospital episode, allowing the child to initiate much of the action. Let him be the doctor, the child, the mother, the father.

A variation on the play session is to tell a story with a happy ending about a ficticious little boy or girl who was brave and unafraid and who went through an operation. Always make the characters in your play or story the same sex as your child.

6. If your child seems unduly nervous about the hospital, and he is over ten, try image desensitization, which we described in chapter 8. Review the chapter first, then, on the day before he is to leave, have the child relax on his bed with his eyes closed. Instruct him to see a big TV screen in his mind. On the screen he sees himself going through the next day: he visualizes himself getting up, having breakfast, dressing, helping his mother to pack his bag, leaving the house, arriving at the hospital, checking in at

the office there, going to his room, and so on. Go through the entire sequence of events that he will actually follow the next day. Be sure to tell him to keep all of his muscles relaxed as he visualizes the scenes.

7. A few days before he is to leave, drop in to the hospital for a brief visit of ten or fifteen minutes. Make this drop-in visit casual and don't announce it. Buy your child an ice cream or a candy bar and then walk through the hospital halls, show him the elevator, the offices, and so forth. Chat in a friendly way with any personnel there. This is an in-life desensitization, which we described in chapter 10.

8. Don't dwell too much on the operation. Your child should carry on as normally as possible with everyday activities until it is time to leave. Of course, you should not let him overhear you having long conversations and tense discussions about his operation or its outcome.

9. Your child should know what his reward will be for going to the hospital. Give him a *concrete* benefit to look forward to as a result of his operation. Don't just say, "Amy, after this is over, you won't have those pains in your tummy anymore," or "You won't have those sore throats in the winter any longer." Instead, try to relate the benefit to what the child values most in everyday life. In addition to the above, say, for example, "After you come home and get well, you'll be able to run a lot faster (play games more easily, etc.)," or "You'll be able to skate (swim, ride your bike, play baseball, jump rope) a whole lot better than before."

10. When the day of departure finally comes, ask him to help you pack his suitcase. Let him pick his favorite toy, clothes, and pajamas. Encourage him to take a favorite toy or game with him. This will be the only familiar "bit of home" he has, and it can offer him some comfort when he is alone.

It is also a good idea, a few days prior to this, to promise to stop at a toy store to buy that "special toy" he's wanted; then, actually stop there on the way to the hospital and buy it for him.

11. If you can manage it, and the hospital permits it, stay with your child at the hospital for the first few days, especially if he's below the age of six. Mother is the preferable parent here. If you can't stay, then visit as often as possible, and always bring a toy or gift when you come.

12. Reassure your child that his friends and relatives at home are thinking about him, and they look forward to having him back to play with.

13. Ask his friends to send cards, letters, and notes. It is preferable that you take these to your child personally. When you visit, read them to him and then jot down any replies he might want to make. Tell him that *you'll* deliver these messages when you get home, and when you return tomorrow to see him you will bring their answers.

If you follow these steps carefully you will impart to your child the proper lifelong attitudes about illness, doctors, and hospitals.

A FINAL WORD

You have just learned about the tools necessary for a happier passage through life. Use them as they are, or alter, expand, or reduce these strategies in any way that makes them more beneficial to you.

I would like to ask that:

1. You feel free to write me (in care of the publisher) about your results with these psychotechniques, so that I can refine them and, perhaps, include them in an even more helpful book in the future.

2. You inform me of any other psychotechniques you find helpful in your day-to-day living, which could be of use to others.

3. Professionals contact me about the results they have with these methods and about others that are succeeding for their clients.

S. V. D.

Bibliography

Ackerman, J. B. 1966. "A New Approach to the Treatment of Bruxism and Bruxomania." *N.Y. State Dental Journal* 32:259–261.

Ayer, W. A., and Levin, M. P. 1973. "Elimination of Tooth Grinding Habits by Massed Practice Therapy." *J. Periodontics* 44:569–571.

Azrin, N., and Nunn, G. 1974. "A Rapid Method of Eliminating Stuttering by a Regulated Breathing Approach, *Behav. Res. & Ther.* 12: 279–286.

Azrin, N., and Nunn, G. 1977. *Habit Control in a Day*. New York: Simon & Schuster.

Azrin, N., and Nunn, G. 1977. *Toilet Training in Less Than a Day*. New York: Simon & Schuster.

Barber, T. X., and Scott, D. C. 1977. "Cognitive Control of Pain: Effects of Multiple Cognitive Strategies." *Psychol Rec.* 2: 373–383. These steps were described by Dr. Theodore X. Barber in a personal communication.

Beck, A.; Rush, A. J.; and Emery, G. 1979. *Cognitive Therapy of Depression*. New York: Guilford Press.

Beck, A. 1976. *Cognitive Therapy and the Emotional Disorders*. New York: International Universities Press.

Belsky, M. 1977. *How to Choose and Use Your Doctor*. New York: Fawcett-Crest.

Benson, H. 1975. *The Relaxation Response*. New York: Morrow.

Berdach, E., and Baken, P. 1967. "Body Position and Free Recall of Early Memories." *Psychother.* 4: 101–102.

Bower, G. 1970. "Analysis of a Mnemonic Device." *Amer. Scient.* 58: 496–516.

———, and Bower, S. 1976. *Asserting Yourself*. Menlo Park: Addison-Wesley.

Carkuff, R., and Truax, C. 1965. "Lay Mental Health Counseling." *J. Consult. Psychol.* 29, no. 5: 426.

Chafetz, M. 1976. *Why Drinking Can Be Good for You*. New York: Stein & Day.

Dreikurs, R. 1964. *Children the Challenge*. New York: Hawthorne Books.

———; Gould, S.; and Corsini, R. 1974. *Family Council*. Chicago: Henry Regnery.

Ellis, A. 1977. *How to Live with and without Anger*. New York: Thomas Crowell.

Freese, A. 1974. *Pain*. New York: Putnam.

Garfield, P. 1974. *Creative Dreaming*. New York: Simon & Schuster.

Glasgow, R. E., and Rosen, G. M. 1978. "Behavioral Bibliography: A Review of Self-Help Behavior Therapy Manuals." *Psychol. Bull.* 85: 1–23.

277

Golla, F. L., and Antonovitch, S. 1929. "The Respiratory Rhythm in its Relation to the Mechanism of Thought. *Brain* 52: 491–509.

Gordon, T. 1970. *Parent Effectiveness Training.* New York: Wyden.

Guareschi, G. 1966. *My Home Sweet Home.* New York: Farrar, Straus &
Giroux.

Handler, L. 1972. "Nightmares in Children." *Psychother: Theory, Res. & Pract.*
9, no. 1.

Hilgard, E. 1975. *Hypnosis in the Relief of Pain.* Los Altos: William Kaufmann.
This method was recommended by Dr. Ernest Hilgard in a personal
communication.

Horney, K. 1950. *Neurosis and Human Growth.* New York: Norton.

Jacobson, E. 1934. *You Must Relax.* New York: McGraw-Hill.

——— 1938. *Progressive Relaxation.* Chicago: University of Chicago Press.

Johnson, Wendell, 1961. *Stuttering and What You Can Do about It.* Danville:
Interstate Publications.

Kelly, C. 1961. *The Natural Way to Healthful Sleep.* New York: Award Books.

Kety, S. 1955. "Sleep." *Jour. Clin. Investigation,* July.

Kline, N. 1977. *From Sad to Glad.* New York: Putnam.

Kunhardt, D. 1933. *Junket is Nice.* New York: Harcourt Brace.

Laird, D., and Laird, E. 1960. *Techniques for Efficient Remembering.* New
York: McGraw-Hill.

Lazarus, A. 1963. "The Results of Behavior Therapy in 126 Cases of Severe
Neurosis." *Behav. Res. & Ther.* 1: 69–79.

——— 1976. *Multi-Modal Behavior Therapy.* New York: Springer.

——— 1978. *In the Mind's Eye.* New York: Rawson.

Levandusky, P., and Pankratz, L. 1975. "Self-Control Techniques as an Alternate to Pain Medication," *Jour. Abn. Psychol.* 84: 165–168.

Leyens, J.-P.; Cisneros, T.; and Hossay, J.-F. 1976. "Decentration as a Means
for Reducing Aggression after Exposure to Violent Stimuli." *European
Jour. Soc. Psychol.* 6: 459–473.

Lindsley, O. R. 1968. *Operant Behavior Management: Background and Procedures.* University of Kansas Press.

Lowen, A. 1975. *Bioenergetics.* New York: Penguin.

Lynch, K. 1960. *The Image of the City.* Cambridge, Mass.: MIT.

Maupin, E. 1969. "On Meditation." In *Altered States of Consciousness,* C. T.
Tart, ed. New York: Wiley.

McGinnes, T. 1976. *Open Family Living.* New York: Doubleday.

Miller, W., and Munoz, R. 1976. *How to Control Your Drinking.* New York:
Prentice-Hall.

Montgomery, G., and Crowder, J. 1972. "The Symptom Substitution Hypo-
thesis and the Evidence." *Psychother: Theory, Res. & Pract.* 9: 98.

Morgan, R., and Bakan, P. 1965. "Sensory Deprivation, Hallucination, and
Other Sleep Behaviors as a Function of Position, Method of Report and
Anxiety." *Percept. and Motor Skills* 20: 19–25.

Nichols, R. 1969. "Listening is a 10-part Skill." In *Managing Yourself* (pamphlet published by *Nation's Business Magazine,* Washington, D.C.).

Novaco, R. 1977. *Anger and Coping with Provocation: An Instructional Manual.* Irvine: University of California Press.

Patterson, C. E. 1964. *Facial Isometrics.* Don Mills, Ontario, Canada: Whiteside.

Phillips, G. M., and Metzger, N. J. 1973. "The Reticent Syndrome: Some Theoretical Considerations about Etiology and Treatment." *Speech Monographs* 40.

Rathus, S., and Nevid, J. 1977. *BT: Behavior Therapy.* Garden City: Doubleday.

Renshaw, S. 1945. "The Visual Perception and Production of Forms by Tachistoscopic Methods." *J. Psychol.* 20: 217–32.

Rogers, C. 1942. *Counseling and Psychotherapy.* Boston: Houghton Mifflin.

Rosen, G. 1976. "The Development and Use of Nonprescription Behavior Therapies." *Amer. Psychol.* 31: 2.

Rothenberg, A. 1971. "On Anger." *American J. Psychiat.* 128: 454–460.

Sears, R. 1937. "Initiation of the Repression Sequence by Experienced Failure." *Journ. Exper. Psychol.* 20: 570–580.

———; Maccoby, E.; and Levin, H. 1957. *Patterns of Child-rearing.* Evanston: Row, Peterson.

Seligman, M. 1973. "Fall into Helplessness." *Psychol. Today* (June).

——— *Helplessness: On Depression Development and Death.* San Francisco: Freeman.

Shah, S. 1967. "Training and Utilizing a Mother as a Therapist." Paper delivered at the Eastern Psychol. Assn. meeting, Boston. (Also in: Guerney, B. G., ed. 1969. *Psychotherapeutic Agents.* New York: Holt.

Shames, R., and Sterin, C. 1978. *Healing with Mind Power.* Emmaus: Rodale Press.

Sheely, C. N. 1976. *The Pain Game.* Millbrae: Celestial Arts.

Shore, N. 1976. *Temporomandibular Joint Dysfunction and Occlusal Equilibration.* Philadelphia: Lippincott.

Skinner, B. F. 1953. *Science and Human Behavior.* New York: Macmillan.

Somers, R. 1978. *The Mind's Eye.* New York: Dell.

Stover, L. 1967. "The Efficiency of Training Procedures for Mothers in Filial Therapy," *Psychother.: Theory, Res. and Pract.* 4: 110.

Stuart, R. B., and Davis, B. 1972. *Slim Chance in a Fat World.* Champaign: Research Press.

Tosti, D.; Loehr, J.; and Homme, L. 1975. *Behavior Mediation in Individual and Group Counseling for Rehabilitation: Training Manual.* Marin County Probation Department.

Wahler, R. 1965. "Mothers as Behavior Therapists for Their Children." *Behav. Res. and Ther.* 3: 113.

Walder, L., et al. 1967. "Teaching Behavior Principles to Parents of Disturbed Children." Paper delivered at the Eastern Psychol. Assn. Meeting, Boston. (See also: Guerney in Shah reference above.)

Wassmer, A. 1978. *Making Contact.* New York: Dial.

Wiggins, J. 1971. *How to Argue Successfully*. Berea: Personal Growth Press.

Wolpe, J. 1958. *Psychotherapy by Reciprocal Inhibition*. Palo Alto: Stanford University Press.

Zane, M. 1977. *I Never Stayed in the Dark Long Enough: Ways to Overcome Phobias*, (A cassette tape). Phobia Educational Materials, PO Box 807, White Plains, N.Y. 10602.

Zimbardo, P. 1977. *Shyness. What It Is. What to Do about It*. Menlo Park: Addison-Wesley.

——— 1978. *Shyness. What It Is. What to Do about It*, (A cassette tape). New York: Biomonitoring Applications.